# Nine College Nines

# Nine College Nines

## A Closeup View of Campus Baseball Programs Today

GREGORY J. TULLY

Bob —

Thanks for your help to
make Chapter 7 possible

McFarland & Company, Inc., Publishers
*Jefferson, North Carolina, and London*

LIBRARY OF CONGRESS CATALOGUING-IN-PUBLICATION DATA

Tully, Gregory J., 1955–
　　Nine college nines : a closeup view of campus baseball
programs today / Gregory J. Tully.
　　　　p.　　cm.
　　Includes bibliographical references and index.

　　**ISBN 978-0-7864-4128-0**
　　softcover : 50# alkaline paper ∞

　　1. Baseball—United States—History.　2. Baseball players—
United States—History.　3. College sports—United States—
History.　I. Title.
　　GV863.A1T85　2009
　　796.323'630973—dc22　　　　　　　　　　2008049594

British Library cataloguing data are available

Cover photographs courtesy of respective schools; background
image ©2008 Shutterstock.

Manufactured in the United States of America

*McFarland & Company, Inc., Publishers*
　*Box 611, Jefferson, North Carolina 28640*
　　*www.mcfarlandpub.com*

To family and college baseball,
especially to those players and coaches
leaving the dugout for the last time

# Acknowledgments

Taking an idea and converting it into 200 pages of words takes a lot of help.

Most of my ideas don't pass the "morning shower" test. Ideas that seem good in the evening are dismissed as stupid by the next morning.

I have my dad to thank for the inspiration to keep the idea for this book afloat. When I was still bobbing in "should I or shouldn't I" indecision, he died. But it was his passing that reinforced how much I enjoy baseball and how much of that is because of him. His grandson, my son, also reminded me of the joy of college baseball as he pursues playing at the college level. I want to share that enjoyment.

I was a zero-tool baseball player as a kid, but that doesn't dampen my enthusiasm for the game almost 40 years after I stopped playing. Some of my most exhilarating spectator sports moments were watching baseball games. Some of those have been watching my son play; some of those have been watching major league baseball. I witnessed two incredible college games in writing this book (I refer to the USC and Miami chapters).

A book on college sports doesn't go very far without the cooperation of the sports information directors. The access they afforded and information they provided was essential. Luke Reid and Teresa Clements at Chico State. Bob Molta at Eastern Connecticut State University. Mike Greenlee at Cal State Fullerton. Bert Sahlberg at Lewis-Clark State College. Bill Franques at LSU. Kerwin Lonzo at the University of Miami. Thomas Dick at the University of Texas. Jason Pommier at USC. I am very grateful for their help.

San Jacinto Junior College's entire coaching staff was very cooperative, especially Tom Arrington and D.J. Wilson.

Once the access is gained, it is very important to contact people who are willing to share their insights. I spoke with players, coaches, trainers, administrators, umpires and others. All of them were wonderful in discussing facts and opinions. Three coaches—Ed Cheff of Lewis-Clark, Bill Holowaty of Eastern Connecticut and Dave Lawn formerly of USC—were very generous with their time.

Lastly, a project isn't enjoyable if others aren't there to share it. My wife, Sue, my son, Scott, my daughter, Megan, my mother, Mary, my brother, Kevin, and my dog Jett, never once said, "Why are you doing this?" They understood. Thanks to everyone. Thanks especially to Sue.

# Table of Contents

# Prologue

I want to take everybody on a road trip that stretches from Fullerton, California, to Willimantic, Connecticut. It's all about college baseball.

Writing about the enjoyment of college baseball to some readers of this book is perhaps like preaching to the bleachers. It's a great game full of passion, excitement and competition. However, when I initially considered the contents for the book, I was driven by the question, "Why isn't college baseball more popular?"

The College World Series produces good ratings and the Southeastern Conference (SEC) succeeds in drawing fans to the game. But it is not a consistent, national phenomenon.

I live in the San Francisco Bay Area and I was a little surprised, but not stunned, to pick up the Saturday morning *San Francisco Chronicle* on May 3, 2008, and not find a single mention of the first game in the series between Saint Mary's College (Moraga, California, about 20 miles east of San Francisco) and the University of Miami. The Hurricanes were ranked number one in the country at the time, but this Bay Area newspaper did not have a summary article, a box score, or even a line score in its seven-page sports section. In some places, I suppose college baseball is not even back page material.

The college baseball experience is not necessarily better than college football or basketball. It's just different. It is like comparing corporate America to a family business. Each has its place. Each has its appeal.

To understand where college baseball is in the pecking order of collegiate athletics, just visit Columbus, Ohio. Although Ohio State athletics are played on a grand scale, their baseball program is representative of what one finds on most college campuses.

Alongside the Olentangy River, after a short right turn off of Woody Hayes Drive, stands Building 082, better known as Ohio Stadium. It is impressive. No one who has seen it will be surprised to learn that this monstrous structure has seating for over 101,000. Over 71,000 attended the 1922 stadium

dedication game against Michigan when its original capacity was 66,000. It
has been just as full ever since.

Just north of the stadium, on the western side of the river, is the Schottenstein Center. Inside, the Value City Arena has a capacity in excess of 19,000,
and it frequently hosts concerts as well as Buckeye basketball games.

In the shadows of the Schottenstein Center is Bill Davis Baseball Stadium. *Stadium* is perhaps too grand of a word. Although it seats over 4,000,
*park* would be more appropriate. Beyond the right field fence stands the Nick-
laus Museum, which honors the great golfer. Beyond the left field fence is the
Jesse Owens Memorial Stadium for track and field, soccer and lacrosse. It can
seat 10,000.

Ohio Stadium, Schottenstein Center, and Davis Stadium are three typical venues for big-time college sports. In a given year, a home game against
rival University of Michigan will likely draw about 105,000 at Ohio Stadium,
18,000 at the Schottenstein Center, and 2,000 at Davis Stadium. With respect
to baseball, that's not apathy; it's reality. College baseball is different and,
frankly, that is part of its appeal.

For college football, the anticipation is everything. There are frequently
13 days of build-up between home games. There is expectation, which builds
as game time approaches and celebratory rites are enacted. Take the "Vol
Walk" from Gibbs Hall to Neyland Stadium two hours before kickoff, for
instance. It's part of what makes University of Tennessee home games memorable. In Columbus, the seemingly simple role of a sousaphone player "dot-
ting the i" in the marching band's script formation of "Ohio State" has been
revered for over 70 years. The USC horse, Traveler, gallops around the Coliseum after each score, too often for most opposing teams.

Tailgating often begins several days before the Saturday kick-off. Some
of these events are legendary, such as the "world's largest cocktail party" held
primarily on the Jacksonville Landing before everyone enters Jackson Municipal Stadium for the Florida-Georgia game.

For college basketball, a great diversion from the inclement weather that
lingers during much of the season, it's all about the game atmosphere. Thousands of fans are crammed inside the arenas, producing thrilling noise levels.

Some of the rivalries equal or exceed the intensity of those of college
football. Duke versus North Carolina. Kansas versus Missouri. Kentucky versus Louisville. Syracuse versus UCONN.

It's hard to match a crowd reaction when the visiting team has just blown
a 10-point lead with minutes to go. It's a wonder that a player can hear any
of the coach's instructions during the final timeouts.

Yes, the college baseball experience is very different than football or basketball.

A college baseball game is usually laid-back and intimate. While one might pay over $300 online for a private sale end zone seat at Ohio Stadium, a $5 general admission ticket gets a good seat at Davis Stadium. Every baseball spectator is close to the action and the emotion. You can hear the third base coach talk. You can see the pitcher wince. You can smell the freshly mowed grass.

It is this proximity to the game that makes college baseball so appealing. Being able to see and hear the players is a unique sports experience. In other sports venues, the fans need binoculars. There are no "velvet ropes" forcing the baseball spectators to keep their distance from the players. To the contrary, college baseball players are generally very accessible.

Like college basketball and football, college baseball often involves the loud, animated support of one's team or alma mater. But baseball can be a contemplative experience too—the sort of activity that can be enjoyed alone.

One aspect of college baseball that differentiates it from the professional game is the very location of the stadium: on the school's campus. A college campus brings back memories: the panic of not being prepared for a midterm; roommates stealing leftovers; staying out until 3 A.M. and having difficulty getting up the next day and deciding whether to start with breakfast or lunch; having an occasional creative thought.

The campus is an everyday forum for problem solving and innovation. At times as I walk towards a college ball field, I think that some student sitting in the library will either be a next-semester dropout or the person who advances, say, alternative energy.

The entire setting is just a little removed from reality. Ending up at the baseball field is the perfect end to a campus-long walk. I don't quite get that same feeling walking towards Oakland–Alameda County Coliseum to watch the Oakland A's play.

This book takes an intimate look at an intimate game. It goes behind the scenes in a different way, using the setting of nine different series, hosted by nine different schools from the various NCAA divisions, incorporating many different points of view and covering nine different topics.

Before I wrote this book, I occasionally attended college games in the Bay Area, having seen Stanford, Cal, Saint Mary's, Santa Clara and the University of San Francisco play home games. I've seen local junior college games. I frequently watch college baseball when it is available on cable TV. I wasn't a hardcore fan, but I thought I knew a decent amount about college baseball. However, there was plenty of information about the college game I did not know. I was determined to have my questions answered and share them with the eventual reader.

College baseball is even more enjoyable the more one has some insight about the game. Recruiting, the fall season, balancing academics, and summer league play are but a few of the activities that are a unique part of college baseball. Professional players don't need to worry about the "satisfactory progress towards a degree" rules. Even the core baseball topics of pitching, hitting and coaching are different at the college level. To better understand some of the nuances of college baseball, I interviewed players, coaches, support staff, and even an umpire.

I wanted to do more than simply explain the things I learned; I wanted to share what I had experienced. I wanted to give the reader some idea of what it is like to watch a game from the park in which I was sitting. I decided there was no better way to discuss both a school's baseball program and a specific topic on college baseball than to weave the two together using games as the backdrop. The approach mimics the natural flow of a baseball game in which spurts of intense action are continually interrupted by moments of inactivity. The latter lends itself to conversation.

I like to think of the reader as the person sitting next to me at these games, someone with whom I can share some insight. It is insight that was mostly acquired during the 2007 season in compiling information for this book.

There are over 1,500 colleges, including community colleges, which have baseball programs. Nine of these were selected for this book because of their history of success. Certainly many other programs are just as worthy of attention and support.

I selected schools that I had never visited, with one exception. For purposes of full disclosure, I graduated from Chico State (in northern California) in the 1970s, but I had never seen a baseball game there. I had veered somewhat away from spectator sports by the time I was fully absorbed into college life. I have no recollection where the baseball field was when I attended Chico. I never knew anyone who played or coached there. In most baseball respects, Chico State was as unfamiliar as any of the other schools featured in this book.

USC was a natural choice to include given the school's outstanding teams and players over decades of seasons. The Trojans may have had some recent sub-par seasons, by their standards, but one cannot ignore history. I linked the topic of recruiting to USC because not only do the Trojans have the disadvantage of dealing with expensive tuition costs with limited scholarship availability, but they have to compete with several other colleges in their Southern California backyard.

In parts, the USC campus is stunning. The Hall of Fame room within the baseball stadium is very impressive. My visit exceeded expectations.

The other California college I selected was Cal State Fullerton. Having attended a sister California State University, in Chico, I am amazed (and curious) how a school with a generally low profile intercollegiate athletic program — and no football team — can reach and maintain a level of national sports prominence in baseball. While the school has a nice but enlarged junior college feel to it, the baseball field is first rate. The topic of conditioning was assigned to Fullerton and it produced a serendipitous result. Besides the usual strength and conditioning coach and trainer, the Titans have regularly used sports psychologist and faculty member Ken Ravizza to enhance their mental game.

The University of Texas and the University of Miami were selected for basically the same reason as USC. When I think of college baseball, in general, one of these two schools most frequently comes to mind.

Texas was used for the topic of collegiate summer ball since its players are scattered throughout the United States during the summer, including the elite leagues in Cape Cod and Alaska. I couldn't have picked a better weekend to visit Austin. It was sunny, but not oppressively hot. The spring practice football game was played just prior to the baseball game. It was not just any baseball series, but the Longhorns were facing Big 12 rival Oklahoma. *Fervor* is the word that comes to mind when I think of Texas fans. It is as if 7,000 vocal, but civil, European soccer fans were transported to Disch-Falk Field. It was one of the most memorable college sporting events I have attended.

Miami was an appropriate choice for the topic of the major league draft since many of the Hurricane high school recruits and undergraduates are consistently selected each June. Miami provided me with my first experience of a game delayed by lightning. During the 2007 season, the renovations to the stadium were in progress but I could see that the improvements would only add to the prestige of one of the nation's best programs.

The other Division I program I chose was LSU. Since the fundamental question I had when I began work on this book centered on the relative popularity of college baseball, it is obvious to profile the Tigers and try to determine how they can continually draw such large crowds. The topic of fan support naturally fits with LSU. I saw games at what will be referred to as the "old" Alex Box Stadium (a new facility will open for the 2009 season). In that series, the team was playing at the end of a disappointing 2007 season, but the fans were still loyal.

I certainly didn't want to limit the colleges I profiled to Division I programs. Chico State, a two-time national champion (and, in 2006, a strike away from capturing a third), was an appropriate choice to cover some of the unique aspects of Division II schools. I used the topic of pitching with the Wildcats because they had returning second and third team All-Americans in starter Nick Bryant and closer Marcus Martinez.

Not only is Nettleton Stadium an impressive and unexpected find, the Chico State campus is an impressive and unexpected find in the northern part of California.

Of course, if one profiles Division I and Division II schools, it is only natural to select a Division III program as well. Eastern Connecticut State University was an appealing choice, not only because of its consistent success, but it also gave me a chance to explore cold weather baseball. Since Division III schools do not offer athletic scholarships, ECSU was a logical choice for exploring the topic of academic balance.

College baseball is not limited to schools governed by the NCAA. The NAIA (National Association of Intercollegiate Athletics) oversees a few hundred schools, generally with small enrollment. Lewis-Clark State College, in Lewistown, Idaho, is a fascinating study in success. Many readers may be unfamiliar with the school, but major league scouts are not. For the topic of coaching it was natural to focus on Warriors head coach Ed Cheff, who has been with the program for 32 years.

Lastly, no book on college baseball is complete without the inclusion of junior colleges. San Jacinto College in Houston, a historically outstanding junior college program, provides the perfect setting to discuss baseball at this level. Since the freshman year can be a big adjustment for hitters facing consistently better pitching than what they saw in high school, I picked the topic of hitting to explore with the Gators' coaches and players.

This book is the cumulation of multiple road trips that I took in the spring of 2007 and will never forget. I walked around college campuses I had never even seen pictures of, and I met some interesting and wonderfully cooperative people. I got to see some great college baseball.

Come on and join me; the first stop is in Los Angeles.

# 1

# University of Southern California Trojans

University of Southern California Trojans *vs.*
Arizona State University Sun Devils
March 23–25, 2007
RECRUITING
White Board Lists

*As USC takes batting practice, it is still two-plus hours before game time. While music blares from the speakers, Dave Lawn is doing something vital to the USC program. He's talking. Lawn is listed in the USC media guide as an assistant coach who "serves as the recruiting coordinator and pitching coach." It is probably not happenchance in which order those two roles are written.*

*He is speaking with a player's parent, part of a group he knows well. As much as a player tries to market himself to USC, Lawn markets USC to the player and his family. He is a "firm handshake, says what he thinks" type of guy.*

A USC baseball recruiter has one of the most challenging jobs in the United States, or, at least, in the greater Los Angeles area. Of course, it is not life or death challenging, just challenging. Competitors have little sympathy.

Young men who wish to play college baseball in the southern part of the state have choices. Within driving distance of the Tommy Trojan statue in the heart of the USC campus, there are several colleges that are or histori-cally have been very competitive in Division I baseball:

- UCLA, 16 miles away
- Loyola Marymount, 17 miles away
- Long Beach State, 24 miles away
- Pepperdine, 29 miles away
- Cal State Fullerton, 33 miles away
- UC Irvine, 44 miles away

- UC Riverside, 60 miles away
- University of San Diego, 123 miles away

In addition to these schools, Cal State L.A. is a good Division II program, and there are several quality junior college teams in the greater Los Angeles area. Although people in Texas and Florida might disagree, a good case can be made for declaring Southern California the capital of college baseball.

USC is located a few miles from downtown Los Angeles, in a tired but not necessarily gritty surrounding neighborhood. The campus is surrounded by a wrought iron fence that serves as much as security as an architectural enhancement. To the east is the 110 Freeway; to the south is Exposition Park. Adjoining the park to the south is the historic Los Angeles Coliseum, which is the home of USC football.

The campus is an impressive 225 acres, consisting of a combination of stately buildings and well-manicured grounds. From the past is the 1921 Bovard Administration Building and, in stark contrast, the distinctive 1964 von KleinSmid Center Tower a couple hundred feet away. In 2006, across the street from the northwest entrance, the Galen Center opened for athletic events and concerts.

*Friday night was not a cause for celebration for the USC men's sports program. In the semi-finals of the NCAA East Regional basketball tournament, the Trojans let a 16-point second-half lead slip away and lost to North Carolina, 74–64. Matching the 10-point defeat, the Trojans baseball team lost 10–0 to Arizona State University. Coming into this series, ASU is ranked 17th nationally, and USC is ranked 19th.*

*Although the sun came out again for the Trojans on Saturday, it was hidden by overcast for much of the morning. The lights are on at Dedeaux Field. The crowd is bigger than the evening before and dozens are seated on top of the roof of the baseball offices, which are set back from the USC dugout along the first base line. Today's crowd is more vocal, too.*

Dedeaux Field is named after the coach who led the Trojans to 11 of their 12 national titles (Mike Gillespie was head coach for the 1998 College World Series victory). Rod Dedeaux died in 2006 at the age of 91; he coached USC from 1942 through 1986, retiring at age 72. He is credited with 1,332 coaching wins at the university.

Just past the first entrance gate to the stadium is Mark McGwire Way. It may be only 40 yards or so long, but it is long enough to capture the glory of the USC program. Twelve maroon banners with yellow lettering hang on poles. Taller palm trees accompany the banners. On one side are the national championship years of 1958, 1963, 1970, 1971, 1973 and 1978. On the other side are the years 1948, 1961, 1968, 1972, 1974 and 1998.

Through the secondary gates, spectators walk up a slight incline to the pavilion, which is surrounded by pine and eucalyptus trees. On the walkway above the grandstand are support columns that have pictures of every current player and to which the overhang is affixed. The overhang, which shields some of the fans from the southern California sun, appears to have been designed by the same person who built structures in Disneyland's "Tomorrow Land."

Dedeaux Field is a comfortable, intimate setting that holds 2,500, featuring individual seats in the grandstand and separate bleachers with bench seating along the foul lines. The facility has been upgraded since it opened in 1974, and the stands and field have a clean, efficient and well-manicured look. A unique feature of the left field fence centers on ten sections that have an "open mesh" look, which shows off neatly planted red and yellow flowers, the school colors. The mound is light tan while the rest of the infield is chocolate brown dirt. Even the four-level parking garage beyond the right field fence is partially hidden by tall pine trees.

*There is a little competition for fan attention this afternoon. Adjoining the baseball field is Howard Jones Field, where the USC football team has an open spring practice. Despite the fact that this football squad has goals of a national championship, the attendance is moderate. There are no stands; spectators simply stand along the sidelines. At any particular time, only a few baseball attendees divert their attention to the football scrimmage.*

*USC pitcher Brad Boxberger starts by throwing three straight strikes to Brett Wallace, the last two of the called variety. One thing is clear — home plate umpire David Rogers is not going to have as tight a strike zone as Jim Garman, who had the duty last night. The first six Sun Devils hitters bat left-handed against the right-handed Boxberger. Eric Sogard follows with a walk before Tim Smith becomes the second strikeout victim, although only the umpire, Rogers, seems to know the count. With a 1–2 count to Ike Davis, Boxberger tries to pick off Sogard at first, but the throw and runner arrive at the base at the same time. The ball goes past first baseman Derek Perren into foul territory and Sogard advances to third. Davis is retired on a pop-up, and Boxberger's error does not hurt the Trojans.*

*Just as they did in the first inning as well as most of the game last night, the Trojans go down one-two-three. Last night they managed only six hits against Josh Satow in his complete-game victory. Satow, at 5'9" and 150 pounds, was hardly an imposing presence on the mound, but he frustrated the Trojan hitters from start to finish. Today it is Mike Leake who is attempting to keep USC off the bases.*

*Last night, five Starter Sport radar guns were aimed in unison at the pitchers by area scouts. Today only one scout, plus an ASU manager, is monitoring the pitch speed. Boxberger has another effective inning in the second, giving up only Kiel Roling's infield hit. Matt Cusick made a diving stop on the grounder up the middle, but he couldn't get enough on the throw to retire the slow running Roling, who was safe by a step. Andrew Romine is the third out when he becomes Boxberger's third strikeout of the game.*

*In the bottom of the inning, Robert Stock and Lucas Duda are quickly retired. Michael Torres, however, times a 1–0 pitch perfectly and hits it just over the fence in straightaway center field. Designated hitter Keith Castillo follows with a strikeout, but the score is 1–0. It's USC's first lead in the series.*

*In the top of the third it is Domino's Pizza's "loudest fan of the game" promotion. For most over the age of ten, it appears to be too much effort to do anything for the possibility of a free pizza. Besides, there are some respectable barbequed selections just in back of the pavilion. The sun finally comes out for good. Before each pitch, catcher Robert Stock looks at pitching coach Dave Lawn, sitting on a folding chair on the far, left-hand side of the dugout. Lawn goes through a series of similar motions each time (multiple touches of the hat and right arm) to convey the requested pitch.*

Lawn is the veteran of the USC staff. The 2007 season is his seventh year as an assistant with the Trojans. Head coach Chad Kreuter and assistants Bill Mosiello and Tim Burton are in their first year at USC. Kreuter became head coach when it was announced in June of 2006 that Mike Gillespie, the 20-year head coach at USC, was retiring. Kreuter is Gillespie's son-in-law.

Prior to coming to USC, Lawn was at Cal for 10 years where he was the pitching coach and recruiting coordinator. He held a similar position with the University of Nevada in Reno for two seasons prior to joining Cal. He has been recruiting college baseball players for almost 20 years.

Division I baseball programs like USC have 11.7 scholarships to use for a roster of 35 players. During conference games and the playoffs, the roster is reduced to 25. The 11.7 is a combined total, a cap, for all players on the team. The peculiar amount was derived in 1991 when the previous limit of 13 baseball scholarships was reduced by 10 percent. No school has to issue the full allotment of scholarships, but presumably all of the major and mid-major colleges do. Prior to 2008, the amount could be sliced and diced in any manner the coaches wanted.

A very good baseball scholarship offer is around 70 percent of the total "cost of attendance" (tuition, fees, books, room and board). A good offer resides in the 50 percent range. Historically, many players received only a fraction of the total cost and some players were given a minimal amount or "book money." It is possible for a player to receive academic financial aid that does not count against the 11.7 limit. In these instances, the academic award must be consistent with that provided to all students, and the athlete must be in the upper 10 percent of his high school graduating class, have a 3.5 or better grade point average, or have a very high SAT or ACT score.

One change the NCAA has mandated effective August 1, 2008, is that scholarship recipients must received at least 25 percent of the "cost of attendance" and a maximum of 27 players can receive baseball financial aid. Thus, no more symbolic "book money" scholarships can be provided.

For Lawn, the basic approach is rather simple in that they recruit what they need. The scholarships he has available in any given year are dependent on who leaves the program as a result of a transfer to another school, the major league draft, graduation, or simply quitting the team. Once an athletic scholarship is provided to a player, it is not guaranteed for each and every year.

A highly skilled catcher, a shortstop, and two to four pitchers are always on his recruiting priority list. He then looks for "the best 'something' to put 'somewhere.'" For example, even if the school doesn't particularly need a second baseman but the best hitter in the area happens to play that position, they will try to recruit him. He may play a different defensive position at USC. The truly prized players, invaluable in a private school program like USC, are those two-way stars who can pitch and hit. Three current Trojans— Robert Stock, Anthony Vasquez and Hector Rabago— have this unique talent.

Lawn sees a recruiting imbalance between public and private colleges that is a result of simple math. If two programs can only offer a 25 percent scholarship (for the private college that means 25 percent of $46,000 and for the public college that means 25 percent of $16,000), many families with a limited college budget may steer their son to the public college. With the latter, the student needs to fund $12,000 rather than $34,500 each year. For 2007, Lawn indicates that 22 of the USC roster players have little or no athletic financial aid.

Lawn contends that for every one premier recruit USC gets with a big percentage scholarship offer, an in-state public college may be able to recruit two good players. Thus, the roster depth at its rival regional public colleges is generally stronger. This also means that a public college can generally take more of a chance on a few players whose skills are still developing. USC generally selects those who appear to be ready to play at a high level immediately.

The imbalance also potentially applies to state-sponsored schools in different states. In states like Georgia (HOPE Scholarship Program) and Nevada

(Millennium Scholarship Program), broad-based academic tuition scholarships can free up portions of athletic scholarships for targeted players. Public schools in states without such programs may have to utilize more athletic scholarships to get the same caliber of player.

Occasionally, when the "do I or don't I" decision after the major league draft occurs, the Major League College Scholarship Plan is discussed. It is not automatic, but instead is a separately negotiated part of the overall agreement. In theory, it is a win-win for the draftee, but it is not necessarily that simple.

The scholarship amount is negotiable. Presumably somebody who wants a USC-level tuition (with tuition, fees and books at about $37,000, before accounting for room and board) for a few years might have to give up a little on the signing bonus. It also means the scholarship may not be available for somebody who would otherwise receive a nominal amount of a signing bonus.

While not a tremendous hurdle, college studies must begin within two years after a player's professional baseball career ends and must continue for two consecutive years, once started, or the scholarship will lapse. The greater hurdle for a former player who has been away from school for a few years comes in finding the motivation to go back to school.

*Wallace comes up after a Matt Hall ground out and Boxberger throws four straight balls. To the next batter, Boxberger finds the strike zone but Sogard likes the looks of it as well and he crushes it. Torres, in right field, barely needs to turn around; he knows the result is not in doubt. Just like that the score is 2–1. On the next pitch, Smith hits a hard grounder that barely eludes Cusick's glove. The last six pitches have not had a good result for the Trojans. Boxberger regroups to get a ground out and a strikeout to escape further damage.*

*USC has a quiet bottom of the third, hitting three consecutive ground ball outs.*

*Matt Spencer leads off the fourth with a line drive that just eludes Perren's glove at first and falls inside the right field foul line. Running hard all the way, Spencer makes it into third with a triple. Roling follows with a hard grounder just to the right of the third baseman, Hector Estrella, who is playing even with the bag. Even though he bobbles the ball momentarily, he is able to hold Spencer at third and throw Roling out. The latter's lack of speed helped the defense. With all of the infielders playing in, Andrew Romine hits a chopper to first. Perren instinctively thinks about throwing home, but he realizes there is probably not enough time and gets the unassisted sure out. ASU ends its at-bat with another run and a 3–1 lead.*

*In the bottom of the fourth, USC has another quick one-two-three inning.*

*For the dozen or so fans on the fourth level of the parking garage beyond the right field fence, there are just enough gaps between the trees to view the game. However, thus far, they have seen little Trojan offense.*

*Wallace leads off an inning for the second time; at 6'1" and 245 pounds, he does not look like a prototypical lead-off hitter. He is effective in the role, however. Wallace is retired on a grounder to second and Sogard follows with a fly out to left. Smith falls behind 0–2 after hitting a deep foul ball. The next pitch he pops up on the right side of the infield and Boxberger, Stock and Perren circle under it. Nobody takes control and the ball falls untouched for a gift single. On the first pitch to Davis, Smith takes off and steals second. To Boxberger's credit, he doesn't give in to the distractions of the past few minutes and gets Davis to fly to center for the third out.*

*USC is looking for a spark, a break to get their offense moving. Although Duda, leading off, falls behind 0–2, he manages to work a walk. A lead-off walk is often the start of something good. Torres looks to sacrifice, but his bunt is popped up and caught by Leake. Castillo gets the count in his favor, 2–0, before hitting a chopper to first base for an unassisted out. He remains in the vicinity of home plate, appealing to umpire David Rogers that he fouled the ball off his foot. He doesn't get the call and, while Duda advances to second, the hope that followed a leadoff walk is looking less promising. Sure enough, Estrella ends the inning with a ground out to short.*

*Boxberger returns the favor of a leadoff walk by giving designated hitter Petey Paramore a base on balls. The walk sends Hector Rabago to start warming up in the bullpen. Spencer is hit by a pitch, and Roling follows by showing his intent to bunt. He takes two straight balls and suddenly the game appears to be at a tipping point. He does lay down a bunt, and Boxberger's only play is to get the out at first. But the inning turns when Andrew Romine drops down a squeeze bunt that Boxberger scoops up and flips underhanded to Stock to get the out at home. Boxberger puts an exclamation point on the turn of events by striking out Matt Hall on three pitches. The 3–1 score is preserved.*

*ASU displays some defense of its own when Perren chops a ball over second base and Sogard goes far to his right, fields it, makes a jump throw to barely get the out. When Grant Green singles with two outs in the inning, it is only the team's second hit. However, he is stranded when Cusick grounds out for the third consecutive time.*

Grant Green is a shortstop out of Canyon High School in Anaheim. He is 6'3" and 180 pounds and *Baseball America* rated him as one of the top high school prospects eligible for the 2006 draft. He was aware that schools were interested in him in the spring of his sophomore year. NCAA rules restrict communication to high school athletes, but there is no restriction on communication initiated by the athlete. Letters or emails from a college can begin on September 1 at the start of a player's junior year. On July 1, between the junior and senior year, telephone calls initiated by the school are permitted. However, text messaging was banned on August 1, 2007, as it was considered an "intrusion" into a student's life.

At first, the challenge for Green was to not get caught up in the whole recruiting process and let it interfere with school or baseball. "The whole deal was kind of hectic at first," he admits. "You have all of those showcases you want to do well in, all of the coaches are there, and after awhile you get used to it. The hardest part for me was to keep playing my game instead of trying to do too much. Once you get used to it, it starts to get more fun." Eventually, he became accustomed to coaches and scouts watching his games, as well as to receiving letters and answering phone calls.

Besides USC, Green was interested in potentially attending UCLA or Long Beach State. The decision was a relatively quick one when USC made an offer in March of his junior year at the level his family had hoped. As with most highly regarded recruits, Green opted to commit at the early signing period in November of his senior year. By signing a national letter of intent, other schools were required to stop recruiting him. Even though the commitment was made well before he played his last season of high school baseball, USC was obligated to its offer and Green was obligated to attend USC if he wanted to receive a Division I college baseball scholarship. The exception could arise if and when the major league draft entered into the equation.

The San Diego Padres selected Green in the 14th round of the June 2006 draft. Teams were reasonably convinced that Green would go to USC, so the late selection made it a self-fulfilling prophecy. Otherwise, he may have been drafted as high as the second round. The only circumstance that may have changed Green's mind was if the Padres offered a signing bonus comparable to that of early-round draft picks.

That result was possible as Drew Rundle, for example, selected four spots ahead of Green, reportedly received a $500,000 bonus. Also, Green had some leverage with the Padres by having committed to a private college with a hefty tuition. His USC scholarship had significant value against which a bonus would be measured. The Padres did not offer a signing bonus that was substantial enough and Green and his family are content to wait until the 2009 draft.

There were a few factors that affected his decision to select USC. He concluded that there was a good chance he could get immediate playing time. He knew of some other local players who were committing to the Trojans and felt the nucleus of a potentially outstanding team was forming. He also was wowed by the prestige of the program and the school.

When Green committed in November of 2005, he was joined by Hank Conger, who gained some national notoriety in the 2000 Little League World Series, Brad Boxberger, who earned the 2006 *Los Angeles Times* Player of the Year award in his senior season, and D'Arby Myers, who had made a verbal commitment. When the following June came, the Los Angeles Angels selected Conger in the first round. He signed for a reported $1,350,000. The Philadelphia Phillies drafted Myers in the fourth round and he signed for a reported $250,000.

Another player who joined Green and Boxberger on the 2007 team was Robert Stock, the *Los Angeles Times* 2005 Player of the Year. He did not attend Agoura High School (northwest of Los Angeles) his senior year, but instead enrolled at USC as a 17-year-old and was red-shirted for the 2006 season. A month prior to his 16th birthday, Stock was named *Baseball America*'s Youth Player of the Year. In prior years, *Baseball America* also considered him the nation's best player at age 13 and 14. By joining other incoming freshman like Keith Castillo, Kevin Couture, and Hector Rabago, Green had every reason to believe that USC would be a quality team throughout his time there. *Baseball America* ranked it as the third-best recruiting class in the nation.

*After having some tense moments in the sixth, Boxberger is in complete control in the seventh. He strikes out the side.*

*Still looking for a spark, Stock leads off with a chopper that first baseman Wallace has to shift to his right to field, but it deflects off his glove into right field. Stock would likely have been safe even if the ball is fielded cleanly. Duda, who looks like he could play tight end for the USC football team still practicing on the adjoining field, rips a double into right. Sensing that every factor is important, Coach Kreuter pinch-runs Spencer Pabst for Duda. No one is out and the tying runs are on base.*

*Michael Torres then hits a hard grounder to Sogard at second. He throws home in plenty of time, with Roling blocking the plate. Roling is unable to catch the ball cleanly, and it rolls towards the backstop. Not only does Stock score, but the speedy Pabst scores without a throw. The game is tied. Torres is on second as the potential leading run. Torres advances to third on a ground out to second. Estrella then hits the third consecutive ground ball to Sogard and this time the runner, Torres, is out at home. After Perren singles to keep the rally going, Nick Buss strikes out on three pitches.*

*With Boxberger's superb inning and the awakening of the Trojan offense, things were looking good for USC.*

*Appearances can be fleeting. As Rabago and Nate Klein warm up in the bullpen, Davis leads off with a single to right. Paramore then fouls off his first bunt attempt, but he gets the next one down on the left side of the infield for a* successful sacrifice. Spencer follows with a fly out to right. Mike Torres sets up under the ball in anticipation of a throw, and makes a fine throw against Davis' tag up and run to third base. Estrella is a few feet away from the bag when he catches the ball; it would have been a close play if he was right on the bag as Torres' throw was that good. Roling then works a 3–2 count before hitting a ball that Estrella dives for but is just beyond his reach. Even if he does stop it, Davis is likely to score anyway given that he is running on contact. After spotting Romine three straight balls, Boxberger comes back with three consecutive called strikes for the third out. However, the Sun Devils have a precious one-run lead.

USC has its best hitters due up in the bottom of the eighth. Leake begins the inning by striking out Green. Cusick, who has had three routine ground outs in his previous at-bats, gets a single. Stock follows with a single that perfectly bisects the infield as it travels into center field. Lucas Duda normally holds the fifth spot in the batting order, but he was removed from the game during the previous inning for a pinch-runner. Pabst, the pinch-runner, played defensively in the top of the eighth. Kreuter decides to pinch-hit Anthony Vasquez for Pabst. ASU counters by bringing in Jason Jarvis.

Third base coach Bill Mosiello reminds Stock to watch Cusick, the runner in front of him, before advancing extra bases. He never gets the chance to do so. Vasquez hits a ball hard to the right of Sogard. The second baseman dives, fields the ball and flips it straight from his glove to shortstop Romine without using his throwing hand. Romine relays a throw to first and ASU turns a demoralizing double play.

Hector Rabago comes out to pitch the ninth inning. Boxberger has competed very well, throwing 147 pitches in the effort. The Sun Devils try to convert a hit batsman (Wallace) and a walk (Jarred Bogany) into a rally, but the half-inning ends on a very long and loud out when Davis flies out to deep right.

It is still a one-run game. Torres starts the inning against Jarvis with a ground out to the pitcher. Castillo keeps hopes alive with an opposite-field single to left. Hoping that little things will make a difference, Roberto Lopez is sent in as a pinch-runner. On the third pitch to Estrella, Lopez takes off running; it is a good decision as Estrella hits what would otherwise be a routine double-play grounder. With two outs, the potential tying run is on second. There is still hope. Perren is at-bat and he quickly falls behind 0–2. There is no dramatic ending this afternoon when Perren hits a routine fly to center to end the game. One senses that the gap between the 17th- and 19th-ranked teams is widening.

Despite all of the national championships and the long history of success, results have been atypical at USC over the past few years. After earning back-to-back PAC-10 championships in 2001 and 2002, the team was 28–28 in 2003 and 24–32 in 2004. However, 2005 was a good year when the Trojans reached the NCAA Super Regional tournament. In 2006, not only was the team 25–33, but the Trojans lost their last ten games of the season as well as 19 of their last 22.

While it may not be the only reason, one explanation does stand out as to why the Trojans have struggled at times in recent seasons: strength of schedule. According to Boyd Nation, who publishes strength-of-schedule ratings, USC has had the most difficult slate in the nation seven of the past nine years. They were rated as having the second-most difficult schedule in the other two years. Given the strength of the PAC-10 Conference and the typical non-conference opponents the Trojans face from the greater Southern California area, it makes sense that USC faces a formidable foe almost every game.

Regardless of the struggles in recent years, no school can match what a recruit will see when a USC coach welcomes him, leaves him in the hall of fame room adjoining the baseball offices, and tells him to wait for a few minutes. The room is six rows up from the first base dugout and has roof-top seating for special groups. Little of the interior space is left unused.

The national championship banners a recruit sees while walking towards the baseball offices are reinforced in this room, with the two cases holding the twelve trophies. Each of the interior support posts are wallpapered with the roster of the championship teams. The area between the windows and the ceiling shows a timeline of USC's baseball success. There are pictures on the wall that are a collage of the famous players who attended the school. On another wall are dozens of *Sports Illustrated* covers containing pictures of former Trojans. Most impressive are the simulated lockers that hold the uniforms of former players.

Several schools can boast of the major league talent they have produced. Even so, it isn't *this* type of talent. Mark Prior pitched in the 2003 All-Star Game. Bret Boone played in three All-Star Games. Dave Kingman hit 442 major league home runs. Barry Zito won the Cy Young Award in 2002. Fred Lynn was the 1975 American League MVP. Randy Johnson is a five-time Cy Young Award winner. Mark McGwire was the American League Rookie of the Year in 1987 and hit 583 home runs in his career. Tom Seaver was inducted into the National Baseball Hall of Fame in 1992 and won three Cy Young Awards. In total almost 100 former USC players have played in the major leagues.

The room is likely the most impressive 150 square feet of college baseball images an 18-year-old has ever seen.

*On Sunday, the game starts on a beautiful sunny day, but it doesn't begin well for USC. Brett Wallace, in his usual lead-off spot, is walked on five pitches.*

*With Sogard up, Wallace is picked off by USC starter Tommy Milone, but a balk is called. On the next pitch, Sogard drags a bunt on the right side of the infield. Milone comes off the mound to field the ball but nobody is covering first; there is no play. Perhaps sensing that the bunt is a good offensive weapon, Tim Smith also bunts. Once again, Milone fields the ball. He looks back at the runner on third, but by the time he throws to first, Smith beats it out. Bases loaded, nobody out.*

*Milone now faces Ike Davis. He gets ahead of the batter 0–2 before throwing three straight outside pitches. In Milone's defense, the fourth and fifth pitches are near-misses. The next pitch doesn't miss — Davis' bat, that is. He smashes the ball over the scoreboard in right-center field. Before the fans have finished their hot dogs, it's 4–0 with nobody out.*

*Milone settles down, yielding only an infield hit before retiring the Sun Devils. It took him 31 pitches to get out of the first and the first 17 were forgettable. Well, at least it is early in the game.*

*Brian Flores starts for the Sun Devils. Matt Cusick, who batted third on Saturday, is back hitting leadoff, as he did on Friday night. He grounds out, but Grant Green follows with a single. He is awarded second base with the second balk of the inning. Stock then hits a pitch down the right field line. Green scores easily, but Stock makes an ill-advised attempt to stretch a double into a triple. He is out by 10 feet on Sogard's relay throw to Matt Hall. The Trojans have recouped one of the runs and there are a lot of innings left to play.*

*Milone's second inning is in sharp contrast to the first. He needs just 13 pitches to retire the Sun Devils, with the only blemish a Wallace single to right. His ball was hit right at Roberto Lopez, who may have been momentarily fooled by the flight of the ball before he short-hopped it.*

*USC mirrors ASU's quiet second inning as Johnny Bowden is the only base runner, reaching first after being hit by a pitch. Bowden is starting at catcher today and Robert Stock is the designated hitter.*

Bowden is not a typical member of the USC roster. He is one of seven seniors on the team, five of whom receive regular playing time. He is one of five junior college transfers and one of five players with an out-of-state hometown. He is only one of two players who qualifies for all three categories. Bowden went to Thurston High School in Springfield, Oregon, which is located on the Willamette River more than 100 miles south of Portland. He came to USC by way of the University of Nebraska and Chandler-Gilbert Community College (located in a suburb southeast of Phoenix).

There was not much recruiting done of Oregon players except for the Pacific Northwest colleges. Bowden's fate changed dramatically after attending the week-long Stanford All-Star Baseball Camp in the summer between his junior and senior years. Soon after the camp ended, Nebraska, Northwestern, Georgetown, Boston College, Kansas and Centenary contacted him.

Bowden took his allotted three official visits to Boston College, Kansas and Nebraska. Even though he had a good experience with the Boston College and Kansas visits, he was seeking a College World Series-caliber program. "Then I went to Nebraska and I was just blown away," Bowden said. "Everything that they had was incredible. They had been to the College World Series the last two years; they were winning the Big 12; the facilities were incredible. That's what really drew me to Nebraska, the winning tradition."

He expected significant playing time during his freshman year at Nebraska, but things changed when catcher John Grose returned for his senior season after an injury in his junior year derailed Grose's major league draft hopes. That situation created a bit of a logjam at the catching position, and Bowden thought a change might be best for him. Grose discussed his experiences at Chandler-Gilbert with Bowden and the latter decided to transfer.

Since the junior college pool of players is much smaller than the high school pool, the opportunities for players like Bowden can expand. He participated in the one-day Sophomore Showcase at the Peoria Sports Complex (the spring training facility of the San Diego Padres and Seattle Mariners) in front of about 50 coaches and scouts. One of those was Dave Lawn, who later expressed USC's interest to Bowden.

During the first weekend in November, Bowden made an official visit to USC. He arrived on a Friday night, and on Saturday he watched the Trojans in a fall baseball workout, received a scholarship offer, and then took in a USC football game. Not a bad day.

He was actively recruited by about 15 Division I schools, but he committed to USC for the same reason he decided to attend Nebraska two years earlier: a winning tradition and a legitimate chance to go to the College World Series.

*The third inning is uneventful for Milone. Davis, who crushed the grand slam two innings earlier, hits a routine pop-up to short. He gives up a two-out single, but needs only 12 total pitches to record the three outs.*

*Flores' third inning is a little dicey. He gives up back-to-back one-out walks to Cusick and Green, yet follows that with back-to-back strikeouts of Stock and Darren Gambol, the number three and four hitters. The game has settled into a competitive contest, with ASU having the advantage.*

*Joe Persichina leads off the fourth as a pinch-hitter for third baseman Matt Hall and singles. Matt Spencer is then sent up to pinch-hit for Mike Leake, who was the winning pitcher in Saturday's game. Today he started in center field. Spencer pops up to short. Back to the top of the order, where Wallace follows* with a single. With Sogard up, Milone bluffs Persichina back to second. After falling behind 2–1 to Sogard, Milone spins quickly and picks off Persichina. Just when most thought the flow of the inning had changed, Sogard hits the next pitch over the right field fence. It is now a 6–1 game.

Perhaps the only fans unaffected by the score are the kids happy to have received the giveaway miniature USC bats and the twenty-plus members of the USC band. They are not in uniform, and they take up four rows in between home plate and the ASU dugout. They continue playing throughout the game, although they have been limited in their opportunities to play "Fight On." The tuba player frequently roams throughout the crowd.

Duda leads off the fourth by pulling a single to right field. Lopez lays a bunt down and beats it out. Bowden then strikes out, but Rabago hits a ball past a diving Persichina at third, down the left field line. Duda scores and Lopez reaches third on the double. After Pabst hits a line-drive out to Wallace at first, Cusick works a walk to load the bases. Perhaps hoping the element of surprise was in his favor, Flores tries to pick off Cusick leading off first. His throw is two feet over Wallace's head and rolls up the right field line. Lopez and Rabago score, and a good idea gone bad lets USC back into the game. Green ends the inning with a deep drive to center, but it is now only a two-run deficit.

Milone's afternoon is done and he makes way for Anthony Vasquez. Vasquez has the unenviable task of facing Ike Davis as his first hitter. Davis singles. Paramore follows with another single. Given the ebb and flow of this game, it appears the tide is moving again towards ASU. Vasquez battles Roling, finally freezing him with a perfect fastball on the inside corner. He then goes 3–0 on the next batter, Romine, who two pitches later hits the ball back up the middle, which Vasquez could have snared with slightly better reactions. The grounder is scooped up by Green at short, and his only play is to first. Davis scores ASU's seventh run of the game. Persichina hits a foul pop-up for the third out.

USC has a similar start to its end of the fifth inning when Stock leads off with a walk and Gemoll follows with a single. However, Stock stops at second on the hit, whereas Davis was able to advance to third in the top of the inning. Ted Aust is brought in to relieve for the starter Flores. When Duda follows with a grounder, it goes up the middle for a double play. Then, just like Persichina, Lopez hits a foul pop-up to first base to end the inning. Unlike the Sun Devils, the Trojans fail to score.

In the sixth, ASU continues the offensive pressure when Spencer leads off with a single. Wallace, who has reached first in each of his previous three at-bats, gets ahead 2–0 and then hits a shot towards the tennis courts beyond the left field fence that lands in the flower bed. Once again, it appears the Sun Devils are on the verge of putting the game away. Vasquez retires Sogard and Bogany, but gives up walks to Davis and Paramore. Kevin Couture is brought in to relieve

*Vasquez and walks Roling on a full count. With the bases loaded, all due to walks, the verge is now closer than ever. On the first pitch, Romine hits a slicing fly ball that Lopez finally catches up with in deep right field. The Trojans have allowed nine runs; it was very close to being 12.*

*Bowden leads off the bottom of the inning by grounding out. Rabago singles and Pabst works the count full until, on the eighth pitch, he singles to center. The center fielder, Bogany, fires the ball too late to third to get Rabago. Pabst tries to advance to second on the throw to third, and the third baseman, Persichina, throws quickly to second hoping to get the putout. Instead, the throw goes into right-center field. Rabago scores and Pabst moves up to third. Back to the top of the order, Cusick falls behind 1–2 when ASU decides to make a pitching change, bringing Parigi in for Aust. Parigi has a three-quarters delivery with a jerky motion that hides the ball well. Cusick strokes a single to right to score the second run of the inning.*

*With Green up and the count 2–2, he takes a very close pitch with Cusick running. The steal is successful. On the next pitch, Cusick is running again, and Green grounds a ball towards third, which almost hits the former. The runner seemingly distracts Persichina, who hurries a one-hop throw that Wallace cannot catch at first. Despite the flurry of action and the sloppy play, ASU stills leads, 9–6. But it is getting interesting again. It gets very interesting when Parigi walks Stock and Gemoll to load the bases and force in a run.*

*Duda comes up and is hoping for anything but a repeat of his double-play grounder from the prior inning. Instead he hits a shot to right-center field that clears the fence over the "Trojans SC" logo. No sooner has the ball landed before an euphoric rendition of "Fight On" comes from the band. Not only is it a grand slam, but improbably USC is now in the lead, 11–9. Parigi's nightmare inning is over after giving up five runs without retiring a batter. Jason Mitchell comes in and promptly walks Lopez. Bowden comes up for the second time in the inning, having made the only out so far by grounding to short. He hits a ball that bounces over the mound and just past the shortstop's glove. His single advances Lopez to third. Bowden then gets frozen on his lead from first and is picked off by the right-hander, giving him the dubious and unusual distinction of committing the first two outs of the inning. Rabago follows with his second single of the inning and drives home a run. Pabst finally ends the inning with a grounder to second that forces Rabago. The same "Tribute to Troy" or "Fight On" instrumentals that have haunted opposing defensive backs for decades must be ringing in the ears of the ASU pitching staff.*

*Eight runs on six hits, three walks, and two errors. USC now owns a 12–9 lead.*

*If there was ever a time in the history of college baseball that a pitcher sought a shut-down inning, this is it. However, given the way this game has gone, nobody is surprised when Persichina leads off with a double. He tags up and goes to third on Spencer's deep fly that Pabst catches in center. Wallace walks, which causes USC to bring in its designated hitter, Robert Stock, as the Trojans' fourth pitcher of the game. Sogard grounds out, but in doing so, the run scores. Pinch-hitter Ryan Sontag ends any further threat with a ground out to short.*

It is likely that every Division I program was familiar with Stock before he began attending USC. Few players have had his exposure.

There are a few different ways a player can get on the recruiting radar of the college of his choice. Exceptional players usually are known at least regionally, if not nationally, on the basis of outstanding high school and summer play. Some are noticed while participating in a college's winter or overnight summer baseball camp. Others receive valuable exposure when they play in showcases and competitive team tournaments.

While an occasional scout or high school coach may provide input, these are rarely an initial source of identifying potential players. "People think we have this network of moles," comments Lawn. "Ultimately we're making the decision based on what we see with our own eyes, 99 out of 100 times. We are not just seeing him for three days at a showcase. We've seen him play for his high school team, his summer league, his scout team. We've seen him. We have lots of information on him."

It may be surprising to some that the primary way USC finds out about a player who is not an elite national or regional recruit is through contact initiated by the player. This fits well with Lawn's philosophy that the first criterion in evaluating a recruit is his desire to attend USC. As the school's name would suggest, Lawn gets most of his talent from Southern California. On the 2006 roster, only five are from out-of-state and two hail from northern California.

In the fall, after the November early signing period has established most of the recruiting class for the following school year, Lawn maintains three lists on his white board. The first is a short list of recruits who have not committed but may be available should anyone from the November signing date change his plans. This most frequently happens when a player signs a letter of intent and becomes such a high draft choice seven months later that he opts to play professional baseball instead of attending college. This scenario occurred with Mike Moustakas in the 2007 draft and Hank Conger in the 2006 draft.

Lawn maintains a second list of about 35 players who are in their junior year. It is a list that will grow. The third list containing current sophomores has about ten names. The second and third lists are indicative of how college baseball recruiting has changed over the past ten years. Whereas the process was always about identifying, evaluating and monitoring high school prospects, it now is done simultaneously for three classes instead of just one.

With respect to showcases, there are several opportunities for the more skilled high school players to get greater exposure, but there is also an investment to make. There are dozens of showcases and tournaments that provide regional and even national exposure. Most have a cost ranging from a few hundred dollars to several hundred dollars to attend as well as travel and lodging.

The Area Code Baseball Games are one of the oldest and most prestigious showcases, having started in 1987. What was started by Bob Williams, who was acquainted with major league scouts, is now run by Student Sports. It has evolved into an event that draws representatives from every major league team as well as agents and about 100 college coaches. USC is a regular attendee. The one-week tournament is held in Southern California and is comprised of high school players from throughout the country who have been invited to try out and have successfully made a regional team.

Other showcases include Perfect Game USA, which coordinates about 40 showcases and tournaments throughout the year across the country. They partner with Sports America, Inc. to produce the AFLAC Classic, a nationally televised event. Grant Green and Hank Conger played in the 2005 game.

Team One. Baseball Factory. Eastern Professional Showcase. The Blue-Grey Classic. USA Baseball Junior National Team. With these events and many more, there is a lot of opportunity for the better players to get on a college's recruiting whiteboard.

*Given all of the action that occurred in the sixth inning, the Trojans were due for a quiet seventh. Matt Spencer, who entered the game in the fourth as a pinch-hitter and left fielder, comes in to pitch. Other than a one-out walk to Green, the eighth free pass the Sun Devils' staff has given, USC has a quiet inning.*

*Stock comes out to pitch the top of the eighth and faces every hitter from the stretch position. He starts his motion in a closed position, with his left foot further to the left (in the batter's eyes) than his right foot. After getting Davis on a deep fly to center, he walks Paramore on four pitches. Stock tries to pick off Paramore, but his throw is off-target and goes by Gemoll. Paramore advances to third. Two pitches later, Stock hits Rocky Laguna, who had come in as a defensive replacement for Roling in the seventh. Romine follows with a fly to center that is deep enough to score Paramore.*

*Raoul Torrez, who was another defensive replacement in the seventh (for Persichina at third base), takes a wild pitch that goes past Bowden behind the plate. He then hits a curving liner that lands just foul down the right field line. Stock walks Torrez, his pitches missing low as they have throughout much of the inning. Chad Kreuter visits the mound and leaves the freshman in. Stock gets ahead of Spencer, now the opposing pitcher, before finally getting him to fly to deep center. He walks confidently off the mound before Pabst makes the catch. USC hangs on to a tenuous 12–11 lead.*

*The Trojans knew almost no lead was safe in this game. With one out, Lopez hits an absolute shot that ricochets off Spencer's glove and reaches first safely. Bowden follows with a walk after falling behind early in the count. The 2–2 pitch is just off the inside corner, and many in the ASU dugout believe it should have been strike three. Spencer is missing high and falls behind Rabago before he hits a deep fly to right that is caught. Pabst walks on five pitches to load the bases, but Spencer comes back to get Cusick to fly out to center to end the eighth.*

*Stock goes back to his DH slot, and Paul Koss comes in to pitch, looking to earn the save. He has an immediate challenge in Brett Wallace, who is 3-for-3 with two walks. On the second pitch, Wallace hits a no-doubter to right center. Game tied. If there is any question that a psyche can be shattered, if even temporarily, Koss walks Sogard on four straight balls. He is missing high. Sontag lays down a successful bunt, and suddenly the go-ahead run is standing on second base. Koss shows his head is clearly in the moment when he runs to cover third after Rabago charged the bunt. The next batter, Davis, walks but Koss comes back to strike out Paramore on three pitches. Home plate umpire Kendall Snyder's call is slightly delayed, and Paramore retorts, "You haven't called that all day." Perhaps he is correct; he has been the Sun Devil catcher, watching pitches all day.*

*Laguna drills a solid single to right and, when Sogard crosses home, ASU has remarkably regained the lead, 13–12. A small but boisterous group of ASU fans are whopping it up along the third base line, while in the USC sections it is so quiet one can hear a hot dog wrapper drop. Romine strikes out for the third out, but a perfunctory "there's still hope" applause can be heard.*

*Jason Jarvis comes in as the seventh ASU pitcher. In a roller-coaster type of game, USC is back at the bottom of the lift hill. Green leads off and is called out on strikes. One pitch later Stock grounds out to the pitcher. The one person standing between an ASU sweep is Derek Perren, who entered the game defensively in the seventh and popped up to third in his only at-bat. He falls behind 0–2 before evening the count and then hitting a single right up the middle.*

*With a glimmer of hope still remaining, Nick Buss comes in as a pinch-runner. Will Chad Kreuter risk a steal attempt with two outs? Buss is not running on the first pitch, which Duda takes as a strike, or on the second pitch, which is taken for a ball. Duda swings at the next pitch and knows instantly he has* timed it perfectly on the sweet spot of the bat. The ball is crushed just to the right of the scoreboard in right field.

Before Duda can finish rounding the bases, the band begins a jubilant chorus of "Fight On." If anyone has classroom assignments due tomorrow, he could not care less right now. Instead, the fans got to witness one amazing college baseball game. Moments later, the band shifts into playing "Conquest" as the USC faithful savor every note. Final score: USC wins, 14–13.

---

### #17 ARIZONA STATE SUN DEVILS VS.
### #19 UNIVERSITY OF SOUTHERN CALIFORNIA TROJANS
### MARCH 24, 2007 AT LOS ANGELES, CALIFORNIA
### DEDEAUX FIELD

**Arizona State (21–7, 2–0 Pac-10)**

| Player | AB | R | H | RBI |
|---|---|---|---|---|
| Wallace, Brett 1b | 3 | 1 | 0 | 0 |
| Sogard, Eric 2b | 4 | 1 | 1 | 2 |
| Smith, Tim cf | 4 | 0 | 2 | 0 |
| Bogany, Jarred cf/lf | 0 | 0 | 0 | 0 |
| Davis, Ike rf | 5 | 1 | 1 | 0 |
| Sontag, Ryan lf | 0 | 0 | 0 | 0 |
| Paramore, Petey dh | 2 | 0 | 0 | 0 |
| Spencer, Matt lf | 3 | 1 | 1 | 0 |
| Laguna, Rocky cf/rf | 0 | 0 | 0 | 0 |
| Roling, Kiel c | 3 | 0 | 2 | 1 |
| Romine, Andrew ss | 4 | 0 | 0 | 1 |
| Hall, Matt 3b | 4 | 0 | 0 | 0 |
| Leake, Mike p | 0 | 0 | 0 | 0 |
| Jarvis, Jason p | 0 | 0 | 0 | 0 |
| **Totals** | **32** | **4** | **7** | **4** |

**USC (16–12, 0–2 Pac-10)**

| Player | AB | R | H | RBI |
|---|---|---|---|---|
| Buss, Nick cf | 4 | 0 | 0 | 0 |
| Green, Grant ss | 4 | 0 | 1 | 0 |
| Cusick, Matt 2b | 4 | 0 | 1 | 0 |
| Stock, Robert c | 4 | 1 | 2 | 0 |
| Duda, Lucas lf | 2 | 0 | 1 | 0 |
| Pabst, Spencer pr/lf | 0 | 1 | 0 | 0 |
| Vasquez, Anthony ph/rf | 1 | 0 | 0 | 0 |
| Torres, Michael rf/lf | 4 | 1 | 1 | 1 |
| Castillo, Keith dh | 4 | 0 | 1 | 0 |
| Lopez, Roberto pr | 0 | 0 | 0 | 0 |
| Estrella, Hector 3b | 4 | 0 | 0 | 0 |
| Perren, Derek 1b | 4 | 0 | 1 | 0 |
| Boxberger, Brad p | 0 | 0 | 0 | 0 |
| Rabago, Hector p | 0 | 0 | 0 | 0 |
| **Totals** | **35** | **3** | **8** | **1** |

**Score by Innings**

| | | | | | | | | | | | R | H | E |
|---|---|---|---|---|---|---|---|---|---|---|---|---|---|
| Arizona State | 0 | 0 | 2 | 1 | 0 | 0 | 0 | 1 | 0 | - | 4 | 7 | 1 |
| USC | 0 | 1 | 0 | 0 | 0 | 0 | 2 | 0 | 0 | - | 3 | 8 | 1 |

2B — Duda (4). 3B — Spencer (1). HR — Sogard (5); Torres (1).

| Arizona State | IP | H | R | ER | BB | SO |
|---|---|---|---|---|---|---|
| Leake, Mike | 7⅓ | 7 | 3 | 3 | 1 | 5 |
| Jarvis, Jason | 1⅔ | 1 | 0 | 0 | 0 | 0 |

| USC | IP | H | R | ER | BB | SO |
|---|---|---|---|---|---|---|
| Boxberger, Brad | 8 | 7 | 4 | 4 | 3 | 9 |
| Rabago, Hector | 1 | 0 | 0 | 0 | 1 | 0 |

Win — Leake (6–1). Loss — Boxberger (1–2). Save — Jarvis (1).

Start: 1:30. Time: 2:33. Attendance: 804

## #17 ARIZONA STATE SUN DEVILS VS.
## #19 UNIVERSITY OF SOUTHERN CALIFORNIA TROJANS
## MARCH 25, 2007 AT LOS ANGELES, CALIFORNIA
## DEDEAUX FIELD

### Arizona State (21–8, 2–1 Pac-10)

| Player | AB | R | H | RBI |
|---|---|---|---|---|
| Wallace, Brett 1b | 4 | 4 | 4 | 3 |
| Sogard, Eric 2b | 5 | 3 | 2 | 3 |
| Smith, Tim lf | 3 | 1 | 1 | 0 |
| Bogany, Jarred cf | 1 | 0 | 0 | 0 |
| Sontag, Ryan ph/lf | 1 | 0 | 0 | 0 |
| Davis, Ike rf | 4 | 2 | 2 | 4 |
| Jarvis, Jason p | 0 | 0 | 0 | 0 |
| Paramore, Petey c | 4 | 1 | 1 | 0 |
| Roling, Kiel dh | 3 | 0 | 2 | 0 |
| Laguna, Rocky cf | 1 | 0 | 1 | 1 |
| Romine, Andrew ss | 4 | 0 | 0 | 2 |
| Hall, Matt 3b | 1 | 0 | 0 | 0 |
| Persichina, Joe ph/3b | 3 | 1 | 2 | 0 |
| Torrez, Raoul 3b | 0 | 0 | 0 | 0 |
| Leake, Mike cf | 1 | 0 | 0 | 0 |
| Spencer, Matt ph/lf | 4 | 1 | 1 | 0 |
| Flores, Brian p | 0 | 0 | 0 | 0 |
| Aust, Ted p | 0 | 0 | 0 | 0 |
| Parigi, Joey p | 0 | 0 | 0 | 0 |
| Mitchell, Jason p | 0 | 0 | 0 | 0 |
| Bailey, Adam p | 0 | 0 | 0 | 0 |
| **Totals** | **39** | **13** | **16** | **13** |

### USC (17–12, 1–2 Pac-10)

| Player | AB | R | H | RBI |
|---|---|---|---|---|
| Cusick, Matt 2b | 4 | 1 | 1 | 1 |
| Green, Grant ss | 4 | 2 | 1 | 0 |
| Stock, Robert dh/p | 4 | 1 | 1 | 1 |
| Gemoll, Darren 1b | 3 | 1 | 1 | 1 |
| Perren, Derek 1b | 2 | 0 | 1 | 0 |
| Buss, Nick pr | 0 | 1 | 0 | 0 |
| Duda, Lucas lf | 6 | 3 | 3 | 6 |
| Lopez, Roberto rf | 4 | 2 | 2 | 0 |
| Bowden, Johnny c | 3 | 0 | 1 | 0 |
| Rabago, Hector 3b | 5 | 2 | 3 | 2 |
| Pabst, Spencer cf | 4 | 1 | 1 | 0 |
| Milone, Tommy p | 0 | 0 | 0 | 0 |
| Vasquez, Anthony p | 0 | 0 | 0 | 0 |
| Couture, Kevin p | 0 | 0 | 0 | 0 |
| Koss, Paul p | 0 | 0 | 0 | 0 |
| **Totals** | **39** | **14** | **15** | **11** |

### Score by Innings

| | | | | | | | | | | | R | H | E |
|---|---|---|---|---|---|---|---|---|---|---|---|---|---|
| Arizona State | 4 | 0 | 0 | 2 | 1 | 2 | 1 | 1 | 2 | - | 13 | 16 | 3 |
| USC | 1 | 0 | 0 | 3 | 0 | 8 | 0 | 0 | 2 | - | 14 | 15 | 1 |

2B — Persichina (3); Stock (4); Rabago (2). HR — Wallace 2 (10); Sogard (6); Davis, I. (4); Duda 2 (5). SF — Romine (1).

| Arizona State | IP | H | R | ER | BB | SO |
|---|---|---|---|---|---|---|
| Flores, Brian | 4 | 6 | 4 | 2 | 4 | 4 |
| Aust, Ted | 1⅓ | 2 | 2 | 2 | 0 | 0 |
| Parigi, Joey | 0 | 2 | 5 | 4 | 2 | 0 |
| Mitchell, Jason | 0 | 1 | 1 | 0 | 1 | 0 |
| Bailey, Adam | ⅔ | 1 | 0 | 0 | 0 | 0 |
| Spencer, Matt | 2 | 1 | 0 | 0 | 3 | 0 |
| Jarvis, Jason | ⅔ | 2 | 2 | 2 | 0 | 1 |

| USC | IP | H | R | ER | BB | SO |
|---|---|---|---|---|---|---|
| Milone, Tommy | 4 | 9 | 6 | 6 | 1 | 1 |
| Vasquez, Anthony | 1⅔ | 4 | 3 | 3 | 2 | 1 |
| Couture, Kevin | ⅔ | 1 | 1 | 1 | 2 | 0 |
| Stock, Robert | 1⅔ | 0 | 1 | 1 | 2 | 0 |
| Koss, Paul | 1 | 2 | 2 | 2 | 2 | 2 |

Win — Koss (2–1). Loss — Jarvis (0–1). Save — None.

Start: 1:00. Time: 3:51. Attendance: 848

# 2
# University of Texas Longhorns

University of Texas Longhorns *vs.*
University of Oklahoma Sooners
March 30–April 1, 2007
COLLEGIATE SUMMER BALL
The Eyes of Texas Are Upon You...

*Chais Fuller's baseball season began ten months earlier, in a city a mere 67-hour drive from Austin, Texas. He played for the Anchorage Bucs of the Alaska Baseball League. Tonight, Fuller isn't thinking about Alaska. His focus is on a state much closer, Oklahoma, and, in particular, its university. The Sooners are a major rival to the Longhorns in the Big 12 Conference.*

*Fuller has been recovering from nagging injuries. His return to the lineup has been delayed due to the solid play of his replacement, Josh Prince. Fuller is a senior and Prince is a freshman; such is the nature of competition. Although Fuller is not in the starting lineup for this Friday night game, he figures to be playing in some capacity in this series.*

*This is a big match-up for Texas. The Longhorns are ranked ninth nationally with a 23–8 overall record, while Oklahoma is ranked 17th with a record of 20–7.*

College baseball has four seasons.

If a 56-game regular season, a few conference championship games and possibly 14 NCAA tournament games weren't enough, structured participation in baseball goes well beyond the spring.

The NCAA limits playing baseball at a college to 132 days, including both the fall practices and the regular season's practices and games. In addition, the players' practice or game-playing time is limited to 20 hours a week, with a maximum of four hours a day, and at least one day off a week (a game counts as three hours, even though most players are at the ballpark for about seven).

In the fall, the team can practice within any 45-day period between September 1 and November 30. In order to stay within the 132-day rule, the team

27

will have approximately 30 practice days within that 45-day period. This expands the fall segment compared to years past. For example, Texas used to practice for about two weeks, from mid-to-late October, and concluded the segment with a two- or three-game Texas Fall World Series in which orange and white teams played each other in inter-squad scrimmages. With the expanded schedule, they added scrimmages against other colleges (Baylor and Texas State in the fall of 2007).

For the remaining portion of the fall leading to the start of the regular season, the players are focused on weight training, flexibility and conditioning. The "outside the playing season" rules restrict the training activities to eight hours per week.

The winter equinox in late December coincides with when the players leave for winter break. Of course, players who return home for a brief winter break continue to work out in their hometowns.

Prior to the 2008 season, most teams played their first games by the end of January or the first week in February. Starting in 2008, team practices cannot begin before January 15, and the first game cannot occur until "the Friday in February that is 13 weeks before the Friday immediately preceding Memorial Day." Although apparently written by the same attorneys that draft revisions to the Internal Revenue Code, what this means is that the first game will be in the latter part of February. This is approximately three weeks later than in 2007 and seasons before.

The rule change shrinks the 56-game season into a more compact period, which will likely mean more travel and more mid-week games prior to the conference contests. It will also likely place a greater premium on pitching and may help to add a little parity to colleges based in cold-weather climates. If a team is talented and fortunate enough to win the national championship, the season ends in late June, usually a month after school has ended.

That leaves the summer. Most players who are not injured or do not have lingering classroom issues participate on a summer team.

College players have more than 40 leagues to choose from. Collegiate summer leagues have flourished, particularly since the 1990s. Prior to then, the two most established and well-respected leagues were the Cape Cod Baseball League and the Alaska League. The Cape Cod League is still considered the premiere circuit, attracting much of the top talent in college baseball.

Aside from Alaska, the more notable leagues in the western United States include the California Collegiate League and the West Coast Collegiate Baseball League (Oregon, Washington and British Columbia). In the middle United States, there are the Northwoods League (Iowa, Minnesota, Michigan, Wisconsin and Ontario), the M.I.N.K. League (Missouri, Iowa, Nebraska and Kansas) and the Texas Collegiate League. Besides the Cape Cod League, on the East Coast there is the Cal Ripken, Sr. Collegiate Baseball League (Maryland and Virginia).

The choices for players are far more expansive than just these leagues. There are even opportunities to play in Hawaii and Canada. Also, a fortunate few are selected to play on the USA national team.

*If Texas did not have the traditional "old school" artificial turf, there is no way a game gets played this Friday night. It has rained heavily at times much of the day and only by mid-afternoon did the rain subside. At 6:07 P.M., Aljay Davis, leading off for the Sooners, sees seven pitches before stroking a solid single to right field. Davis is the quintessential lead-off hitter in that he can hit for a high average, draw walks and steal bases.*

*James Russell, the starter for the Longhorns, is well aware of Davis' running ability. He throws over to first three times before getting the number two hitter, Aaron Reza, to fly out to right. But before Russell strikes out Joe Dunigan for the second out, Davis steals second. Two pitches into Devin Shepherd's at-bat, Davis steal third. Shepherd flies out to end the inning, and Davis' efforts go unrewarded.*

*Texas mounts a similar threat in the bottom of the inning. Chance Wheeless is on first with two outs and goes towards third on Bradley Suttle's single to right. When right fielder Dunigan fires the ball to shortstop Reza, Wheeless is caught between second and third. Reza, holding the ball, runs at Wheeless toward third base, and then flips a throw to Bryant Hernandez covering the bag. Somehow, someway, Wheeless ducks under Hernandez' tag before even reaching the dirt cutout in the AstroTurf. Suttle advances to second during the rundown and Oklahoma is faced with one of those "what just happened here?" moments. However, the Sooners' starter, Stephen Porlier, gathers himself to get Kyle Russell, an All-American candidate, to pop up and end the inning.*

*After a one-two-three top of the second for Oklahoma, Texas starts the bottom of the inning with Russ Moldenhauer getting hit by the fourth pitch. He is quickly replaced as the runner at first when Preston Clark grounds into a force out with an unsuccessful sacrifice bunt attempt. Josh Prince follows with a first-pitch single, which lands just in front of Aaron Ivey in left and Joseph Hughes in center. Clark is running hard and makes it to third just in front of the tag. As the number nine hitter, Nick Peoples, comes up, most of the 4,000-plus in the crowd begin staccato clapping. It's spontaneous and loud. Peoples takes the count to 3–2 before popping up to first baseman Aaron Baker in foul territory. Could this be another futile threat, as in the first inning?*

*Travis Tucker gets hit by a pitch to load the bases for Chance Wheeless. On the first pitch, taking the Sooners by surprise, he lays a perfect bunt down the third base line. There is no play to be made, Texas takes a 1–0 lead, and the bases are still loaded. Within moments, thousands are yelling the chorus of the Texas fight song:*

> *Yea Orange! Yea White!*
> *Yea Longhorns! Fight! Fight! Fight!*
> *Texas Fight! Texas Fight,*
> *Yea Texas Fight!*
> *Texas Fight! Texas Fight,*
> *OU Sucks!*

*Just as quickly, the excitement dissipates when Jordan Danks takes three straight strikes for the third out.*

After Texas A&M, most Texas fans save their athletic disdain for Oklahoma. The teams are in the same league, but the rivalry predates decades before the current Big 12 Conference was formed for competition, starting in 1996. The Longhorns and Sooners were originally charter members of the now-defunct Southwest Conference and have engaged in a rivalry that is heading towards 100 years. They now compete in the Big 12, a conference that is a misnomer when it comes to baseball: neither Colorado nor Iowa State has baseball programs.

If a word association test was given to sports fans throughout the country, "Texas" might be the most common response to the phrase "college baseball." The notoriety stems from a winning tradition. Coming into the 2007 season, according to the *NCAA Baseball Records Book*, Texas has the highest winning percentage, at .740. Their 3,000-plus total wins are second only to Fordham University, but the Rams had a 36-year head start. To Texas' credit, the team has bounced back well from the disastrous 1–4 season in 1898.

In the "what have you done for me recently" category, the Longhorns have won the College World Series (CWS) twice in the current century (six times overall), and since the ESPN-CWS era began in 1980, they have been to the Omaha event 14 times. That results in viewers seeing and hearing about the burnt orange and white many times over the years. Head coach Augie Garrido has led Texas to the NCAA regionals in all but the first two of his ten seasons in Austin.

*Joseph Hughes leads off the third inning, falling behind quickly 0–2. He then looks at three straight balls before fouling off three pitches. The last two pitches have him fooled and he barely makes contact. He is not fooled on the ninth pitch of the at-bat and drives the ball deep over the left field fence. Score tied. Russell regroups and retires the next three batters in order.*

*Texas has had a lot of offensive action in the first two innings and Bradley*

*Suttle, leading off, continues the trend as he doubles just to the right of the Long-horn logo, below the 405 mark in right-center field. Kyle Russell follows with a single to right, but Suttle cautiously does not try to score as third base coach Tommy Harmon plays it safe with no outs. The designated hitter, Russell Mold-enhauer, walks to load the bases, which starts the recorded organ music and gives a willing audience of clappers another opportunity to make noise. Preston Clark grounds into a force out, and Suttle scores, but Oklahoma cannot get two out of it. The Sooners do, however, two pitches later when Prince grounds into a standard 6–4–3 double play. Just three innings have elapsed, 11 different Long-horns have been on base, but only two have scored. That's a lot of clapping with-out much to show for it.*

*After retiring the first two hitters in the top of the fourth, Russell falls behind Baker 3–0. He gets the perfunctory strike and then fools Baker with the next pitch. Baker checks his swing half-way and manages to bloop a hit into left field. It is the type of result an experienced pitcher like Russell can shrug off. The next bat-ter, Jackson Williams, falls behind 0–2 before hitting a ball along the third base line. It hits the bag and careens into left field. Williams winds up on second and Baker reaches third. An experienced pitcher like Russell can shrug that off as well. He goes right after Aaron Ivey and gets ahead 0–2 before Ivey hits a line drive that Russell instinctively reaches for, and deflects, with his bare hand. The ball falls harmlessly to the ground, but Russell has no play; the game is tied. Rus-sell lets everyone know that he is unharmed and then strikes out Joseph Hughes to end the inning.*

*After all of the action in the first three innings, Texas was due to have a relatively quiet inning. Porlier retires the side, allowing only Wheeless on base (for the third time) on a hit-by-pitch.*

*Russell's fifth inning is a pitcher's dream: three batters, nine pitches, three outs.*

*After Suttle leads off the bottom of the fifth by striking out, Russell crushes a pitch to deep center field. For those in the crowd asking, "Did you see that!?" it is not a rhetorical question — it's an exclamation. The clapping, chanting and music is brought back to life. For Russell it is his 17th home run of the season, which not only leads Division I hitters, but it is only one less than the rest of the Texas team has collectively. Porlier regroups to strike out Moldenhauer and retire Clark on a foul pop-up to the catcher, Williams.*

*As Joe Dunigan leads off the sixth, he looks not to his third base coach but directly to the dugout for signs. It is the routine for Oklahoma hitters. He singles and Russell is concerned about him stealing to move into scoring position. He throws over to first three times while Devin Shepherd is at-bat. Although Shep-herd strikes out swinging, Dunigan goes on the swing and steals second. Russell gets ahead of Baker 0–2, but he throws a wild pitch, allowing Dunigan to move to third. He strikes Baker out on the next pitch.*

*Despite Russell's nine-pitch fifth inning, he has thrown 102 pitches. With Williams, a right-handed batter, coming up, head coach Augie Garrido decides to pull the left-handed Russell and bring in Pat McCory. Russell gets a loud ovation as he leaves the field. McCory does his job but not without a scare, as Williams flies deep to center field to end the inning and strands Dunigan at third.*

*The bottom of the sixth is uneventful for the Longhorns. Nick Peoples singles and steals second with one out, but Tucker and Wheeless both fly out. Going into the seventh, Texas is holding onto a 3–2 lead, but it seems like its offense has produced more than that. Oklahoma is but a rally away from tying the score or going ahead.*

Peoples has started every game for Texas this season. He is a senior from Round Rock, which is only 20 miles from Austin. In fact, Dell (as in the computer company) Diamond is located in Round Rock and is the home for the Triple-A affiliate of the Houston Astros. It also was the home field for the Longhorns at the start of the season while renovations were made at UFCU Disch-Falk Field. ("UFCU" stands for University Federal Credit Union; "Disch" is Billy Disch and "Falk" is Bibb Falk, both former Longhorn baseball coaches. UFCU gets top billing, given its $13 million multi-year contribution.)

Peoples is a versatile player, having split time between third base and right field the prior season. This year he plays center field. Although he bats right-handed, he experimented with hitting left-handed during the summer.

For the past two summers, he played for the Santa Barbara Foresters. In between his freshman and sophomore years, he played for the Beatrice (Nebraska) Bruins in the M.I.N.K. League. After a player's freshman year, there are usually more options for a summer program choice. Assistant coach Tommy Harmon coordinates the summer teams for the Longhorn players. He gets calls as early as July from summer team managers seeking to set their rosters for the following summer. Harmon follows two basic rules in assisting players onto specific teams: (1) the player needs to be with a team in which he will have a chance to play; (2) the level of play must be appropriate for the player. For Harmon, there is a balance between challenging a player's skill and keeping a player's confidence intact.

Peoples, Chance Wheeless, reserve infielder Clay Van Hook, and pitcher Drew Bishop chose the fun and sun of the Southern California coast. The team uses the field at the University of California Santa Barbara. It is near the beach and, for many players, it is the best summer baseball weather they have experienced, featuring consistent sunshine after the morning fog, no rain, no humidity, temperatures in the seventies or low eighties, and gentle breezes.

The Foresters are part of the California Collegiate League, which is made up of seven teams either on the coast or close inland. The league formed in 1994, and teams in Santa Barbara and San Luis Obispo are original members.

Although Santa Barbara is stereotyped as a retirement community, the host families for most of the players are couples with younger children. As can be expected, it is a thrill for kids to have a Division I athlete living in their house for a couple of months.

Although Peoples did not pursue switch-hitting once the Longhorns' season started, summer programs provide an opportunity to refine skills or try new things. The environment is competitive but not as serious as they experience during the regular college season.

Peoples thinks wood bats, which are used in most summer leagues, require about a two-week adjustment from the aluminum models. He feels there is a "wood bat swing" and a "metal bat swing." "What I like about the wood bat is that you can really tell how your swing is just by how you hit the ball," Peoples said. "A lot of times with a metal bat you can't exactly tell how your swing is; you just have to judge how the ball takes off of it."

The Foresters' season started before Texas' season ended, and since Peoples was nursing a broken nose, he took a few weeks off before joining the team. He hit .320 in the 25 games he played, about half of the summer season. However, the Foresters' success provided Peoples with some additional games.

Summer baseball ends in mid–August with the National Baseball Congress (NBC) World Series. The tournament has its roots from the 1930s in which the participants were members of semi-pro teams, often made up of former professional players. The teams were sponsored by businesses in local towns. Over the years, the teams became increasingly stocked with current college players rather than ex-professionals.

Twenty-two leagues produce a combined 42 teams that funnel into Wichita, the home of the NBC World Series, via 17 regional tournaments. In the 2006 championship game, the Santa Barbara Foresters defeated the Derby Twins, a team from Wichita that plays in the Jayhawk Collegiate League in Kansas. In the 8–7 win, Peoples went 2-for-3 including a three-run homer.

Wichita is not the only site of a baseball championship in August. Huntsville, Texas, hosts the American Amateur Baseball Congress (AABC) Stan Musial World Series. The Stan Musial division is comprised of teams that have a mixture of college, junior college and ex-professional players. There is a limit of five ex-professional players per team.

*At this point in the game, the outfield is still a dark green due to the ear-*

*lier rains. The infield surface is a light green because it was covered with a tarp during the day. McCory's one-out walk to Joseph Hughes doesn't create a problem as Hernandez flies out and Hughes is officially out "caught stealing." The catcher, Clark, throws to first and Wheeless relays the throw to shortstop Prince, who applies the tag.*

*Porlier has pitched well enough for Oklahoma to keep the Sooners in the game. He has gotten into a rhythm since the third inning, and his only big mistake since then was the Russell home run. Danks, who has had a quiet game so far, hits a full-count single. He steals second and then advances to third as he runs on contact when Suttle grounds to the shortstop. Hernandez is now splitting his attention between Danks at third and Russell at the plate. A classic manufactured run materializes when Hernandez flinches during his motion and Harmon, the third base coach, and the home plate umpire, Randy Wetzel, spot the balk simultaneously. The run appears all the more fortuitous once Russell strikes out and Moldenhauer grounds out to third.*

*After the disruption Aljay Davis caused as the first batter of the game, he has not been an offensive factor since. He grounds out to begin the inning. Reza singles to left field before McCrory starts out the number three hitter, Dunigan, with a ball. With Dunigan being a left-handed hitter, Coach Garrido calls on Keith Shinaberry to likely face just this one batter. The Texas squad is predictably loaded with Texas citizens, but Shinaberry is the only Austin native.*

*Once Shinaberry takes his sign, he bends over almost 90 degrees before he begins his delivery. He looks like he either just got punched in the stomach or his hamstrings need to be stretched right then and there. The stance is unusual and deceptive. Dunigan fouls off two of Shinaberry's pitches and then misses the third. It's a nice three-pitch outing for the hometown boy.*

*With two outs and a runner on first, the Longhorns go with their closer, Randy Boone. He owns all seven Texas saves but also has an 0–5 record and a 4.18 earned run average. His 26:5 strikeout-to-walk ratio is very good, but he has also allowed 36 hits in 32 innings. He jumps ahead on the designated hitter, Shepherd, 0–2, but then bounces a wild pitch that allows Reza to move up to second. Shepherd singles to right and Reza scores. Boone gets Baker to ground to first for the third out.*

Boone is an established senior on the team. In 2005, a national championship year for the Longhorns, Boone pitched in five post-season games. He has experience both as a starter and a reliever.

Boone was a standout three-sport athlete (baseball, football, basketball) for Yoakum High, located in the small town east of San Antonio in which many of the residents are employed in leather manufacturing.

With Boone's athleticism and size (6'3", 210 pounds), it figures that he will get some serious attention along with a few of his teammates when the major league draft occurs in early June. His fastball can reach the low 90s and he supplements it with a slider. He focused on improving the slider when he arrived to play last summer for the Coppell Copperheads in the Texas Collegiate League. Coppell is a suburb northwest of Dallas. The prior two summers he pitched for the Hyannis Mets in the Cape Cod League.

While the experienced Boone was looking to fine-tune one pitch over the summer, Hunter Harris had very different goals. Having red-shirted the 2006 season, Harris was looking to get some innings, build confidence and continue to improve all of his pitches. It worked. Playing for the Youse Orioles, Harris earned pitcher of the year honors for the Cal Ripken, Sr. Collegiate Summer League.

Given the competitive nature of the summer leagues, pitchers are expected to be effective, but they can still work on improving mechanics or specific pitches. "Usually your pitching coach will come up to you in the first couple of days you are there," says Boone, "and ask and make sure you are on the same page with everything. He'll ask, 'Is there one thing you want me to keep an eye on or help you with?' You build on that relationship for the rest of the summer."

Boone was very effective for Coppell, going 6–0 with an ERA of 1.13 while being used exclusively as a starter. He was named the Texas Collegiate League Pitcher of the Year. Although the Cape Cod League in prior years gave him the opportunity to meet new people, broaden his horizons and trade baseball ideas, he liked being closer to home in his final collegiate summer baseball season.

*Nich Conaway relieves Porlier to begin the bottom of the eighth. He retires Clark, Prince, and Peoples in order to keep it a one-run game.*

*Boone comes out for the ninth and does what closers do: a ground out and two strikeouts. Game over. Cue the Texas fight song music and have "The Eyes of Texas" ready after that. For the Texas fans, it is nice that the rain cleared.*

*Saturday's game is in marked contrast to Friday night's game. The sun is shining brightly. The damp stains on the outfield turf have still not completely evaporated, but they fade with each passing minute.*

*There is a lot of activity near the eastern side of the campus and Interstate 35. Today is the spring football intersquad scrimmage that will draw more than 30,000 to Texas Memorial Stadium. More than a few of these fans will first get a pre-season taste of football and wash it down with baseball.*

*Most of the pre-game activity is the same as what occurs in college parks throughout the country. The home team takes the field three hours before game time and completes a mixture of warm-up calisthenics, defensive drills and batting practice. Once the home team is finished, they pack up the dozens of base-*

*balls scattered around and vacate the field so that the visiting team can go through the same routine.*

*There is one piece of equipment at Disch-Falk Field that is different. It is the zamboni-like vehicle that vacuums up the dirt that has inadvertently spread on top of the artificial turf. Light green AstroTurf completely covers the playing surface except for the pitcher's mound, batter's area, warning track and each of the bases. From the stands, it is not readily apparent if the Tennant 6400 Rider Sweeper effectively completes its assigned task as dirt still seems to have discolored the edges of the turf.*

Even baseball purists, who want nothing less than Kentucky Bluegrass on the infield and outfield, can find things to like about the setting at Disch-Falk. An overhang covers much of the grandstand with stadium seats, and provides welcomed shade. The stadium is undergoing several improvements and, when finished, will have the overall look of a very good minor league park. Fans can find nearby parking and the adjoining lots are ample enough to accommodate numerous tailgaters. Five rooftop buses provide unique seating for dozens of generally rowdy spectators on Comal Street, not far from the right field fence. Most of all, it is the passion of the fans and their numbers that provide a great college baseball experience.

With an enrollment of just under 50,000, Texas is among the five largest universities in the United States. To walk to the main campus from Disch-Falk, one heads east under Interstate 35 and quickly approaches Memorial Stadium. One of the most lasting images of the Austin campus is how huge the Memorial Stadium scoreboard is. Perhaps it was originally designed to be the size of a football field and then was scaled back ever so slightly.

Heading further east, the central part of campus becomes hillier and includes the Tower. University literature does not attempt to hide the building's infamous past of the Charles Whitman shootings (16 killed, 30 injured) some 40 years ago. When the Longhorns won the 2005 College World Series, the Tower was lit up burnt orange. Many of the nearby buildings are built of limestone and have a stately "government issued" architectural style. It's a large campus, impressive overall.

*Adrian Alaniz gets the start for the Longhorns. He is 7–1 with an earned run average of 1.89 in his seven starts and two relief appearances. He is a veteran on the staff, having pitched in the College World Series in 2005. Oklahoma has made a few changes to its lineup, but the first five hitters are the same as the night before; only Baker and Shepherd have been flipped-flopped in the order.*

*For Texas, designated hitter Chais Fuller is back in the lineup for the first time in almost a month. Josh Prince continues to start at shortstop, one ahead of Fuller in the batting order.*

Fuller is an atypical Longhorn. He was born and raised in Fairfield, in between San Francisco and Sacramento, and was home-schooled until he attended Fairfield High. That makes Fuller, along with freshmen Josh Prince and Michael Demperio, the only three non–Texans on the roster.

Although he was recruited by Miami and Oklahoma, "everything felt right" during his visit to Austin, and he was understandably impressed with the game atmosphere at Disch-Falk. He came from Sacramento City College and was the starting shortstop for the Longhorns in the prior season.

His goal for the summer prior to his senior season was to develop hitting skills, particularly on the mental approach to hitting. He wanted to gain more confidence in his at-bats, "not going up there thinking too much, not worrying about anything at that time."

He had his opportunity to work on that approach with the Anchorage Bucs of the Alaska Baseball League. In the small world of college baseball, the Bucs coach was Mike Garcia, who was a member of the Augie Garrido-coached 1979 national championship team at Cal State Fullerton. When Garrido met up with Garcia at a baseball meeting and the latter indicated he needed a middle infielder, Fuller became the solution. But Fuller was apprehensive of what he would experience in Alaska.

"When I first got the letter from Coach Harmon, I didn't know what to expect," Fuller said. "Alaska, you're thinking it's probably freezing there, terrible. When I got up there it was the complete opposite. There's great baseball. There's a lot a great competitive baseball players up there, great league. You're traveling everywhere, all over Alaska, anywhere from two hours to about eight hours on a bus and you are going from 'this' side all the way over to 'this' side. It was a great chance to play baseball and have the good outlook of scenery."

Fuller roomed with a catcher from Rice, Adam Zornes, in a spacious basement of the host family. His neighbors included bears and moose. He got a job cleaning his baseball home, Mulcahy Stadium, to earn a little spending money.

His playing 40 games for the Bucs was not the end of summer baseball. The Bucs lost their final game to the Kenai Oilers, 1–0. The next day Fuller received a call from the Havasu Heat, an aptly named team playing its summer ball in western Arizona. A Bucs teammate who played for the Heat the previous year passed along Fuller's name to the Heat's coach.

The Heat needed a reserve infielder as they headed for Wichita and the National Baseball Congress World Series. When the starting second baseman was unable to play, Fuller unexpectedly took over that role and played for another two weeks. The 42-team tournament necessitates "on call" baseball. With weather and time delays, games were shifted. Fuller recalls once that a

10 P.M. scheduled start did not begin until 1:30 A.M. He learned to sleep in his uniform so that he could get to the park quickly.

Fuller felt his baseball summer came to a successful close when the mental hitting focus he was striving to achieve came together in Wichita.

*Alaniz gets through the first inning unscathed. The only unusual play occurs when catcher Preston Clark's mitt nicks Joe Dunigan's bat when he swings. The rule allows the batter to either be awarded first base automatically or accept the result of the play. Since Dunigan fouled the ball, he opts for the former. Clark is charged with catcher interference and an error.*

*In the bottom of the inning against starter Heath Taylor, the Longhorns manage just a Chance Wheeless single. The hit is almost an excellent defensive play as, after the ball glances off diving first baseman Aaron Baker's glove, second baseman Aljay Davis suddenly changes direction to field the ball and tosses to a hustling Taylor covering first. Close, but not quite.*

*An underrated skill that is apparent even in the first inning is how the Texas student managers know how to position themselves just right when balls fouled straight back hit the backward angled protective screen. The ball rolls down the screen, falls to the artificial surface and bounces once into the hands of the manager. They make it look effortless.*

*The next four innings feature consistent action: Oklahoma's first three batters are retired; Texas gets two runners on but cannot score.*

*Joseph Hughes did manage an infield single for the Sooners in the third. However, he is picked off first when Preston Clark throws behind him, with Wheeless applying the tag. During this stretch, the Texas defense is very effective, although not necessarily elegant. Devin Shepherd hits a deep drive to start the fifth. Russell circles under the ball at the warning track, battles the sun, stumbles, catches the ball and lands face down to end the play.*

*The Longhorns have three consecutive two-out rallies in the second through fourth innings. In the fifth, they get their first base runner of the inning with one out, but the result is the same.*

*In the sixth, Alaniz allows his first lead-off runner when Jarod Freeman singles to left. He is stranded at first. Alaniz retires the three, four and five hitters in the seventh to earn the compliment of "a great game so far." To illustrate what good stuff he has, Shepherd completely turns away from the first pitch he sees only to have it called a strike. Alaniz has given up no runs, allowed but two singles, has walked nobody, and has not allowed a runner to reach second base.*

*By contrast, Heath Taylor is pitching a shutout despite having allowed nine base runners. The game has a feeling similar to the one on Friday night — Texas has had its opportunities, but they haven't scored much.*

*The bottom of the seventh has an uneventful start when both Travis Tucker*

*and Chance Wheeless ground out. Jordan Danks, who manufactured the win-*
*ning run the previous night, singles up the middle and then steals second. Bradley*
*Suttle follows with a single but the left fielder, Dunigan, charges the ball aggres-*
*sively and makes a strong throw to home. The ball is ever so slightly high and*
*to the third base side of home, which allows Danks to slide under Jackson*
*Williams' tag. On the throw, Suttle goes to second.*

The previous summer, Suttle received a call from the general manager
of the Wareham Gateman in the Cape Cod League with an invitation to join
the team. Suttle's decision was an easy one because he wanted to play against
the best competition. He felt he learned a lot by being exposed to different
philosophies of hitting while playing for the Gateman.

Suttle concluded that the quality of summer pitching was probably a little better than the overall pitching he faced during the Longhorns' regular season. "Up in the Cape every starter is a Friday or Saturday starter at a really
good school," Suttle said. "They have some guys who go to D II's [Division
II colleges] or smaller schools, but they're really good pitchers. You are facing really good pitching every single night."

Not only was the pitching consistently challenging, but so was hitting
with a wood bat. Although he used the same approach to hitting as he did
with an aluminum bat, he found the wood bat a little heavier with a smaller
sweet spot. Given the challenges of hitting, offensive strategies in the Cape
steered away from hoping for home runs and playing for the big inning.

Baseball at the Cape is a serious endeavor. "It is a really busy summer,"
says Suttle. "It's not a 'go up to the Cape, have nights off, play a little bit of
baseball and have a lot of fun.' My typical day was to wake up at 8 o'clock,
eat breakfast and you'd go work up at the Cape, whether it be at the grocery
store or at the field. I worked the camps with the kids around the area. You
work from 9 to 12, you'd go eat lunch and you come back to the ballpark at
2 o'clock and take BP (batting practice). You would then start getting ready
for the game, and the games don't get over until 10 o'clock. By then you are
dead tired and you go straight to bed. It's not an easy, relaxing summer."

*Oklahoma coach Sunny Galloway decides to intentionally walk the nation's*
*leading home run hitter, Kyle Russell, to take his chances with Preston Clark*
*with two outs. The strategy does not work as Clark doubles down the left field*
*line, driving in both runners. Reza's relay throw home is too late to get Russell.*
*Finally, the key two-out hit happens. It's time for a chorus of "Deep in the Heart*
*of Texas."*

*With the three runs and the manner in which Alaniz is throwing, things*
*are looking good for Texas. The Sooners' designated hitter, Mike Gosse, leads off*

*the eighth. He hits a routine deep fly that Russell once again has difficulty see-*
*ing. The ball goes over his glove and bounces to the wall. Gosse makes it all the*
*way to third; maybe this isn't going to be easy for the Longhorns. The next hit-*
*ter, Jackson Williams, pops a foul ball beyond the Oklahoma first-base dugout.*
*Wheeless, Tucker and Russell all sprint from their first, second and right field*
*positions, respectively. Tucker dives and makes the catch. He has the presence of*
*mind to immediately jump up in case the runner from third decides to tag and*
*tries to score. Gosse didn't.*

At the end of the Longhorn's previous regular season, nobody could have foreseen the starting second baseman would be Travis Tucker.

Tucker finished his first season of college baseball at McLennan Community College in Waco, Texas. Waco is about an hour's drive from Tucker's hometown of Killeen; both are south of Dallas. He had a very good year, hitting .382 and earning an all-conference first-team selection.

Early in the season at McLennan, Tucker wanted to finalize his plans for the summer. When the plans stagnated, he decided to seek the help of his cousin and his high school baseball coach, both Texas alumni. The latter was able to arrange a contact with the Beatrice Bruins' head coach, who informed Tucker that he had a roster spot available for an infielder. The Bruins are in the M.I.N.K. League, and Beatrice is a small town about 40 miles south of Lincoln, Nebraska.

Unlike some summer teams that use college or well-maintained municipal stadiums, Christenson Field, the Bruins' home, is more modest. It is home to two other youth baseball leagues in Beatrice and has an honest, no-frills look to it. About 15 to 20 spectators attended the weekday games; that number tripled for the weekends. It is safe to say that the ground balls did not have the consistent true hop that infielders expect at Disch-Falk.

During the summer he had a team-high 46 runs and 22 stolen bases. Besides focusing on hitting the ball harder (by hitting the sweet spot) and with more confidence, Tucker learned some of the nuances of infield defense. "It was a real good learning experience," said Tucker. "I learned to read hitters. If they're open (in their stance) when they hit the ball, they're going to pull the ball a little more; if they're closed they're going to try to fight the ball off, hit the ball the other way. I've learned how to read where the pitch is. If the pitch is called for outside, I learned to cheat a little 'over there' because that's where the ball is going to go. That has helped me out tremendously coming into this year."

His most memorable road trip was up to Alaska where, unbeknownst to him, he watched and played against his future teammate — Chais Fuller with the Anchorage Bucs. He also played in the Midnight Sun Game in front of a few thousand fans with a 10:30 P.M. start.

Most of Tucker's generation has a stressful preoccupation about the college admission process. For him, things fell into place like a routine single. He was convinced that he was headed back to McLennan for his sophomore year. "I didn't realize I was going to Texas until the end of the summer, until about three or four weeks before the fall (semester) started," Tucker said. "Coach Harmon flew up to Beatrice and was just checking in on Shinaberry and Danks and just saw me out there playing. Coach Harmon ended up calling me the next day."

After a spirited competition with Michael Demperio for the second base job in the fall, Tucker earned the spot and started the first game of the season. He has started every game since leading up to the series with Oklahoma.

*The next batter, Jarod Freeman, grounds to short to score Gosse. Alaniz then strikes out Hughes to end the inning.*

*Garrett Richards replaces Taylor on the mound and proceeds to sandwich three walks around two outs. The Sooners make a pitching change and bring in Nich Conaway, who has the unenviable task of facing the number three hitter, Bradley Suttle, and his .432 average. He is up to the challenge as Suttle falls behind 0–2 before popping up to center field.*

*Alaniz takes the 3–1 lead into the ninth. Coming into today, he is the only Texas starter with a complete game. The first pitch of the ninth is a searing line drive right back at Alaniz. He instinctively puts his glove up, doesn't quite catch it, but the ball lands close enough for the putout. The next hitter, Reza, also hits the ball right back at Alaniz. Alaniz easily fields the grounder for his second putout of the inning. Dunigan then follows with a deep fly out to center and 2 ½ hours after he started the game, Alaniz completes a three-hitter against his conference rivals.*

*Within minutes, the Texas team faces the stands and joins the crowd in singing "The Eyes of Texas." There is no mistaking the genuine reverence afforded the song. As the final lyrics, "...the eyes of Texas are upon you, 'til Gabriel blows his horn" drift into the Austin air, the mingling players in the visitors dugout cannot help but be impressed and slightly intimidated by the atmosphere. After all, this isn't summer ball.*

## #17 UNIVERSITY OF OKLAHOMA SOONERS VS.
## #9 UNIVERSITY OF TEXAS LONGHORNS
## MARCH 30, 2007 AT AUSTIN, TEXAS
## UFCU DISCH-FALK FIELD

### Oklahoma (20–8, 2–2 Big 12)    Texas (24–8, 6–1 Big 12)

| Player | AB | R | H | RBI | Player | AB | R | H | RBI |
|---|---|---|---|---|---|---|---|---|---|
| Davis, Aljay 2b | 4 | 0 | 1 | 0 | Tucker, Travis 2b | 3 | 0 | 0 | 0 |
| Reza, Aaron ss | 4 | 1 | 1 | 0 | Wheeless, Chance 1b | 3 | 0 | 2 | 1 |
| Dunigan, Joe rf | 4 | 0 | 1 | 0 | Danks, Jordan lf | 4 | 1 | 1 | 0 |
| Shepherd, Devin dh | 4 | 0 | 1 | 1 | Suttle, Bradley 3b | 4 | 1 | 2 | 0 |
| Baker, Aaron 1b | 4 | 1 | 1 | 0 | Russell, Kyle rf | 4 | 1 | 2 | 1 |
| Williams, Jackson c | 4 | 0 | 1 | 0 | Moldenhauer, Russell dh | 2 | 0 | 0 | 0 |
| Ivey, Aaron lf | 2 | 0 | 1 | 1 | Clark, Preston c | 4 | 1 | 0 | 1 |
| Williamson, Cory ph/lf | 2 | 0 | 0 | 0 | Prince, Josh ss | 4 | 0 | 1 | 0 |
| Hughes, Joseph cf | 3 | 1 | 1 | 1 | Peoples, Nick cf | 4 | 0 | 1 | 0 |
| Hernandez, Bryant 3b | 2 | 0 | 0 | 0 | Russell, James p | 0 | 0 | 0 | 0 |
| Gosse, Mike ph | 1 | 0 | 0 | 0 | McCrory, Pat p | 0 | 0 | 0 | 0 |
| Biancamano, V. 3b | 0 | 0 | 0 | 0 | Shinaberry, Keith p | 0 | 0 | 0 | 0 |
| Porlier, Stephen p | 0 | 0 | 0 | 0 | Boone, Randy p | 0 | 0 | 0 | 0 |
| Conaway, Nich p | 0 | 0 | 0 | 0 | | | | | |
| Totals | 34 | 3 | 8 | 3 | Totals | 32 | 4 | 9 | 3 |

### Score by Innings

| | | | | | | | | | | | R | H | E |
|---|---|---|---|---|---|---|---|---|---|---|---|---|---|
| Oklahoma | 0 | 0 | 1 | 1 | 0 | 0 | 0 | 1 | 0 | - | 3 | 8 | 0 |
| Texas | 0 | 1 | 1 | 0 | 1 | 0 | 1 | 0 | X | - | 4 | 9 | 0 |

2B — Williams (8); Suttle (10). HR — Hughes (1); Russell (17).

| Oklahoma | IP | H | R | ER | BB | SO |
|---|---|---|---|---|---|---|
| Porlier, Stephen | 7 | 9 | 4 | 4 | 1 | 4 |
| Conaway, Nich | 1 | 0 | 0 | 0 | 0 | 2 |

| Texas | IP | H | R | ER | BB | SO |
|---|---|---|---|---|---|---|
| Russell, James | 5⅔ | 6 | 2 | 2 | 0 | 7 |
| McCrory, Pat | 1⅔ | 1 | 1 | 1 | 1 | 1 |
| Shinaberry, Keith | ⅓ | 0 | 0 | 0 | 0 | 1 |
| Boone, Randy | 1 | 1 | 0 | 0 | 0 | 2 |

Win — Russell (6–2). Loss— Porlier (4–2). Save — Boone (8).

Start: 6:08. Time: 2:57. Attendance: 4,681

## #17 UNIVERSITY OF OKLAHOMA SOONERS VS.
## #9 UNIVERSITY OF TEXAS LONGHORNS
## MARCH 31, 2007 AT AUSTIN, TEXAS
## UFCU DISCH-FALK FIELD

Oklahoma (20–9, 2–3 Big 12)      Texas (25–8, 7–1 Big 12)

| Player | AB | R | H | RBI | Player | AB | R | H | RBI |
|---|---|---|---|---|---|---|---|---|---|
| Davis, Aljay 2b | 4 | 0 | 0 | 0 | Tucker, Travis 2b | 5 | 0 | 0 | 0 |
| Reza, Aaron ss | 4 | 0 | 0 | 0 | Wheeless, Chance 1b | 4 | 0 | 1 | 0 |
| Dunigan, Joe lf | 3 | 0 | 0 | 0 | Danks, Jordan lf | 3 | 1 | 2 | 0 |
| Baker, Aaron 1b | 3 | 0 | 0 | 0 | Suttle, Bradley 3b | 4 | 1 | 1 | 1 |
| Shepherd, Devin rf | 3 | 0 | 0 | 0 | Russell, Kyle rf | 2 | 1 | 0 | 0 |
| Gosse, Mike dh | 3 | 1 | 1 | 0 | Clark, Preston c | 4 | 0 | 1 | 2 |
| Williams, Jackson c | 3 | 0 | 0 | 0 | Prince, Josh ss | 4 | 0 | 1 | 0 |
| Freeman, Jarod 3b | 3 | 0 | 1 | 1 | Fuller, Chais dh | 2 | 0 | 0 | 0 |
| Hughes, Joseph cf | 3 | 0 | 1 | 0 | Moldenhauer, Russell ph | 0 | 0 | 0 | 0 |
| Taylor, Heath p | 0 | 0 | 0 | 0 | Demperio, Michael pr | 2 | 0 | 0 | 0 |
| Richards, Garrett p | 0 | 0 | 0 | 0 | Peoples, Nick cf | 3 | 0 | 1 | 0 |
| Conaway, Nich p | 0 | 0 | 0 | 0 | Alaniz, Adrian p | 0 | 0 | 0 | 0 |
| Totals | 29 | 1 | 3 | 1 | Totals | 31 | 3 | 7 | 3 |

### Score by Innings

| | | | | | | | | | | | R | H | E |
|---|---|---|---|---|---|---|---|---|---|---|---|---|---|
| Oklahoma | 0 | 0 | 0 | 0 | 0 | 0 | 0 | 1 | 0 | - | 1 | 3 | 1 |
| Texas | 0 | 0 | 0 | 0 | 0 | 0 | 3 | 0 | X | - | 3 | 7 | 1 |

2B — Clark (9); Peoples (11). 3B — Gosse (2).

| Oklahoma | IP | H | R | ER | BB | SO |
|---|---|---|---|---|---|---|
| Taylor, Heath | 7 | 7 | 3 | 3 | 4 | 6 |
| Richards, Garrett | ⅔ | 0 | 0 | 0 | 3 | 0 |
| Conaway, Nich | ⅓ | 0 | 0 | 0 | 0 | 0 |

| Texas | IP | H | R | ER | BB | SO |
|---|---|---|---|---|---|---|
| Alaniz, Adrian | 9 | 3 | 1 | 1 | 0 | 5 |

Win — Alaniz (8–1). Loss — Taylor (5–1). Save — None.

Start: 2:05. Time: 2:32. Attendance: 5,228

# 3

# California State University Fullerton Titans

California State University Fullerton Titans *vs.*
Long Beach State University 49ers
May 25–27, 2007
CONDITIONING
It's One Pitch at a Time

*After Fullerton takes the field to start the game, Evan McArthur receives warm-up throws at his third base position. He and fellow infielders Corey Jones and Joe Scott wear their pinstripe pants legs just below the knee, showing their navy blue socks. Tonight the team wears blue shirts with "Fullerton" written in an ascending "9 to 2 o'clock" manner. Below the name, the player's number is in orange. McArthur has number 11. The throws he makes are routine, but the process McArthur took to be able to take these throws tonight is hardly commonplace.*

McArthur spent his first year of collegiate baseball at Eastern Arizona, a community college not far from the New Mexico border. His arm was important to the Gila Monster program as he was used as both a starting shortstop and a closer to begin the season. However, due to injuries to the starting rotation, he became a starting pitcher in addition to his shortstop duties. This use likely developed into overuse. When everyday motions like rubbing soap in the shower caused pain, he knew something was wrong. Besides lathering with his right arm, he used the shoulder to throw and bat.

The following year he transferred to Fullerton. He spent the entire season on medical hardship status because about 18 months were needed to heal the damage to his labrum in his right shoulder. His primary focus initially was to strengthen his legs and maintain his optimal playing weight. Gradually, he took on specific shoulder strengthening exercises under the supervision of a physical therapist.

The injury had an unexpected benefit. By having a year to observe and really understand Fullerton's approach to maintaining an elite Division I program, McArthur had a somewhat easier time making the transition from junior college ball.

McArthur saw limited action in his first playing season at Fullerton, primarily used as a pinch-hitter and designated hitter. In his junior baseball season, he was the starting third baseman and hit .303 with seven home runs and 36 RBIs. He had high expectations coming into his senior season because his hitting had never been better. Just as his final season was beginning, however, he fractured the hamate bone at the bottom of his left hand. In early February, after the Titans had played only three games, he had surgery to remove the bone.

He initially lost considerable strength in his left hand and wrist. The left hand is critical for a right-hand hitter to generate bat speed. As soon as the cast was removed, he began strengthening his wrist and forearm. But he knew this wasn't a season-ending injury and he understood the patience required to rehab back into the lineup.

By mid–March, he was back in the starting lineup. During the time McArthur was healing, fellow senior Bryan Harris was the primary replacement at third base, while Billy Pinkerton also got some playing time there.

*Wes Roemer gets the pitching start on this Friday night. Friday night is usually reserved for the ace of the pitching staff. A quick glance at the back inside cover of the Cal State Fullerton media guide indicates that Roemer is the ace for this season. The page is an old western-style photograph showing Roemer wearing his baseball uniform and a holster. Across the bottom is the bold print "Gunslinger."*

*Although his record is a solid but unspectacular 9–6, it is difficult to live up to his sophomore season. He was 13–2 with an excellent 2.38 earned run average. He was a first-team All-American and Collegiate Baseball's co–National Player of the Year. He played on the U.S National Team.*

*On the first pitch of the game, the gunslinger hits his target; that is, the opposing batter. T.J. Mittelstaedt jogs down to first, immediately reinforcing the unofficial Long Beach State nickname, the "Dirtbags." The moniker is meant to signify getting the job done offensively and defensively by simply doing whatever it takes to get it done. Style points are irrelevant.*

*After throwing over to first five times, Roemer fields a Matt Cline sacrifice bunt. Two pitches later Shane Peterson hits a shot to deep center field. Clark Hardman first dekes that he'll catch the ball, but it is over his head. It's a double, easily scoring Mittelstaedt. Danny Espinosa goes full circle in his at-bat, starting off with three balls before striking out on three straight strikes. Roemer jumps ahead of Robert Perry 0–2 before Perry pulls a single that is perfectly placed in between a diving Matt Wallach at first and Corey Jones at second. The hit scores Peterson. Brandon Godfrey, the fifth left-handed batter of the inning, flies out to right for the third out.*

*Fullerton has nothing to show for its half of the inning. Manny McElroy, a right-hander, starts for Long Beach State. Both Clark Hardman and Josh Fellhauer fly out to deep center field and Nick Mahin grounds out to third.*

Goodwin Field is a good venue to watch college baseball. The first season was played at the facility in 1992 (business administration graduate Kevin Costner threw out the first pitch at the dedication game that season), and it was renamed from Titan Field to honor benefactors Jerry and Merilyn Goodwin. It is located in the northeast part of the campus, between Titan Stadium and the Fullerton Arboretum.

This section is clearly the nicest part of the campus. In general, the campus has an expansive California community college look to it. The buildings are largely of 1960s and 1970s design that in general look architecturally tired. There are a few exceptions, including the Performing Arts Center (2006) and the new Mihaylo Hall (2008), the home of the College of Business and Economics.

The east and west sides of the campus are bound by the Orange Freeway (State Route 57) and the heavily traveled State College Boulevard. To the northwest are affluent, but not spectacular, homes in the surrounding hills. About a mile from campus, BreitBurn Energy, a California oil and gas company, maintains well number 28 at the corner of State College and East Bastanchury Road. While that well remains, the orange trees that once completely covered the campus and surrounding acreage have mostly vanished. To see an aerial view photo of what is now the school compared to 60 years ago is astonishing.

The Fullerton Arboretum is a 26-acre botanical garden that shows off plants and trees from around the world. There are four primary collections: cultivated plants, woodlands, desert and Mediterranean. When strolling along the paths, hidden among the trees and with the sound of a stream, one quickly forgets that Goodwin Field's outfield fence is only yards away.

If any college in the U.S. deserves the label of a "commuter school," it is Fullerton. A parking space inventory chart indicates there are a total of 11,414 spaces on campus. That covers only a portion of the 35,000-plus students who attend the university either full- or part-time.

Titan Stadium, a foul ball away behind the third base dugout, was largely built for the now-defunct football team. Fullerton is probably the largest Division I school without a football program. In its final season in 1992, the

Titans lost back-to-back to UCLA (37–14) and Georgia (56–0) en route to a 2–9 record. The latter was the annual "body-bag" game in which Fullerton would go on the road to face a heavily favored opponent. In exchange for a lopsided loss, the school would receive a sizable check that significantly helped the athletic department budget.

Ironically, after much effort, Titan Stadium was built in time for the 1992 season. Four home games were played before the football program vanished. At least the soccer program has a nice field.

As unusual as it is for a school as big as Fullerton to not have a football program, the success the Titans have had in baseball is just as striking. If one excludes the baseball program, the school has little national sports prominence. In its infancy, Fullerton competed in the National Association of Intercollegiate Athletics (NAIA). It then moved into the California Collegiate Athletic Association, which today is a respected Division II conference that includes such state university brethren as Chico State, Sonoma State and Cal State L.A. Fullerton made the transition to the Big West Conference (formerly named the Pacific Coast Athletic Conference) in 1974.

Today the Big West is a California-only conference. The Big West name, which became official in 1988, made sense at the time since the conference included Utah, Nevada and New Mexico. From a baseball perspective, the conference today is highly respected as it includes the solid programs of Fullerton, Long Beach State, UC Irvine and UC Riverside.

How does a California state university rise in national baseball prominence? Two reasons: Southern California talent and Augie Garrido. It is the same Garrido that has had success at the University of Texas. Within two years of arriving for the 1973 season, Garrido took the Titans to the College World Series for the first time. In 1979, with Garrido in charge, a Tim Wallach-led team won its first national championship.

The second national title came in 1984. By the time Garrido left after the 1987 season for the head coaching job at Illinois, he had taken the Titans to the College World Series four times, and on seven other occasions he led them to a NCAA regional tournament. Garrido returned for the 1991 season and remained through the 1997 season, until leaving for Texas. In his second stint, returning after Larry Cochell departed for Oklahoma and with Titan Field under construction, Garrido helped the Titans to three more trips to the College World Series. They won the national championship again in 1995 (with USA Baseball Golden Spikes award winner Mark Kotsay) and at least made it to the NCAA regionals every year but 1991.

As good a coach as Garrido is, he also needed talent, and Southern California had, and still has, plenty of it. The difficult challenge is to compete with other outstanding Southern California schools (USC, UCLA, Long Beach

State, Pepperdine, UC Irvine, UC Riverside, University of San Diego, etc.) to get that talent to commit.

Garrido's replacement, George Horton, continued the tradition and captured the title in 2004. He had been a player for Garrido in 1975 and 1976 and was an assistant coach at Fullerton during Garrido's second coming. Prior to that, Horton was a very successful coach at Cerritos College, in Norwalk, about a dozen miles northwest of Fullerton.

Hence, for more than 30 years, Fullerton, as incongruous as it may be, has been a national baseball power.

*Roemer strikes out Travis Howell to start the third, but Jason Tweedy pulls a drive down the right field line that lands about six inches fair and rolls all the way to the fence. Tweedy ends up on third with a triple. Roemer then throws six straight strikes, including three consecutive foul balls, to Chris Nelson before striking him out. Mittelstaedt hits a chopper that Corey Jones fields going into the hole, but he cannot get much on the throw. Mittelstaedt gets the infield single and Tweedy scores. His first pitch to Cline is wild, allowing Mittelstaedt to advance to second. Not wanting things to get out of hand so early in the game, Coach Horton goes out to speak with Roemer. The pitcher ends the two-out threat by striking out Cline.*

*The Titans have another quiet inning in which a lead-off walk to John Curtis doesn't lead to anything. The inning ends with McArthur taking three consecutive strikes.*

*Despite giving up three early runs, Roemer clearly has good stuff. In the third, he strikes out Peterson and Perry, sandwiched around a pop-up out by Espinosa.*

*The bottom of the third brings more offensive futility for Fullerton. McElroy gives up a one-out bloop hit to Joe Scott, but he is left stranded at first.*

*Godfrey leads off the fourth with a soft, opposite-field double towards the left field line. Howell likewise goes opposite field with a double that lands in the right-center field gap and bounces off the fence. Godfrey scores easily and the 49ers take a 4–0 lead. Roemer, however, limits the damage again when he gets a pop-up, a bunt putout and a strikeout.*

*Nothing in the bottom of the inning leads one to believe that McElroy is vulnerable tonight. It takes him just 10 pitches to retire the heart of the order. Drives by Mahin and Curtis are deep to right and center field, respectively, but are only deep outs. Perry catches Mahin's ball with a leaping catch at the right field fence.*

*Roemer, who has had threats in all but the third inning, breezes through the two through four hitters, matching McElroy's ten-pitch effort a half-inning before.*

*McElroy strikes out Wallach to begin the fifth. He gets ahead of McArthur 1–2 before battling to a full count. On the next pitch, McArthur hits a shot that clears the left field fence to the right of the scoreboard and equal to the height of it. The damage is minimum given that it is a solo home run. It appears to be a one-pitch aberration. After striking out Jones, McElroy gives up a solid single to Scott. He runs on the first pitch to Hardman and is thrown out by Powell.*

*Perry leads off the sixth with a single up the middle. Fullerton, concerned about Perry running, has Roemer throw over to first a couple of times and also throw a pitch-out. Perry is running on a hit-and-run in which Godfrey pulls a double down the right field line that drives in the run. The 49ers settle for manufacturing the second run of the inning. Godfrey moves over to third on a ground ball out and then scores on a sacrifice fly that Tweedy hits to deep center. Although Roemer strikes out a batter for the third out for the fourth time this game, he and his Titans are facing a 6–1 deficit.*

*Hardman leads off the bottom of the sixth since he was at-bat the prior inning when Scott was thrown out stealing. He is hit by the first pitch. After falling behind 0–2, Fellhauer hits a ball to third, where Tweedy commits an error. Mahin follows with a high chopper that Tweedy has to wait for and makes a good strong throw. But Mahin is hustling and just beats out the throw. He spins around with a quick celebration. The bases are loaded and nobody is out. On the next pitch, Curtis hits a deep drive to right field that easily scores Hardman for the sacrifice fly. On the first pitch to Chris Jones, McElroy hits him, the second hit batsman of the inning.*

*Wallach hits a 2–2 pitch deep to right. Perry times his leap and appears to have snagged the ball the way he did in the fourth inning on a drive by Mahin. First base umpire Rorke Kominek's initial signal, from a distance, seems to indicate an out. The Long Beach fans are momentarily delighted until everyone finally realizes that Perry doesn't have the ball. It cleared his glove for a grand slam. Shockingly, the success that McElroy had for five innings has completely disappeared. David Roberts comes in from the right field bullpen and retires the side without any further scoring. It's now a tied game.*

Chris Jones is a red-shirt sophomore who went to Mission Viejo High School, about 30 miles southeast of Fullerton. The high school is a sports powerhouse in Orange County. His first year of college was at Texas A&M, and he pitched a total of 7⅔ innings and batted four times for the Aggies. He transferred to Fullerton the following year and sat out while on red-shirt status.

As a former high school football player in a highly respected program, Jones is familiar with athletic conditioning outside the sport of baseball. He feels weight training has had a "huge impact" on his hitting, enabling him to stay strong throughout the season. His goal is to have his bat stay quick and not feel heavy. While he was bench pressing a little in excess of 200 pounds in high school, that load is now up to 340 pounds.

Jones echoes many of his teammates when he recounts the training. He considers the fall "a grind; it is probably one of the most difficult couple of months a baseball player can go through." Running is the foundation of the conditioning program and it can take the form of 10 timed laps around the perimeter of the baseball field, a five-mile street run, or nine "innings" (repetitions) of stadium stairs. In the weight room, Jones, being a position player, focused on heavy bench presses and squats.

For Jones, there may have been a greater emphasis on weight training at Texas A&M, but that could have been a by-product of the available facilities at a major football school. He observes that Fullerton emphasizes general conditioning over weight training, not that the latter is ignored by any means.

*Roemer has to work against the top of the order in the seventh. Given the Titans' effort to match Long Beach's six runs, a shut-down inning would give Fullerton a big lift. They get it. The ball doesn't leave the infield; a pop-up to second, a line drive to third and a strikeout gets the defense off the field quickly.*

*Fullerton has a similar result in the bottom of the inning as its one, two and three batters are retired in order. Hardman pops up, Fellhauer strikes out, and Mahin flies out to left. The game has evolved from an almost blow-out to one that may be decided by the slightest break or mistake.*

*As quickly as Roemer recorded the three outs in the seventh, the eighth was doubly as impressive. Danny Espinosa, who had been retired in his three prior at-bats, lined out to the shortstop on the third pitch. Perry popped up to shallow left for the second out, and Godfrey followed with a ground out to second on the first pitch. Godfrey's grounder is to the left of Corey Jones, who makes a sliding stop and throws to Wallach at first from his knees. Roemer needs only five pitches to retire the 49ers. For those who are believers in momentum, it is clearly with Fullerton.*

*In the bottom of the eighth, Curtis leads off with a fly out to center and Chris Jones makes the second out by striking out. Wallach, whose grand slam instantly changed the game in the sixth, pulls a pitch down the right field line and reaches second with a double. Roberts is facing his first threat, particularly when he falls behind McArthur 2–0. After a called strike, McArthur hits a ball that mirrors Wallach's. It slices fair down the third base line and Wallach scores easily. Jon Wilhite pinch-hits for Corey Jones and hits a line drive to end the inning. The Titans are ahead for the first time tonight, 7–6.*

*Although Fullerton has a one-run lead, it is still precarious despite the fact that Roemer has retired nine batters in a row. He starts the ninth by striking out Howell. Tweedy follows and strikes out on three pitches. Long Beach sends up Jason Corder to pinch-hit, which cannot be an easy task. He takes the first pitch for a strike. The next pitch he hits to deep left and, as it travels, many of the Titans fans gasp, either literally or mentally. Fellhauer retreats, but he has room to make the catch. The gunslinger may not have been outstanding early on, but he competed throughout the evening. His ninth win of the season is well earned.*

*After Friday night's exciting win, Fullerton was disappointed with the 10–7 loss on Saturday in which the 49ers scored a total of seven times in the eighth and ninth innings.*

*Sunday is another day, the last game of the regular season. It is about an hour before game time and the Fullerton players are mingling around in front of the dugout. They assemble in groups of two or three, chatting among themselves. A few of them hold their gloves loosely in their hands.*

*The batting cage is already in place along with a blue tarp that covers a triangle area in between home plate and the pitcher's mound. A portable pitcher's mound, with wheels and a slight incline, is set up about 10 feet in front of the pitching rubber.*

*A cut-away screen is in front of the mound and full screens are in front of each base and in shallow center field.*

*Head coach George Horton appears and the group jogs out en masse to center field. Horton speaks to his team for about five minutes. When he finishes speaking, within seconds, the pre-game music begins. The entire sound system for Goodwin Field is comprised of three speakers affixed to a single pole behind the center field fence. An hour or two before this moment several players had visited head trainer Chris Mumaw or his graduate assistants.*

Like head coach George Horton, Mumaw is a Fullerton alumnus. He grew up locally, "not athletic at all," and owes his career in part to the French horn. While in high school, he played the horn "not very well" and discovered that to avoid after-school music practice he needed another activity. After going out for sports teams as a sophomore, he became a student manager, first for football and then for baseball and basketball. Thus, at age 15, he began taping ankles.

He has a part in 17 sports, with more than 400 student-athletes assisted. Grad assistants help him with the baseball program. He has covered just about every sport, including the less-publicized sports of fencing, gymnastics, wrestling and tennis. He also was the head trainer for the football program before it ended 15 years ago.

Mumaw views the dynamics among players, coaches and trainer as a "very delicate balance." He must have the confidence of both players and coaches in order to gain their trust. Usually the last decision a player wants to hear is that he cannot play. Thus, a player's tendency is not to be forthcoming about injuries. Mumaw assures the players that his job is to keep them on the field and will only not do so if playing will put the player at further risk of developing longer-term health issues. At the same time, Mumaw occasionally needs to assure a suspicious coach that a minor injury is indeed legitimate and that the player needs a period of rest.

There is a distinct difference between pitchers and position players when it comes to health maintenance issues. Position players tend to be a little more reactive than proactive compared to pitchers when it comes to preventative maintenance.

Pitchers generally self-monitor their body so closely that they border on being quirky in terms of both their habits to keep their arms injury-free and their concerns when something doesn't feel right. Their primary concern is their shoulder and elbow. The pre-game routine typically involves a combination of ultrasound, hot packs and assisted stretching. A pitcher like Roemer, for example, likes to have his hamstrings and lower back stretched about 35 minutes before game time. Ultrasound is administered by a device that produces high frequency sound waves that vibrate in the muscle tissues. The post-game routine varies among pitchers, but it includes some combination of ice, heat, massage and stretching.

While position players can have issues with overuse in the preseason (e.g., an outfielder can make hundreds of throws in a long fall practice), they suffer a broader spectrum of injuries due to getting hit by pitches, diving for fly balls and sliding into bases. For Mumaw, 2007 became the "year of the hand." Mumaw first dealt with four separate hand injuries on the men's basketball team. Then, three infielders (McArthur, Scott and Vasquez) had a fracture in their hand, while a fourth, Joel Weeks, had an ankle fracture. While most sprains and strains take a week to ten days to heal, fractures can take six to eight weeks.

Fullerton usually provides Mumaw with post-regular season challenges. The starting pitchers, who are used to throwing once every seven days, with their habitual pre- and post-game routine, do not have that comfort anymore. In these often do-or-die situations, the pitchers are asked to perform more frequently than they are accustomed to. He will often get a little more aggressive in his treatment and rehabilitation to decrease soreness and have a pitcher ready as soon as possible. His experiences in these situations may be useful beginning with the 2008 season, when the more condensed regular season will place a premium on pitching and likely produce some overuse injuries.

In recent years, Mumaw has seen innovations in preparing for and reacting to injuries. The amount of weight training that players now do, without sacrificing range of motion or flexibility, plays a significant role in avoiding overuse injuries. On the diagnosis-side of injuries, he believes that "old has become new again" because arthrograms (dye-injected x-rays) are being used to supplement MRIs to provide a much better look at an injured area.

*Bryan Harris gets the start for the Titans. It is his first start of the season and he makes every pitch from the stretch. He had no pre-game treatment with the training staff because this is an uncharted adventure for him. He starts his motion slightly hunched over with the heel of his left foot in line with the toe of his right foot. The first batter, Mittelstaedt, poses an initial challenge of patience. He takes the first five pitches thrown and runs the count full. He fouls off the sixth and then takes strike three. Bryan has gotten three calls on pitches on the outside part of the plate.*

*Cline then hits a ball to deep left center. Hardman loses the ball in the bright, early afternoon sun. Fellhauer hustles over from left field but he cannot get there in time. The ball lands at the base of the fence and Cline has a double. Peterson, who was the starting first baseman Friday night and the designated hitter Saturday night, is the starting pitcher tonight. He grounds in between Billy Pinkerton playing second and Matt Wallach playing first. Pinkerton fields the ball and tosses to Harris, who hustles over to cover first. Cline is stranded at third when Espinosa grounds out to Wallach.*

*Wallach technically did not start the game. As part of Senior Day, Jake Vasquez took the field initially but came out before the first pitch was thrown. He looked like he might have trouble fielding his position with a cast on his glove hand. Vasquez fractured his left wrist and hand when he collided with a Cal State Northridge runner in the Big West Conference opener back in March.*

Harris has had two distinct roles on the team, serving as a relief pitcher and playing third base. He started 12 of the 19 games that Evan McArthur did not start at third base while the latter was recovering from his wrist injury. Harris began his college career at Santa Ana College, a little over ten miles due south of Fullerton. He then transferred to LSU but sat out a year due to a medical hardship after incurring a knee injury and hernia before the season started. The following year he was used sparingly before transferring to Fullerton. In his junior year, the Titans used him as a designated hitter, third baseman and relief pitcher.

Harris is a student of himself, literally. His graduate kinesiology paper on the subject of dealing with adversity and injuries was fundamentally based on his own experiences. His past injuries have led him to be more conscientious of taking care of his own body. "If you let your legs go, then your arms go," said Harris. "What I really learned from my knee surgery was that I need to keep my legs strong in order to keep my arm strong."

Whereas Harris believes LSU emphasizes strength (under former coach Smoke Laval), Fullerton emphasizes endurance, quickness and agility. He believes the heavy lifting he was exposed to at LSU may have been counter-productive for pitchers. It may have been an aberration, but the LSU pitching staff during Harris' time there was suffering frequent arm injuries, particularly when compared to the Fullerton program. Harris is partial to stadium steps to keep his legs in shape. He certainly had more to run in LSU's Tiger Stadium, but Fullerton's stadium steps also work. For his pitching arm, he likes the arm band exercises as well as long toss.

The toughest part about being a two-way player is balancing the throwing demands of a fielder versus those of a pitcher. For Harris, it was primarily a mental process of determining what he needed to do to feel prepared for each position.

*As Peterson takes the mound, he is about seven miles away from Disneyland in neighboring Anaheim. However, the "happiest place on earth" for now is right on this pitcher's mound. His first inning is memorable as he strikes out the first three batters.*

*Harris has a memorable inning of his own in the second, needing just seven pitches to retire the side. He is aided by a 6-4-3 double play after a Godfrey single.*

*As the bottom of the inning begins, the shadows cast from the outfield speakers look like two church steeples, complete with crosses against the hitter's backstop in straight-away center field. Peterson is equally impressive in the second as he was in the first. He gets Curtis on a routine ground out, Chris Jones on a strikeout, and Wallach on a foul pop-up to Travis Howell behind home plate. Peterson has yet to allow a ball past the infield, but, of course, the game is still early.*

*Before the inning starts, Bobby, a local pre-teen, is selected to try to hit plastic golf balls off Fullerton's dugout roof into a hula hoop. He lacks the touch and is unsuccessful. If he were an adult, certainly the derision of the fans would have rained upon him. However, being a kid, he is cut some slack.*

*Harris starts off the third by striking out Tweedy. Chris Nelson is then hit by the first pitch and Harris becomes preoccupied with keeping him anchored at first. He throws over a couple of times before falling behind Mittelstaedt 3–1. On the next pitch Nelson is running and Curtis unloads a strong throw that beats the runner. Unfortunately for the Titans, it's ball four and there is no play at second. The threat ends with Cline flying out to left and Peterson grounding out to second.*

Little happens in the bottom of the inning. Although Pinkerton manages a single past a diving Cline, he is stranded. Peterson adds two more strikeouts to his tally and gets Hardman to hit a lazy pop fly to right.

Espinosa leads off the fourth and the second baseman, Pinkerton, is very familiar with the result. Similar to the ball he hit in the prior inning, Pinkerton dives to his right but cannot stop the grounder from going into right field. Espinosa is set to run and goes on the second pitch to Perry, which he hits foul. Perry hits four consecutive foul balls, the last of which is a very close call when Wallach fields the ball right along the first base line. After Harris throws over to first for the fourth time, he hits Perry with a pitch.

On the first pitch to Godfrey, the batter shows bunt and at the last moment swings away, grounding to short. With the runners going, Scott doesn't hesitate and throws to first to get the sure out. Howell follows with another grounder to short, which is as productive as the preceding one with Espinosa scoring and Perry moving up to third. Tweedy then hits one into the gap in right-center field and advances to third for a triple. After Nelson hits a deep drive to left for the third out, the 49ers have struck first with a 2–0 lead.

Fellhauer leads off the bottom of the inning by getting hit by the pitch. His effort to avoid the offering is minimal, at best. On the very next pitch Mahin hits a deep drive just to the left of the 385-foot sign in left-center field. Arriving at the fence just as the ball does, Mittelstaedt crashes into the wall, creating an audible thud. His collision leaves an imprint on the fence. At first, it looks as though the ball may have died and Mittelstaedt makes the catch. He doesn't. It's a home run and a siren begins to blare.

Mittelstaedt is all right, and Peterson walks the next batter, Curtis, who ultimately is standing on third after a sacrifice and an unassisted ground out to first. Although McArthur becomes the second hit batsman of the inning, the runners are stranded when Pinkerton hits a soft pop fly to right.

Mittelstaedt leads off the fifth with a single up the middle. Cline is looking to sacrifice, but his bunt is too easy for Harris to field quickly, and the latter alertly spins and throws to Scott covering second for the force play. That's the last batter for Harris. For a third baseman/reliever-turned-starter, it has been a good effort. One person who missed Harris' effort from the dugout is his professor, Ken Ravizza. He usually watches the Titans' games in the dugout, but not tonight. Ravizza feels more comfortable not being in the Fullerton dugout or even at the park during this series.

Ken Ravizza is a professor of Applied Sport Psychology in the Kinesiology Department at Fullerton. His involvement with the Fullerton baseball team began back in the 1980s when he worked with the gymnastics team and began having frequent conversations with Augie Garrido. He also began working with then pitching coach Dave Snow (who moved on as head coach of Loy-ola Marymount from 1985 to 1988 and then as the head coach of Long Beach State from 1989 to 2001). He developed ties with Marcel Lachemann with the California Angels (pitching coach from 1984 to 1992), and with Snow's replacement at Long Beach, current head coach Mike Weathers.

With ties to both the Fullerton and Long Beach programs, it is under-standable that Ravizza feels awkward being at the games in which they play one another.

Ravizza is the author of *Heads Up Baseball Book: Playing the Game One Pitch at a Time*. The book is an easy read but very informative in explaining the optimum mental approach that baseball players should use.

According to Ravizza, one key is "trying to get the players more com-fortable being uncomfortable" or "to embrace adversity." Put another way, Ravizza comments, "Are you that bad that you have to feel great to perform well?" Baseball "adversity" can range from coming back from an injury to unfavorable game situations. Performing well is not about being in the "zone." He believes that the "zone" is overrated because a player is in such a state a small percentage of the time, perhaps only 10 percent to 15 percent. Thus, peak performance is not about being perfect; it's about compensating, adjust-ing and just competing with what one has that day, that moment.

Ravizza preaches that players must strive for quality during practices and have a sense of purpose while training. Once the game begins he believes it is no longer about mechanics, but all about simply competing, which may well be 100 percent mental. He emphasizes that each player must be "in the moment," focused on just that pitch and not be results-oriented.

For a pitcher, Ravizza explains he should not be thinking about pitch-ing a shutout or getting out of an inning. For a batter, it's not thinking about going 4-for-4 or hitting a home run. Those are results. The pitcher should only be focused on the next pitch in terms of selection and location. The bat-ter should only be focused on the next pitch and commit to his plan for that pitch (for example, hit to the opposite field).

Two tools Ravizza provides the player to continually get back "into the moment" are the focal point and the breath. The focal point is some unique object at the ball park, perhaps the flag pole, which can be used as a reminder to remain calm ("controlled intensity") and simply focus on the next pitch when adversity occurs.

To Ravizza, the breath is more than the physiological mechanism to bring oxygen into the body. It helps one think clearly. It will pull the player to the present moment. The inhale brings in energy; the exhale allows a player to let go while serving as a release. Ravizza sees the breath as an important way to control oneself, which is crucial to controlling one's performance.

To explain and reinforce the concepts of playing one pitch at a time, he addresses either the entire team or a split between pitchers and position players in a classroom once or twice a week. The sessions can last anywhere from 20 minutes to an hour. Ravizza will attend many games and provide feedback as part of the discussion.

*With Harris now out of the game, the heart of the order is about to appear and Paul Canedo has been warming up since the previous inning. Canedo looks smaller than the 5'10" as he is listed, and his first pitch to Peterson is smacked towards the right field line for a double. He doesn't look terribly comfortable pitching to the cleanup hitter, Espinosa. His first pitch is really high; his second is really outside; his third is really low. Not surprisingly, he is told to make the fourth pitch an intentional walk. With the bases loaded, Canedo's participation ends after he falls behind Perry 2–0.*

*Adam Jorgenson comes in, hoping to shake off last night's performance in which he gave up four runs and five hits in just two-thirds of an inning. He doesn't have much chance to think about Friday when Perry launches his first pitch to deep center for a bases-clearing double. Two pitches later, Godfrey drives in Perry, and the former advances to second when the throw to home is too late and then to third when Curtis makes an error. Jorgensen regroups to get a routine ground out from Howell that scores Godfrey. The half-inning ends when Tweedy hits a foul pop-up to third. Five runs score for the 49ers and it is suddenly a 7–2 game.*

*After Scott's bunt is pushed too hard towards second and results in a putout, Hardman follows with a drive to right. He has an easy double, but he makes an ill-advised attempt to stretch the hit into a triple. The relay from Perry to Espinosa to Tweedy is in plenty of time to tag out Hardman. The decision stings the Titans a bit more when Fellhauer lines the very next pitch up the middle. Peterson tries to snag the ball but his glove goes flying in the air and lands in foul territory beyond the first base line. The ball goes into center field. Mahin comes up to the plate and is hit by the pitch. The two-out rally dies when Curtis grounds to the right of second baseman Cline, and Peterson races over to cover first in time.*

*Before the top of the sixth, a quartet of freshmen — Dean McCullough, Travis Kelly, Ryan Ackland and Michael Morrison — manually drag the infield dirt smooth with mesh mats. Nelson leads off with a deep fly out to center, but Mittelstaedt reaches first for his third consecutive time with a walk. It is a relatively quiet inning, however, once Cline and Peterson line out and pop-up to third base, respectively.*

*Being down five runs in the sixth is hardly insurmountable in college baseball. Peterson is done for the day, although he remains in the lineup as the designated hitter. Omar Arif comes in to relieve and Chris Jones hits the first pitch just to the right of left-center field. The ball is cut off quickly near the fence, but Jones is easily in at second standing up with a double. Wallach follows with a walk and the fans smell a rally of sorts,— or perhaps it is just the funnel cakes frying along the third base side mezzanine. McArthur officially makes it a rally when he hits a single just over Arif's glove and just past Cline diving near second base. Jones comes in to score. Khris Davis comes up to pinch-hit for Pinkerton and, after falling behind 0–2, he loads the bases after being hit by a pitch.*

*Arif ends his "it's not my day" outing and hands the ball over to David Roberts. His first opponent is the number nine hitter, Scott, who hits a fly to medium-deep center field. It is deep enough to score Wallach and allow the other runners to move up as well. Hardman follows with a fly ball; this one is deep enough in left field to allow McArthur to score. With Davis still on second, Fellhauer hits the second pitch he sees off the KCET (local PBS affiliate) sign above the fence, about 25-feet high and just to the left of the 385-foot marker. The Titans have come all the way back, and the game is tied at 7–7. Mahin ends the inning with a deep drive to left that is caught just short of the fence.*

A game in May is a long way from the training in the fall. But as players like Chris Jones and Evan McArthur can attest, that intense training is never forgotten. Along with assistant coach Rick Vanderhook, strength and conditioning coach Andy Williams is responsible for those memories. Williams refers to the fall Saturdays as "death days." Williams, along with two graduate assistants, covers all of Fullerton's sports.

Williams was raised in the small town of Sedalia, Missouri, about 95 miles east of Kansas City. After serving as what he considers to be "not even an average college player" on the Missouri Western State University football team, he received an internship with the Kansas City Chiefs and, shortly thereafter, with the nearby Kansas City Royals. His resume was built on experiences in NFL Europe, Middle Tennessee State and the Somerset Sports Performance and Rehabilitation Center in New Jersey. When Fullerton's strength and conditioning coach moved on to UC Irvine, Williams took the position. Before the 2007 regular season began, Williams moved on to become the New York Yankees strength and conditioning coordinator.

While he exchanged ideas with Coach Horton, he was given full responsibility and was not micro-managed. The overall philosophy to the players was rather simple: "train hard, eat right, and rest and recovery." Since Williams had little control over the latter two rules, his focus is naturally on the training. His primary job was "prehab," the opposite of "rehab," in which he hopes players can bounce back from inevitable injuries quicker.

The second goal was to increase work capacity. Williams describes the process as "building postures, not parts" with focus on the body's core, that area between the chest line and above the mid-line of the thighs. Also, there was emphasis on working the "braking" muscles to counteract the natural muscle imbalance at birth in which the muscles in the front of the body are dominant relative to those in the back.

On a typical fall Saturday, Williams believed, "On that day we are the hardest working team in the nation." The conditioning consists of a circuit of running with medicine balls for 100 yards before throwing them, split jumps, duck walks, rotational push-ups and stadium stairs running. In the preseason, the position players are training four days a week, pitchers three days a week.

During the regular season the training was cut to two times a week and the volume of weight training is cut in half. During this portion of the year, "dynamic flexibility" was emphasized. The position players, unlike the pitchers, did weight training that impacts chest muscles, such as the bench press and clean pulls. Pitchers are more concerned with shoulder stabilization exercises, often using light dumbbells (so-called Jobes exercises, named after orthopedic surgeon Frank Jobe, who pioneered tendon transplant surgery, a.k.a. Tommy John surgery, in the elbow) and elastic bands. All players consistently did squats, usually a mixture of heavy weights, box squats or band squats.

Williams' view was that the myths surrounding weight training for baseball have almost, but not entirely, died out. The belief that weight training makes one slow or inflexible has gradually dissipated. With an emphasis on explosive movements, flexibility and attention to the core body area, today's player may well be better conditioned.

The use of kettle bells is one trend that Williams sees continuing to gain popularity. The process of innovation is important. "You need to keep shocking the system because the body is so smart, that, if you do the same workout two times in a row, what will happen is that it will find a more efficient way to do the second workout so it's not as tough." The innovation does not necessarily have to be worldly unique, just something new to a particular player.

*Jorgenson, whose pitching motion is right over the top, is going through the order for the second time. He starts off the inning hitting Espinosa. The Titans are concerned about Espinosa running, and Jorgenson throws over to first three consecutive times. His second pitch to Perry is in the dirt and Curtis makes a fine block to keep the ball in front of him and to hold Espinosa at first. Perry quickly changes the strategy when he pulls a line drive down the right field line. It is deep enough to score Espinosa and, just like that, the 49ers have their third lead of the game. Godfrey follows with another single to right, yet Perry holds at third, not taking a chance to score when there are no outs. His cautiousness is rewarded when Howell follows with the third consecutive hit to right field.*

*With Perry scoring and the Titans now trailing by two, Michael Morrison is brought into the game. He was dragging the infield just an inning before. Pitching coach Rick Vanderhook remains on the field throughout the warm-up and passes along some encouragement to Morrison with the game at a critical stage. Morrison comes in throwing strikes, and he gets Tweedy to ground to Corey Jones, who came in at the start of the inning to play second base. Jones' best option is to simply get the force out at second and Godfrey comes into score. Morrison then gets Nelson to hit into a 4-6-3 double play to retire the 49ers.*

*The Titans come up trailing, 10–7, but they know they have three offensive half-innings remaining. They know this game is not over. Curtis leads off hitting a line drive that ricochets off Godfrey's glove down the right field line. The crowd gets a "here we go again" feeling when Curtis ends up with a double. Chris Jones grounds out to short for the first out and Long Beach brings Jason Markovitz in to relieve. He battles Wallach to a full count before getting a called third strike. McArthur then hits a deep drive to left that dies on the warning track. A breeze is blowing in as indicated by the direction of the American flag directly behind the flight of the ball and Mittelstaedt catches the third out. It deflates the hometown crowd for the moment.*

*Every inning this game the 49ers have put offensive pressure on Fullerton by getting either the lead-off or the second batter of the frame on base. Mettelstaedt leads off with a single right over second base. Content to play for one run, Cline sacrifices the runner with a bunt that Morrison fields to record the out himself. Peterson, in his designated hitter role, pulls a single to right, driving in Mittelstaedt. Although Morrison comes back to get Espinosa and Perry to pop out and ground out to third, respectively, he is now looking at a four-run deficit.*

*Dustin Garneau, pinch-hitting for Corey Jones, grounds out to short to start the bottom of the eighth. Scott flies to right for the second out. Hardman then hits a high shot down the right field line that hits one of the ten advertising signs suspended above the fence. While the home run gets the crowd back into the game, Fellhauer provides a little more optimism when his slow grounder to short is fielded cleanly by Espinosa, who cannot get enough on the throw to record the out. With the right-hand hitting Mahin coming up, Long Beach counters by bringing in right-hander Dustin Rasco. With a bit of a jerky motion, he gets ahead of Mahin, 0–2, before unleashing a wild pitch that allows Fellhauer to move to second. Rasco gets Mahin to swing and miss for strike three and Fullerton will have at least a three-run deficit to make up in the ninth.*

*Morrison has a good battle with Godfrey to start the ninth, needing nine pitches before finally getting the strikeout. Howell follows with a ground out to* short. Finally, the Titans have retired the first two batters of the inning. However, a one-two-three inning, something that hasn't occurred since the sixth inning last night, is not to be. Tweedy nails a double down the right field line for the 49ers' 20th base runner of the game. Morrison comes back with his first strikeout of the game, getting Nelson on three pitches.

Curtis, the clean-up hitter, leads off the bottom of the ninth facing the sixth Long Beach pitcher of the game, Bryan Shaw. Curtis hits a hard one-hopper back to Shaw, who snags it as he recoils and looks almost tauntingly into the Fullerton dugout before throwing to first for the out. Chris Jones then hits a chopper up the middle that Espinosa fields before his throw sails well over Godfrey's head at first. Wallach follows by getting hit by the first pitch from Shaw. McArthur then comes up as the potential tying run. The potential is indeed present given the 49ers' lack of crisp defense and pitching in the inning so far. On the first pitch, he grounds into what appears to be a game-ending double play, but his hustle down to first beats the relay throw. Fullerton is down to their final out.

Jon Wilhite comes up as a pinch-hitter in the eighth slot, becoming the sixth player to occupy that spot in the batting order for the Titans in this game. With a 1–1 count he is hit by the pitch. Unbelievably, he is the ninth batter hit by a pitch this afternoon. Both teams are seemingly defying the adage that "nobody pitches inside in college baseball." It not only loads the bases, but it gets the crowd back into the game. Scott, hitless in four previous at-bats, comes up and falls behind 1–2. Shaw's next pitch is taken for strike three. Game over.

This is not how Fullerton expected the game to end. It is not how the Titans expected the regular season to end. It is not how the seniors expected their final home game to end. But it did.

---

#22 LONG BEACH STATE 49ERS VS. CAL STATE FULLERTON TITANS
MAY 25, 2007 AT FULLERTON, CALIFORNIA
GOODWIN FIELD

---

| Long Beach (35–18, 13–6) | | | | | Fullerton (33–21, 10–9) | | | | |
|---|---|---|---|---|---|---|---|---|---|
| *Player* | *AB* | *R* | *H* | *RBI* | *Player* | *AB* | *R* | *H* | *RBI* |
| Mittelstaedt, TJ lf | 3 | 1 | 1 | 1 | Hardman, Clark cf | 3 | 1 | 0 | 0 |
| Cline, Matt 2b | 3 | 0 | 0 | 0 | Fellhauer, Josh lf | 4 | 1 | 0 | 0 |
| Peterson, Shane 1b | 4 | 1 | 1 | 1 | Mahin, Nick rf | 4 | 1 | 1 | 0 |
| Espinosa, Danny ss | 4 | 0 | 0 | 0 | Curtis, John c | 2 | 0 | 0 | 1 |
| Perry, Robert rf | 4 | 1 | 2 | 1 | Jones, Chris dh | 3 | 1 | 0 | 0 |
| Godfrey, Brandon dh | 4 | 2 | 2 | 1 | Wallach, Matt 1b | 4 | 2 | 2 | 4 |
| Howell, Travis c | 4 | 0 | 1 | 1 | McArthur, Evan 3b | 4 | 1 | 2 | 2 |
| Tweedy, Jason 3b | 3 | 1 | 1 | 1 | Jones, Corey 2b | 3 | 0 | 1 | 0 |
| Nelson, Chris cf | 3 | 0 | 0 | 0 | Wilhite, Jon ph | 1 | 0 | 0 | 0 |

| Player | AB | R | H | RBI | Player | AB | R | H | RBI |
|---|---|---|---|---|---|---|---|---|---|
| Corder, Jason ph | 1 | 0 | 0 | 0 | Pinkerton, Billy 2b | 0 | 0 | 0 | 0 |
| McElroy, Manny p | 0 | 0 | 0 | 0 | Scott, Joe ss | 3 | 0 | 2 | 0 |
| Roberts, David p | 0 | 0 | 0 | 0 | Roemer, Wes p | 0 | 0 | 0 | 0 |
| Totals | 33 | 6 | 8 | 6 | Totals | 31 | 7 | 8 | 7 |

### Score by Innings

| | | | | | | | | | | | R | H | E |
|---|---|---|---|---|---|---|---|---|---|---|---|---|---|
| Long Beach | 2 | 1 | 0 | 1 | 0 | 2 | 0 | 0 | 0 | - | 6 | 8 | 1 |
| Fullerton | 0 | 0 | 0 | 0 | 1 | 5 | 0 | 1 | X | - | 7 | 8 | 0 |

2B — Peterson (9); Godfrey 2 (7); Howell (8); Wallach (6); McArthur (7). 3B — Tweedy (1). HR — Wallach (4); McArthur (3).

| Long Beach | IP | H | R | ER | BB | SO |
|---|---|---|---|---|---|---|
| McElroy, Manny | 5$\frac{1}{3}$ | 5 | 6 | 5 | 1 | 3 |
| Roberts, David | 2$\frac{2}{3}$ | 3 | 1 | 1 | 0 | 2 |

| Fullerton | IP | H | R | ER | BB | SO |
|---|---|---|---|---|---|---|
| Roemer, Wes | 9 | 8 | 6 | 6 | 0 | 11 |

Win — Roemer (9–6). Loss— Roberts (3–1). Save — None.

Start: 7:07. Time: 2:48. Attendance: 2995

---

### #22 LONG BEACH STATE 49ERS VS. CAL STATE FULLERTON TITANS
### MAY 27, 2007 AT FULLERTON, CALIFORNIA
### GOODWIN FIELD

**Long Beach (37–18, 15–6)**                    **Fullerton (33–23, 10–11)**

| Player | AB | R | H | RBI | Player | AB | R | H | RBI |
|---|---|---|---|---|---|---|---|---|---|
| Mittelstaedt, TJ lf | 3 | 1 | 2 | 0 | Hardman, Clark cf | 4 | 1 | 2 | 2 |
| Cline, Matt 2b | 4 | 1 | 1 | 0 | Fellhauer, Josh lf | 4 | 2 | 3 | 2 |
| Peterson, Shane p/dh | 5 | 1 | 2 | 1 | Mahin, Nick rf | 4 | 1 | 1 | 2 |
| Espinosa, Danny ss | 3 | 3 | 1 | 0 | Curtis, John c | 4 | 0 | 1 | 0 |
| Perry, Robert rf | 4 | 3 | 2 | 2 | Jones, Chris dh | 4 | 1 | 2 | 0 |
| Godfrey, Brandon 1b | 5 | 2 | 3 | 1 | Wallach, Matt 1b | 3 | 1 | 0 | 0 |
| Howell, Travis c | 5 | 0 | 1 | 3 | McArthur, Evan 3b | 4 | 1 | 1 | 1 |
| Tweedy, Jason 3b | 5 | 0 | 2 | 2 | Pinkerton, Billy 2b | 2 | 0 | 1 | 0 |
| Nelson, Chris cf | 4 | 0 | 0 | 0 | Davis, Khris ph | 0 | 1 | 0 | 0 |
| Arif, Omar p | 0 | 0 | 0 | 0 | Jones, Corey 2b | 0 | 0 | 0 | 0 |
| Roberts, David p | 0 | 0 | 0 | 0 | Garneau, Dustin ph | 1 | 0 | 0 | 0 |
| Markovitz, Jason p | 0 | 0 | 0 | 0 | Weeks, Joel 2b | 0 | 0 | 0 | 0 |
| Rasco, Dustin p | 0 | 0 | 0 | 0 | Wilhite, Jon ph | 0 | 0 | 0 | 0 |
| Shaw, Bryan p | 0 | 0 | 0 | 0 | Scott, Joe ss | 4 | 0 | 0 | 1 |
| | | | | | Harris, Bryan p | 0 | 0 | 0 | 0 |

| Player | AB | R | H | RBI | Player | AB | R | H | RBI |
|---|---|---|---|---|---|---|---|---|---|
| | | | | | Canedo, Paul p | 0 | 0 | 0 | 0 |
| | | | | | Jorgenson, Adam p | 0 | 0 | 0 | 0 |
| | | | | | Morrison, Michael p | 0 | 0 | 0 | 0 |
| Totals | 38 | 11 | 14 | 9 | Totals | 34 | 8 | 11 | 8 |

### Score by Innings

| | | | | | | | | | | | R | H | E |
|---|---|---|---|---|---|---|---|---|---|---|---|---|---|
| Long Beach | 0 | 0 | 0 | 2 | 5 | 0 | 3 | 1 | 0 | - | 11 | 14 | 1 |
| Fullerton | 0 | 0 | 0 | 2 | 0 | 5 | 0 | 1 | 0 | - | 8 | 11 | 1 |

2B — Cline (6); Peterson (11); Perry 2 (12); Tweedy (4); Hardman (3); Curtis (17); Jones, Ch. (12). 3B — Tweedy (2). HR — Hardman (3); Fellhauer (2); Mahin (9).

| Long Beach | IP | H | R | ER | BB | SO |
|---|---|---|---|---|---|---|
| Peterson, Shane | 5 | 4 | 2 | 2 | 1 | 6 |
| Arif, Omar | 0 | 2 | 4 | 4 | 1 | 0 |
| Roberts, David | 1⅓ | 2 | 1 | 1 | 0 | 0 |
| Markovitz, Jason | 1⅓ | 2 | 1 | 1 | 0 | 1 |
| Rasco, Dustin | ⅓ | 0 | 0 | 0 | 0 | 1 |
| Shaw, Bryan | 1 | 1 | 0 | 0 | 0 | 1 |

| Fullerton | IP | H | R | ER | BB | SO |
|---|---|---|---|---|---|---|
| Harris, Bryan | 4⅓ | 5 | 3 | 3 | 1 | 2 |
| Canedo, Paul | 0 | 1 | 2 | 2 | 1 | 0 |
| Jorgenson, Adam | 1⅔ | 5 | 5 | 4 | 1 | 0 |
| Morrison, Michael | 3 | 3 | 1 | 1 | 0 | 2 |

Win — Roberts (4–1). Loss — Jorgenson (3–2). Save — Shaw (10).

Start: 1:07. Time: 3:42. Attendance: 3,047

# 4

# Lewis-Clark State
# College Warriors

Lewis-Clark State College Warriors *vs.*
Albertson College Coyotes
April 20–22, 2007
COACHING
Practice with Effort


*"Hey Mike, would you hit something to his backhand instead of right at him?"*

*"Mike" is assistant coach Mike Madrid, who is hitting ground balls to the Lewis-Clark State College infielders before their game with Albertson College.* *"Him" is Zach Evangelho, a senior infielder from Fresno, California. His uniform is dirty after his first dive for a ball hit to his glove side at third base. In minutes, other infielders' uniforms will be dirty as well.*

*Head coach Ed Cheff is making the request. He stands to the left of the second base bag where he yells out instructions to a batter, infielder or outfielder. His instructions and constructive criticisms are constant. In about a half-hour, the Warriors take on the Coyotes (or Yotes) in a National Association of Intercollegiate Athletics (NAIA) Region I conference game. Cheff's teaching does not end with the pre-game preparation; he frequently instructs the team during the game.*

*"Don't hit hippity-hop grounders!" yells Cheff minutes later. This time his request is to Brad Schwarzenbach, a junior pitcher who has taken over hitting fungos to some of the infielders. Schwarzenbach begins to hit balls harder and only within diving distance of Brian Bollwitt's glove.*

*From a distance, Cheff can easily be mistaken for a player. He is very trim. The only visual hint that it is not a player is that his navy blue jersey is slightly*

---

* *In October 2007 it was announced that the college was changing back to the original name of the school, the College of Idaho.*

64

*faded compared to that of his players. Cheff is in his 31st year of coaching the Warriors.*

Lewis-Clark State College (LCSC) is easily confused with Lewis & Clark College. The difference between a "hyphen" and "ampersand" is about 350 miles and $26,000. The school with the hyphen is a public college in Lewiston, Idaho, and the one with the ampersand is a private college in Portland, Oregon. "Hyphen" has an enrollment of 3,400 and has tuition costs of about $3,900 for in-state students; "ampersand" has about 2,000 students and costs $30,000. If "hyphen" were to play baseball against "ampersand," a Division III program, the former would be a prohibitive favorite.

Lewiston is in north central Idaho, where the Snake and Clearwater rivers join, a "confluence" as described by those with an understanding of geographical terms. It is a town of about 30,000. Heading west on either the Southway Bridge or the Main Street Bridge, one crosses the Snake River and arrives in Clarkston, Washington. The University of Idaho in Moscow is about 30 miles due north and Washington State University in Pullman is about the same distance away, slightly northwest.

At the northeast end of town, along the Clearwater River, Potlatch runs a large mill that produces paperboard and tissue. Both its buildings and treatment ponds are distinctly visible from views across the river looking back south at Lewiston. Potlatch, along with many other local businesses, has an advertisement on LCSC's outfield fence.

The campus is a compact 44 acres. By comparison, the University of Connecticut is 4,100 acres, Stanford is 8,200 acres and the U.S. Military Academy (Army) is 16,100 acres. Although LCSC's grounds are relatively small, the campus does not appear cramped or void of open spaces.

Reid Centennial Hall, built in 1895 with the lettering "State Normal School," indicating that it was a teachers' college, has a beautiful brick exterior and clock tower. It is the showcase building on campus, although Spalding Hall on the opposite side of campus is equally appealing. In the center of the grounds is a fountain with sculptures of Lewis and Clark pointing and looking like two coaches discussing ground rules at home plate.

Surrounding the campus are well-maintained craftsman and occasionally larger Victorian homes. The combination of wide streets, lawns and pink or white dogwood trees gives the neighborhood a very tranquil feel. Not far from campus, larger homes built on a bluff overlook the Snake River.

The baseball field is on the south end of campus. An impressive, curved entrance sign indicates "Harris Field — The Warriors Play Here." It is large and sits on top of bronze poles. It gives a visiting fan a hint that this is not just another small-college baseball program. Beyond the outfield bleachers a six-foot-high gray picket fence encloses the field along 11th Avenue. Just behind the third base line bleachers runs Sixth Street, and the cyclone fence is hidden by shrubs.

Affixed to the bleachers behind home plate are twelve four-by-four posters of some of the more notable Lewis-Clark players. Heading that list of those who made it to the major leagues are Keith Foulke (Chicago White Sox, Oakland and Boston), Steve Decker (primarily San Francisco), Tom Edens (seven different teams), Steve Reed (primarily Colorado and Cleveland), Jason Ellison (primarily San Francisco), and Marvin Benard (San Francisco).

*The prior evening Chris Kissock improved his record to 10–0 and Beau Mills and Paul Martin each hit home runs in the 13–4 win over Albertson. When Kent Bradshaw steps to the plate to start Saturday's game, there is one thing missing: a batter's box. Coach Cheff's grounds-keeping philosophy is simple. If something is going to disappear quickly, why bother to create it? Bradshaw lays down a bunt but pitcher Mike Miller easily retires him. Pat Burke, the Yotes catcher, has a much "patterned" at-bat. He takes three straight balls, takes two strikes, fouls off three straight pitches, and then takes a called third strike. Miller ends the inning getting Casey Oliver to fly out to right.*

*Andrew Brock gets the unenviable task of pitching against the Warriors and their .357 team batting average against right-handed pitching coming into this series. Brock, who is listed as 5'10" and 150 pounds, looks like he also competes in Little League. He gets through the first inning unscathed aside from hitting Beau Mills on the first pitch. If done intentionally, what it lacks in sportsmanship is made up for in strategy. Mills is hitting .491 with 23 home runs. He is a hitter one would rather not face under any circumstances.*

If one sarcastically wonders as to whether LCSC is playing a grocery store team, it is not too far off. Albertson College, with an enrollment of just 800, got its name in 1991 in recognition of its benefactors, Kathryn and Joe Albertson. The latter started his first grocery store in 1939 in Caldwell, Idaho, having attended what was then called the College of Idaho a few years before. His single store eventually expanded into a national chain. The college's earliest roots were tied to the Presbyterian Church, but currently it simply identifies itself as "Idaho's Liberal Arts College."

Caldwell, home to Albertson College, is about 30 miles west of Boise in the southwestern part of the state. It is about a 275-mile drive north near the Oregon and Washington borders to reach LCSC in Lewiston.

*Mike Miller picked up his second and third strikeouts in retiring the side in order in the second. Tyler Smith was one of those strikeouts, and when strike three fell to the dirt, first baseman Kyle Greene yelled "inside," a reminder to the catcher, Travis Georgius, to throw the ball to the left side of first base to get the putout. It is a simple fundamental, but obviously one for which Greene has been trained to react.*

*Andrew Brock retired his three batters in the second, but two of them hit balls hard to right field. Before the top of the third, the Happy Day Bingo numbers are read: I-28, G-58, O-61, B-12 and N-37.*

*After Miller has his third consecutive one-two-three inning, Brock gets two quick outs in the bottom of the frame. The lights have been turned on, and there is a very light, intermittent rain that falls. Mark Thompson then singles to left, the first hit of the game. Brent Wyatt follows with a double to right and Ed Cheff, coaching third base, does not hesitate to send Thompson home. He scores easily. Beau Mills comes up and is walked intentionally. Under NAIA rules, the intentional walk does not require the pitcher to throw four balls. This is a win-win situation: the fans don't have to sit through four high and outside pitches and the pitcher neither has to disrupt his rhythm nor have four balls count against his ball/strike pitch ratio. Once again, not letting Mills swing at a pitch pays off as Jessie Mier ends the inning with a fly out.*

In most college programs the head coach does not coach third base. Ed Cheff does. Since there are many decisions that must be made during a team's at-bat, Cheff feels it is the head coach's responsibility and that is where he believes he can most effectively coach. He feels it gives him instantaneous flexibility should he decide to take off a sign, such as when he senses a pitchout after the original sign is to steal. He also feels it slows down the game unnecessarily if every sign is relayed from the bench.

*Miller continues his success against the Coyotes by retiring the side in order. Brock gets three pop-up outs in the bottom of the inning. However, in between these outs, Paul Martin hits one deep over the left field fence. For Martin, it is his second home run of the season; his first was hit last night.*

*In the top of the fifth, Miller retired all three batters, just as he had done in the prior four innings. He has thrown an economical 50 pitches and has struck out five. Despite the outstanding effort so far, there are sounds of somebody warming up behind the Warriors' dugout. Although Miller was nowhere near his pitch count limit of 100, the bullpen was purely precautionary in case the coaches noticed anything labored or unusual in his arm action. He is coming off of an injury.*

Gus Knickrehm carefully monitors the pitching staff. He was a pitcher on the 1986 and 1987 LCSC teams, the latter winning the NAIA national title.

He became the pitching coach starting with the 2007 season after former pitching coach Gary Picone became the LCSC athletic director. Knickrehm not only has been part of the coaching staff since 2003, but he also had a six-season stint with the coaching staff after his Warriors playing days ended 20 years ago.

Cheff believes in allowing his assistants to be put in position to one day become a head coach if that is their goal. Wanting the coaches to take ownership of their roles, he tries to give them responsibility so that they can show initiative and independence. Knickrehm works collaboratively with Cheff in terms of teaching mechanics and deciding game strategy for the pitching staff.

Knickrehm describes Cheff's playing philosophy, saying, "Everyday, you (the player) are going to come out and demonstrate (skills), no mater if it's batting practice or a regular practice, and you are going to go out and put it into a game-type setting. You are going to compete at everything you do. It's a commitment to playing hard every pitch."

Athletic director Gary Picone knows something about Ed Cheff's coaching. He was a player at LCSC from 1973 through 1975, prior to Cheff arriving as the coach. He has had two stints as both an assistant LCSC baseball coach and as the athletic director. Just last season he was the pitching coach. Picone believes three things have contributed to Cheff's success: he has a passion for teaching; he believes in players and their ability to improve; he is involved in virtually every aspect of the program, from fundraising to administration.

While other programs may say they practice with a game pace, Picone speculates that may not be entirely true. "One of the first drills they do every year, one of the first practices of the year, we put the bases loaded with a 3–2 count and have the catchers call it (whether the pitch is a ball or strike). He doesn't believe in working you in slowly; he tries to put you in the fire so that anything that happens in a game is almost easy."

It goes with a coaching approach and belief that a player is more likely to succeed if he has experienced a situation before. Picone queries, "Take the guy who pitches the most innings for us. He's going to have 15 appearances and maybe 100 innings. How many times is he really going to be in a situation with a runner on second and nobody out? If he doesn't get it in practice, where does he get it?" It is a rhetorical question. It will happen in a Warrior practice.

*Despite his small frame and youthful appearance, it is not surprising that Andrew Brock is pitching well. When Albertson and LCSC met a month earlier in Caldwell, he gave up just one run in 7⅓ innings and earned a no-decision. He retires the leadoff hitter in the fifth, just as he has all game. Mark Thompson*

…nd one pitch later he steals second. Brent …pson moves over to third on the second out. …'s surprise, he is intentionally walked again. …and has seen one actual pitch — the one that …itch to Jessie Mier, but the latter flies out to …hompson and Mills.

…at opposing teams can be competitive with …a surprise. The Warriors are that good. They …les heading into the 2007 season. Between 1982 …consecutive title games and won eight of those. …on, they are 36–3, losing one-run games to Gon- …pping a conference game to British Columbia, …AA Division I opponents Air Force, Southern Utah …t anyone think a NAIA school cannot match up …ool, LCSC provides at least one program's answer. …CSC Region I conference competitors include the University of British Columbia, Concordia (Portland, Oregon), Corban (Salem, Oregon), and Oregon Tech (Klamath Falls).

The NAIA is an athletic organization that is an alternative to the National Collegiate Athletic Association (NCAA). There are slightly less than 300 participating NAIA colleges, which is smaller than the NCAA Division III membership. The two levels are often compared since both contain smaller colleges. In fact, numerous NCAA Division III (and Division II, for that matter) schools were once members of the NAIA.

The NAIA was formed in 1937, a by-product of a small-college national basketball tournament. In 1948, while operating under the name National Association of Intercollegiate Basketball (NAIB), it became the first national athletic organization to provide a post-season tournament in which black student-athletes could participate. By 1952 the group evolved into the NAIA and soon thereafter added national championships in other sports.

With respect to baseball, some famous major leaguers have come from the NAIA ranks:

- Lou Brock — Southern, Louisiana
- Norm Cash — Sul Ross State, Texas
- Chris Chambliss — Montclair State, New Jersey
- Mike Hargrove — Northwestern Oklahoma State
- Tommy John — Indiana State
- David Justice — Thomas More College, Kentucky
- Harmon Killebrew — College of Idaho

- Tony LaRussa — University of Tampa
- Tim McCarver — Christian Brothers, Tennessee
- Joe Morgan — Oakland City University, Indiana
- Phil Niekro — West Liberty State, West Virginia
- Gaylord Perry — Campbell University, North Carolina
- Lou Piniella — University of Tampa
- Tim Salmon — Grand Canyon University, Arizona
- Don Sutton — Whittier College, California

To show how things have changed, of these aforementioned colleges, Campbell, Indiana State and Southern are now NCAA Division I programs; Christian Brothers, Grand Canyon, Oakland City, Tampa and West Liberty are Division II programs; Montclair State, Sul Ross State, Thomas More and Whittier are Division III programs. For this select group of players and their respective colleges, that leaves only the College of Idaho (Albertson) and Northwestern Oklahoma State as remaining members of the NAIA.

While today the NAIA generally seems to be on a par with NCAA Division III programs in terms of athletic talent, the rules for the former are more similar to the Division II level. Specifically, NAIA schools are permitted to offer the equivalent of 12 full athletic scholarships for baseball. Nine scholarships are permitted at the NCAA Division II level, and no athletic financial aid is available at the Division III level. From a coach's and administrator's perspective, the NAIA has its advantages over the NCAA. The NAIA has fewer recruiting, eligibility, and participation rules to follow, and those that it maintains are generally less burdensome.

While the NAIA Baseball National Championship has been held at different locations throughout the country, LCSC received a 10-year commitment that began in 2000 and ends after the 2009 season. The school also had hosted the national championship for an eight-year period from 1984 through 1991. If competing teams do not relish the thought of potentially playing the tournament favorite on their home field, they at least have to concede that the community does a great job of supporting the event. In 2006, the championship game drew almost 5,500 spectators.

*Bryan Champ leads off the sixth and falls behind in the count 1–2. He then hits a line drive that deflects off Miller to his left. Miller can't get to the ball quickly enough, and it is too shallow for the second baseman, Zach Evangelho, to retrieve. Miller's perfect game is ended with a ball settling 75 feet from home plate. The next pitch hits Dane McGrady.*

*Drew Cauffman enters the game as a pinch-runner for the catcher McGrady, as a NAIA speed-up rule afforded to catchers. Coach Cheff gets Miller's attention and points to his own head. He is signaling to Miller to be aware of the game situation, two runners on and nobody out. A bunt rotation play is on. With number nine batter Camron Hammond up, the infield anticipates a bunt. Sure enough, Hammond lays down a bunt that Miller quickly picks up and throws to third to get the force out. However, the good defensive decision is neutralized one pitch later when a passed ball advances both runners.*

*Cheff goes out to visit Miller and the catcher, Dick Knutz (who entered the game at the top of the inning), and makes sure that Miller realizes the catcher's signs have changed. The change was made with the runner on second, who potentially could steal the signs. Knutz had been crossed up on the previous pitch. Nearly 90 percent of the time the LCSC catchers call the game. This process is rather unusual in college baseball, where a coach in the dugout usually calls each pitch. "If you can pass high school algebra, you can pass pitch calling," comments Cheff. The one exception will be when LCSC is in the national tournament and the catcher is unfamiliar with the opponent.*

*The Coyotes are one hit away from tying the game. Kent Bradshaw hits a ball to medium-deep right field. Mike Rivera makes the catch and sets himself for a throw to the plate. The pinch-runner, Cauffman, tags up and races towards home. Rivera's throw is slightly high but Knutz applies the tag and Cauffman is out. The perfect game is gone, but the shutout is still intact.*

*In the bottom of the inning, Brock gets his usual lead-off out, getting Greene to pop up the first pitch to shallow center. When he returns towards the dugout, Cheff reminds him that his pitch selection was inconsistent with the game plan. The conversation is brief and Paul Martin follows with a single to right. In the Warriors' typical aggressive approach to base running, Martin steals second on the first pitch. Once the count is 2–0, Evangelho hits a bomb over the right field fence. LCSC ends the inning with a four-run lead.*

The right field fence is the same as the rest of the fence at Harris Field in that it is covered in advertisements. In fact, business sponsorship is so popular at the park, there is a second set of advertisements slightly above and behind the outfield fence. The right field scoreboard is complete with a message board. The ballpark gives the feeling of a nice blend of a small college facility and a minor league park. The stadium is predominately bleacher-style seating with the exception of platform areas along both the first and third base lines in which spectators bring folding chairs to comfortably watch the action. It is a well-manicured field with light brown dirt in the infield and mound, contrasted with dark brown dirt leading from the dugout.

*In the sixth, Miller shows the first signs of vulnerability. He starts the seventh inning by hitting Pat Burke. After Casey Oliver lines out to Paul Martin in left, Richie Snider has a bloop hit land fair by inches down the left field line. Miller gets Smith to hit a pop-up to right field and he is one out from getting out of the inning.*

*Luke Howarth, who has struck out and grounded back to the pitcher in his previous at-bats, singles to center field. Burke comes around to score and Snider stops at second. Miller comes back with a strikeout to end the inning.*

*Brock takes the mound in the seventh trailing by three runs. He yields three fly ball outs to Luke Howarth in center field with a single to right in between. The solid single does not amount to anything, but is noteworthy for one reason: it is the first time all game that Beau Mills had the opportunity to swing at a pitch.*

*Miller finishes the game even more effectively and efficiently than he started it. He retires the last six batters in a row and only needs 17 pitches in doing so. His pitching line is superb: one run, three hits, no walks and six strikeouts. Brock did a nice job for Albertson, but it is difficult to be matched against a team that wins 92.5 percent of its games.*

Ed Cheff's coaching path has had few zigzags. Ironically, Cheff graduated from Lewis & Clark (Portland) and soon became a football coach and English teacher at Tillamook High School in Oregon. He followed that with a successful five-year baseball coaching stint at Lower Columbia College (a junior college in Longview, Washington). In 1977, he became head coach at LCSC. Thirty years later, it is the same job, same place.

Cheff is the exception to the rule. Most coaches do not arrive on campus and stay for a few decades. In contrast to Cheff, for some college coaches, it is a circuitous path they follow to arrive at their current job. It is a path largely dictated by where one is and who one knows. Such is the case, for example, for Chico State's Dave Taylor.

Taylor played collegiately at the University of Arizona after two years at Oxnard College, a community college about 60 miles northwest of Los Angeles. Before his sophomore year at Oxnard, Taylor was moved from an infielder to a catcher. The move likely had a significant impact on his career. At the new position, he was good enough to attract Arizona's attention, and he could better understand some of the nuances of the game.

In both years Taylor attended Arizona, the team went to the College World Series, winning the title in his senior season (1986). Winning meant more than just a championship ring. "Winning the national championship as a player opened up a lot of doors for me from there on out. Everybody likes to be associated with a winner," says Taylor.

Although Taylor was not drafted into major league baseball after he graduated, he went to play professional baseball for the Salt Lake City Trappers, an independent team not associated with any major league team. After the season, he signed a free agent contract with the Milwaukee Brewers, rising briefly to the level of AA.

"I didn't want to be one of those guys I was on the bus with every five days that was thirty years old with three kids. I thought it was time that I finish my degree and get on with coaching. My father was a coach, a football coach, and I think I had that in my blood; I knew I was going to do that." He earned his degree at Cal Lutheran, a small college in Thousand Oaks (40 miles northwest of Los Angeles), and became a part-time coach working with the catchers and pitchers. The part-time hitting coach was Lindsay Meggs, who eventually became Chico State's head coach, from 1994 through 2006. Beginning with the 2007 season, Meggs became the head coach at Indiana Statue University, a Division I program that plays in the Missouri Valley Conference.

The summer after the Cal Lutheran season, Jim Gattis, his manager in Salt Lake (and an assistant at Pepperdine), was also a manager in the Florida State League (an advanced Class A minor league). Gattis asked Taylor to join him as a player-coach, mainly doing the latter. When Gattis had business commitments back in California that required his attention, Taylor became the manager, at age 25, exchanging lineup cards with the likes of Felipe Alou, Clete Boyer and Clint Hurdle.

When Meggs left Cal Lutheran to work at Oxnard Community College in 1989, Taylor followed him there. When Meggs left Oxnard for Long Beach City College (a junior college, not be confused with Long Beach State, the Division I program), Taylor took over at Oxnard. The following season he rejoined Meggs at Long Beach City.

Taylor then decided at that time that he had enough moving around and, having earned a California teaching credential, took a job teaching eighth grade history at Sequoia Junior High in Simi Valley. He also was the pitching coach for Simi Valley High, a nationally ranked program a mile away.

Gattis then became the head coach at the University of Wyoming and he asked Taylor to join him there as the pitching coach for the 1994 season. Wyoming was a Division I program in the Western Athletic Conference (the school is now a member of the Mountain West Conference). When Gattis once again had to attend to business matters back in California, Taylor was promoted to head coach of the Cowboys. At an elevation of 7,200 feet, it was a hitter's paradise and a challenge to recruit pitchers.

After his third season in Laramie, Wyoming dropped the baseball program and Taylor circled back as a pitching coach for Meggs at Chico State in 1997. Although it was discouraging to no longer be a head coach at a Division I program, it was either that or perhaps sell life insurance with his father-in-law. He chose baseball.

Meggs gave Taylor autonomy with the pitchers and catchers and the pair lasted for eight seasons, winning the NCAA Division II championships in 1997 and 1999, and finishing runner-up in 2002.

Eventually, the head coaching position became available at Cal State L.A. for the 2005 season and Taylor accepted the job. In his second season (2006), the Golden Eagles lost to Chico State in the championship game of the NCAA West Regionals. When Meggs left Chico for the Division I opportunity at Indiana State University, Taylor accepted the position back at Chico.

By contrast, Ed Cheff found a place to stay early in his career. His family, including his wife and three sons, enjoyed growing up in the Lewiston area. His wife was a long-time elementary school teacher. He likes the small-school environment and a very supportive administration and community. Cheff admits that he has never really sought a "bigger stage" in which to coach; however, he has been able to schedule numerous games against Division I schools over the years. The opportunities for such games still exist, although it has curtailed in recent years.

In fact, of *Collegiate Baseball's* 30 highest-rated teams in 2007, only Rice scheduled a non–Division I opponent. The Owls played one game against the University of Central Missouri, a Division II college that plays in the Mid-America Intercollegiate Athletics Association. Even though the Mules are a highly respected program, Rice had little to gain by playing them. Whether it is a genuine concern about power rankings or simply an unwillingness to face potential embarrassment, Division I coaches schedule games against lower division schools infrequently.

The Cheff name certainly is recognized within the baseball community. In 2006, he was inducted into the American Baseball Coaches Association Hall of Fame. Besides coaching at LCSC, he has twice assisted with the USA Baseball national team and has coached several summer seasons in the respected Alaska League with the Anchorage Bucs and the Fairbanks Gold Panners.

His coaching ideas are included in *The Baseball Coaching Bible* (2000, Jerry Kindall and John Winkin), *The Baseball Drill Book* (2003, by Bob Bennett), and *Dugout Wisdom: The Ten Principles of Championship Teams* (2003, by Jim Murphy). He has contributed to such videos as "Correcting Common Hitting Faults," "Pitching: Ideas to Control the Short Game" and "Catching, Receiving, Blocking & Throwing."

*Sunday's finale is played under a bright sun that suddenly changes with intermittent dark clouds.*

*Albertson has changed the batting order for Sunday's game, but only three of the starters are different. On the home dugout wall, two of the LCSC starters have changed. As is often the case, the designated hitters have changed for both teams.*

Even the umpire crew has changed. Today they wear black shirts and are part of the Central Washington Umpires Association. Yesterday's crew wore light beige. LCSC is in its familiar white pants (with red and blue trim) and navy blue shirts (with white numbers and red and white trim). "Warriors" is written in block letters on the jerseys. The caps are navy blue with a red bill and the initials "LC" in white block letters.

Matt Fitts takes the start for the Warriors. He is 5–0 with one no-decision and an earned run average of 2.76, having started three games and relieving in three others. To dispel any idea that LCSC is unknown outside of western Idaho and eastern Washington, Fitts is one of seventeen Californians on the roster, having transferred from Long Beach State. By contrast, Albertson has one player from California.

After Bradshaw leads off and takes a called third strike, Howarth reaches first on a four-pitch walk. Fitts is aware that Howarth might be running and throws over to first before he makes a pitch to Oliver. The number three hitter for the Yotes hit the ball hard a few times yesterday, but all resulted in fly ball outs. The second pitch he crushes into the bleachers, but it is only a long foul. Fitts then throws a pitch-out, but even though Howarth is not running, he is nearly picked off with a strong throw from the catcher, Mier. Mier has another opportunity to show off his arm when Howarth runs on a 3–2 count and is thrown out on the foul-tip strikeout.

The public address announcer lets the crowd know that there is a car illegally parked in the university lot. The lot is so close to the field the guilty fan can be back in his or her seat in a couple of minutes. Carson Taysom starts for the Coyotes but things don't begin very well. He strikes out Mark Thompson, but the third strike is a wild pitch that allows Thompson to reach first. Thompson, who chokes up on the bat and gives every impression that he is a tough out, seems to purposely swing at the ball in the dirt given his immediate run towards first after the miss. He steals second and Brent Wyatt moves him over to third with a single to center. With the center fielder, Howarth, charging the ball quickly and unleashing a throw to home, Ed Cheff decides to hold Thompson at third. Beau Mills, who saw four pitches he could swing at yesterday, falls behind 0–2 before he hits a home run that clears the upper part of the fence in center field.

Taysom gets Jessie Mier to pop out to second but then gives up a double down the left field line to Paul Martin. He then falls behind Kyle Greene 2–0 before Greene hits one in a spot close to where Mills' ball landed. With one out, the score is 5–0. To his credit, Taysom does not melt after the rocky start and strikes out Jesse Roehl and has a nine-pitch battle with Kyle Merton before getting him to pop out to the catcher. However, this is not the team one wants to spot five runs.

The strength of LCSC's program is the consistency of the teaching and expectations the players understand. It is a year-round process.

The summer is generally more of an opportunity for the players to get additional playing experience on club teams rather than a time to make mechanical adjustments in one's swing or pitching delivery. Cheff believes there is no substitute for live pitching to develop hitting, defensive and pitching skills. He does not subscribe to a theory that a summer schedule of 50 ball games may cause baseball burnout. Although he doesn't do it every summer, he or one of his assistant coaches might coach a collegiate summer team and include some Warriors on the roster. NAIA rules do not preclude a coach from coaching some of his own players on an independent summer team.

The fall is spent working on mechanics and plays, and the intellectual and emotional side of the game is developed as well.

Cheff believes that good things happen when the people involved truly care about each other. Team Chemistry 101. Many of the Warriors are transfers from either junior colleges or four-year schools and they meet each other for the first time in the fall. In the past, the team has gone on camping trips with the goal of initiating friendships among the team. In mid–October, the team takes on the "firewood project" in which the players collectively split, deliver and stack about 150 cords of wood. It not only brings the players together off the field, but serves as a fundraising effort that brings in about $15,000. These monies, along with the advertising revenue and annual donations, help the program make up for a budget shortfall.

Cheff also coordinates the team boxing matches in the fall, which is designed to have players address the fear of the unknown, the fear of failure, and once again, to bond as a team. The boxing is not designed to reinforce a fighting mentality to carry over into the season, as Cheff has no tolerance for group conflict on the field; he insists that the umpires and coaches deal with any issues that may arise.

According to Cheff, there is a difference between an "educated" player and a "trained" one. The trained player is generally capable of success provided he does not have to deviate from what he has practiced doing. The educated player has an intellectual appreciation of the game and embraces the unexpected. Similarly, coaches who accept the educated player concept see a flipside to it and are more open-minded in dealing with mechanical adjustments. They do not believe everyone has to fit a specific approach to hitting, pitching or defense.

The biggest innovation in his years of coaching is video, being able to help the players who are visual learners. It also helps to dispel faulty teaching. For example, with respect to baseball mechanics, Cheff believes, "What really happens and the sequence in which it happens has been mis-coached forever because we didn't have the DVD; we had myths. We had myths on the pitching delivery. We had myths on hitting." Cheff is incredulous how many youth coaches let "experts" tell them, erroneously, how things work. Instead, he concludes that they should be able to study video and draw the proper conclusions on their own.

The fall is when Cheff instills in the newcomers the practice concept of "a high level of intensity and game-level enthusiasm." Basic skills may be taught at a low-key level, but the application of those skills is done in an intense, game-like situation. It is the segment of the year that allows the coaches to determine if a player can handle a different position or command a new pitch. "The philosophy of the program has to be ingrained in the players in the fall," says Cheff. "They have to understand how you want things done mechanically, how you want them to emotionally react to things, the mental toughness part of it, the physical toughness part of it. All of those elements have to be spelled out. When fall is over, those players have to understand exactly what we do on a first and second bunt rotation and just as well as what we do in certain types of hitting situations, pitching situations, and the type of response that we want from our players."

Cheff's favorite part of coaching is the practices, particularly the small group practices in which he can provide suggestions that hopefully lead to individual development.

Practices start with structured and monitored stretching, running and warm-up throwing.

For throwing, the drills may vary. For example, each of the four catchers might occupy a base and work on pick-off throws to first or third. Corner infielders might practice relay throws or cutting off the throw and throwing to second.

When it comes to hitting, the coaching staff likes to simulate certain types of pitching. For instance, knowing the tendencies of collegiate left-handed pitching, the batters will look for outside fastballs in the mid–80s and curveballs that break towards the right-handed hitter in the low–70s. To practice this, the coaches will set up "five-station" hitting drills. Beyond the right field fence, an enclosed aluminum building houses three parallel hitting chutes. Two more are located outside the entrance to the large shed. Here, the machines are set to simulate what is being done with the live batting practice. Station one has machines set to throw curveballs from the same trajectory as a left-handed pitcher. Station two uses other machines to throw fastballs to the outer, first-base side of the plate. Station three is on the regular field where left-handed batting practice is thrown from the mound, but the batter is five feet in front of home plate in order to decrease reaction time. Behind the left-field bleachers is a small practice infield, station four, in which left-handed position players throw to batters who practice bunting. Lastly, station five is in the bullpen where hitters get into a batter's stance and watch the left-handed LCSC pitchers throw to get a better sense of timing and rhythm.

In addition to the five-station hitting, the Warriors hold team batting practice. It is not a stand-around, enjoy-the-clouds process. This is a three-station approach in which the hitters on the field move onto bunting in the bullpen and hitting off a tee near the dugout. The defense is expected to make a play on every pitch hit during batting practice. Infielders are expected to dive for ground balls and outfielders are expected to go full-speed for every fly ball. While this is going on, players are assigned as runners on each base and are trained to react to wherever the ball is hit.

The Warriors do a combined team defense and base-running drill. A coach in the batter's box hits fungo after a thrown pitch. Runners are at various bases and a pretend batter stands at home plate. Once the coach hits the ball, the defense and runners are expected to give maximum effort, both mentally and physically.

The players will frequently participate in a "controlled scrimmage," which is designed to eliminate as much inactivity as possible. It is a little of Cirque du Soleil baseball style. The time between innings is a two-minute drill in which every second is put to good use. The infielders turn simulated double plays against a stopwatch and outfielders are challenged to make three difficult catches. The pitcher has a designated selection of pitches to throw and the catcher is to assume that each pitch is delivered with runners on first and third. The batter up first in that inning stands in the box during the warm-up throws to maximize realism. To turn up the intensity, the coaches play six "three-inning games" (assumed to be the seventh, eighth and ninth innings), in lieu of two traditional nine-inning scrimmages. Often these innings begin with a runner already on first just to add some pressure.

Practice is not just for practice. Cheff likes the infielders to practice double plays in between innings of real games in lieu of just having the first baseman roll pretend grounders. The way he figures is that it gives his defense a chance to turn an additional 4,000 practice double plays than if the infielders just did the traditional "field and throw" routine between the innings.

*After Fitts has an uneventful top of the second, Joey Zubizarreta comes in to relieve Taysom. If anyone wanted a quality long-relief assignment, this was it. Zach Evangelho pulls the first pitch he sees to right for a single. After Mark Thompson grounds into a fielder's choice, forcing out Evangelho, his presence as a base runner gives Zubizarreta some concern. He throws over to first before each of his deliveries to Brent Wyatt — a pitch-out followed by two other balls.*

*On the 3–0 count, Thompson steals second and moves onto third when catcher Pat Burke's throw goes into center field. Wyatt hits the next pitch into center field, scoring the Warriors' sixth run. They can beat a team with the long ball; they can beat a team with aggressiveness.*

*Fitts has a one-two-three top of the third and is doing what a pitcher is supposed to do with a six-run lead — he's throwing strikes. The bottom of the third starts innocently enough with a fly out and a Paul Martin infield hit off Zubizarreta's glove. Kyle Greene doubles to the wall in left-center and Martin scores from first. After Roehl flies out for the second out, the Warriors get three consecutive base runners on a single (Kyle Melton), a hit batter (Zach Evangelho), and a double by Mark Thompson. Melton scores on the double, and although the two other runners are stranded, it is now 9–0. About the only suspense that remains is whether the margin of victory would be more lopsided than Friday night's 13–4 game.*

Having a roster heavily dependent on junior college transfers places a premium on effective recruiting. First, Cheff looks for those prospects that have certain "characteristics of play" that can be implemented all of the time (for example, infielders who routinely dive for every ground ball in their area). The Warriors generally recruit for power and speed, but they will adapt their game to whatever they have. Cheff has had teams that have collectively hit as few as 35 home runs in a season or as many as 140. He has won national championships with both. Ultimately, there are a lot of ways the game can be played and that is dictated by the nature of the players on the roster.

There is no one way that players end up at LCSC. On one occasion a scout may pass along information; in another instance, it might be a former player who makes a recommendation. However, the Warriors don't leave the recruiting process to chance. The coaching staff diligently follows the progress of players in California and the Northwest and the statistics reinforce discussions the staff will have with coaches, particularly at the junior college level. Each year about 40 pitchers and 40 to 50 position players are on LCSC's radar as realistic recruits.

*At the end of the fifth, with the score still 9–0, Matt Fitts' day was done. He threw 58 pitches, allowing just two hits and a walk. Brad Schwarzenbach comes out to pitch the sixth. Perhaps it is a case of one upmanship for the Warriors as they counter the Yotes' Zubizarreta with a pitcher with twelve letters.*

*Schwarzenbach gets the first two outs on routine grounders to short. Kent Bradshaw singles up the middle and advances to second on a wild pitch. Luke Howarth follows with a single also right up the middle, scoring Bradshaw, and Howarth steals second. Oliver follows with a single, scoring Howarth. Three*

*straight singles is out of character for the way the series has evolved this week-*
*end. When Roach delivers a fourth straight single, it is nothing short of aston-*
*ishing. It is also astonishing to think that this is considered astonishing. That is*
*how impressive LCSC's dominance has been over the years.*

*The Warriors find a way to end the Yotes' feel-good moment when Paul*
*Martin scoops up the single in left and fires it back into the infield with*
*Schwarzenbach as the cutoff. Oliver, running hard from first with two outs,*
*rounds third as the throw comes in. He freezes once he realizes the throw has*
*been cut off. Schwarzenbach quickly flings the ball to Beau Mills at third and*
*Oliver cannot get back to the bag in time. He is the third out.*

*Lest Albertson has forgotten the offensive strength of LCSC, Mark Thomp-*
*son responds in the bottom of the sixth with a one-out single. He steals second,*
*and one pitch later he is standing on third after Brent Wyatt's single. Mills*
*grounds to first with Drew Echanis' only option to underhand a toss to*
*Zubizarreta. Thompson scores. At the end of the sixth, the score is 10–3. It is the*
*24th time this season the Warriors have scored 10 or more runs. It is only their*
*41st game.*

LCSC is Idaho baseball. There are but four public Idaho colleges: Boise
State University, Idaho State University, Lewis-Clark State College and the
University of Idaho. With respect to the major men's sports, there is generally not much debate as to which college is superior in Idaho. The bragging
rights are well established.

In football, Boise State University is the clear leader. The school's memorable 43–42 Tostitos Fiesta Bowl win over Oklahoma in 2007 was a plus sign
on a report card of good football grades over eight recent seasons. That game,
the most memorable of the 2006-2007 bowl season, featured a hook-and-lad-
der play for a touchdown, followed by a Statue of Liberty play for the winning two-point conversion. Boise State, playing its home games on blue
"Smurf Turf" (AstroPlay turf), typically battles Fresno State and the University of Hawaii for the Western Athletic Conference (WAC) championship.

In basketball, one looks to the WAC and, once again, Boise State has had
recent superiority over its league rival, the University of Idaho. The conference's top basketball teams are usually the University of Nevada and Fresno
State.

In baseball, it is not even a topic for debate. Of the four state-run four-
year colleges, only LCSC has a baseball program. Boise State and the University
of Idaho dropped their baseball programs and operate only as a club sport.

*The final run of the series scores in the top of the seventh. It occurs with*
*little drama. Pat Burke reaches first on an error and David Brigham comes in*

*as a courtesy runner for the catcher. Brigham reaches second on a wild pitch before a four-pitch walk to Bryan Champ. Brigham advances to third on a groundball double play. Camron Hammond's single to center scores Brigham.*

Only a few fans filter out. The game is not in doubt, and hasn't been since the first inning. Tim Bourner comes in to finish the game for the Yotes. Over the seventh and eighth inning he gives up a walk and a couple of hits, but otherwise does not allow a base runner past second. Schwarzenbach pitches the eighth. Despite giving up a lead-off strikeout/wild pitch, followed by a single, no runners score. When he heads towards the dugout, Coach Knickrehm comments to Schwarzenbach that his arm angle is better than the prior innings.

In the bottom of the eighth, a one-out Brent Wyatt single is quickly erased when Bourner gets Mills to ground into an inning-ending double play. While it is a relief to retire Mills without him doing damage, it cannot be too satisfying given the overall results of the series.

Brian Parker comes in for the ninth and brings the inevitable to a close. After back-to-back strikeouts, he gets Camron Hammond to ground out to second to end the game.

The fans that stayed for the whole game appreciate that the drizzle has gone away and that LCSC provided entertainment on a Sunday afternoon in a small town in Idaho.

---

ALBERTSON COLLEGE COYOTES VS.
LEWIS-CLARK STATE COLLEGE WARRIORS
APRIL 21, 2007 AT LEWISTON, IDAHO
HARRIS FIELD

---

Albertson (24–12, 14–9)   Lewis-Clark (37–3, 17–1)

| Player | AB | R | H | RBI | Player | AB | R | H | RBI |
|---|---|---|---|---|---|---|---|---|---|
| Bradshaw, Kent rf | 4 | 0 | 0 | 0 | Thompson, Mark ss | 3 | 1 | 1 | 0 |
| Burke, Pat 1b | 3 | 1 | 0 | 0 | Wyatt, Brent cf | 4 | 0 | 1 | 1 |
| Oliver, Casey ss | 4 | 0 | 0 | 0 | Mills, Beau 3b | 1 | 0 | 1 | 0 |
| Snider, Richie dh | 4 | 0 | 1 | 0 | Mier, Jessie dh | 4 | 0 | 0 | 0 |
| Smith, Tyler lf | 3 | 0 | 0 | 0 | Greene, Kyle 1b | 4 | 0 | 0 | 0 |
| Howarth, Luke cf | 3 | 0 | 1 | 1 | Martin, Paul lf | 4 | 2 | 3 | 1 |
| Champ, Bryan 3b | 3 | 0 | 1 | 0 | Evangelho, Zach 2b | 4 | 1 | 1 | 2 |
| McGrady, Dane c | 2 | 0 | 0 | 0 | Rivera, Mike rf | 4 | 0 | 0 | 0 |
| Cauffman, Drew pr | 0 | 0 | 0 | 0 | Georgius, Travis c | 2 | 0 | 0 | 0 |
| Hammond, Camron 2b | 3 | 0 | 0 | 0 | Knutz, Dick c | 1 | 0 | 0 | 0 |
| Brock, Andrew p | 0 | 0 | 0 | 0 | Miller, Mike p | 0 | 0 | 0 | 0 |
| Totals | 29 | 1 | 3 | 1 | Totals | 31 | 4 | 7 | 4 |

### Score by Innings

| | | | | | | | | | | | R | H | E |
|---|---|---|---|---|---|---|---|---|---|---|---|---|---|
| Albertson | 0 | 0 | 0 | 0 | 0 | 0 | 1 | 0 | 0 | - | 1 | 3 | 0 |
| Lewis-Clark | 0 | 0 | 1 | 1 | 0 | 2 | 0 | 0 | X | - | 4 | 7 | 0 |

2B — Wyatt. HR — Martin (2); Evangelho (1).

| Albertson | IP | H | R | ER | BB | SO |
|---|---|---|---|---|---|---|
| Brock, Andrew | 8 | 7 | 4 | 4 | 2 | 1 |

| Lewis-Clark | IP | H | R | ER | BB | SO |
|---|---|---|---|---|---|---|
| Miller, Mike | 9 | 3 | 1 | 1 | 0 | 6 |

Win — Miller (3–0). Loss — Brock (4–3). Save — None.

Start: 2:00. Time: 1:38. Attendance: 265

---

## ALBERTSON COLLEGE VS. LEWIS-CLARK STATE COLLEGE
## APRIL 22, 2007 AT LEWISTON, IDAHO
## HARRIS FIELD

---

### Albertson (24–13, 14–10)

| Player | AB | R | H | RBI |
|---|---|---|---|---|
| Bradshaw, Kent lf | 4 | 1 | 1 | 0 |
| Howarth, Luke cf | 3 | 1 | 3 | 1 |
| Oliver, Casey ss | 3 | 1 | 3 | 1 |
| Garsez, Jacob ph/ss | 1 | 0 | 0 | 0 |
| Roach, Adam dh | 3 | 0 | 1 | 0 |
| Burke, Pat c | 4 | 0 | 1 | 0 |
| Smith, Tyler pr/ph | 1 | 0 | 0 | 0 |
| Brigham, David pr | 0 | 1 | 0 | 0 |
| Champ, Bryan 3b | 2 | 0 | 0 | 0 |
| McGrady, Dane ph/2b | 1 | 0 | 0 | 0 |
| Echanis, Drew 1b | 4 | 0 | 0 | 0 |
| Hammond, C. 2b/3b | 4 | 0 | 1 | 1 |
| Cauffman, Drew rf | 3 | 0 | 0 | 0 |
| Taysom, Carson p | 0 | 0 | 0 | 0 |
| Zubizarreta, Joey p | 0 | 0 | 0 | 0 |
| Bourner, Tim p | 0 | 0 | 0 | 0 |
| Totals | 33 | 3 | 8 | 3 |

### Lewis-Clark (38–3, 18–1)

| Player | AB | R | H | RBI |
|---|---|---|---|---|
| Thompson, Mark ss | 5 | 3 | 2 | 1 |
| Wyatt, Brent cf | 4 | 1 | 3 | 1 |
| Mills, Beau 3b | 5 | 1 | 1 | 4 |
| Mier, Jessie c | 4 | 0 | 0 | 0 |
| Georgius, Travis c | 0 | 0 | 0 | 0 |
| Knutz, Dick c | 0 | 0 | 0 | 0 |
| Martin, Paul lf | 3 | 2 | 2 | 0 |
| Greene, Kyle 1b | 4 | 2 | 2 | 3 |
| Roehl, Jesse rf | 4 | 0 | 1 | 0 |
| Melton, Kyle dh | 3 | 1 | 1 | 1 |
| Briggs, Joey ph | 1 | 0 | 0 | 0 |
| Evangelho, Zach 2b | 3 | 0 | 1 | 0 |
| Fitts, Matt p | 0 | 0 | 0 | 0 |
| Schwarzenbach, Brad p | 0 | 0 | 0 | 0 |
| Parker, Brian p | 0 | 0 | 0 | 0 |
| Totals | 36 | 10 | 13 | 10 |

### Score by Innings

| | | | | | | | | | | | R | H | E |
|---|---|---|---|---|---|---|---|---|---|---|---|---|---|
| Albertson | 0 | 0 | 0 | 0 | 0 | 2 | 1 | 0 | 0 | - | 3 | 8 | 1 |
| Lewis-Clark | 5 | 1 | 3 | 0 | 0 | 1 | 0 | 0 | X | - | 10 | 13 | 2 |

2B — Thompson, M; Martin; Greene. HR — Mills (23); Greene (5). SF — Wyatt.

| Albertson | IP | H | R | ER | BB | SO |
|---|---|---|---|---|---|---|
| Taysom, Carson | 1 | 4 | 5 | 5 | 0 | 2 |
| Zubizarreta, Joey | 5 | 7 | 5 | 4 | 0 | 0 |
| Bourner, Tim | 2 | 2 | 0 | 0 | 1 | 0 |

| Lewis-Clark | IP | H | R | ER | BB | SO |
|---|---|---|---|---|---|---|
| Fitts, Matt | 5 | 2 | 0 | 0 | 1 | 5 |
| Schwarzenbach, Brad | 3 | 6 | 3 | 2 | 1 | 3 |
| Parker, Brian | 1 | 0 | 0 | 0 | 0 | 2 |

Win — Fitts (6–0). Loss— Taysom (6–4). Save — None.

Start: 12:00. Time: 2:10. Attendance: 195

# 5
# Chico State Wildcats

Chico State Wildcats *vs.*
Cal State Los Angeles Golden Eagles
March 9–11, 2007
PITCHING
Pitching Line: 1 run, 1 run earned...

*The home plate umpire Scott Lentendre points his index finger towards the mound and simply says, "Play." Chico State pitcher Nick Bryant stands just in front of the pitching rubber looking into catcher Lorin Nakagawa's target. Bryant appears confident.*

Chico, with a population of 80,000, is in northern California, less than a three-hour drive from San Francisco and about 90 miles due north of Sacramento.

*Everything about the start of the game is neat and crisp. The home plate area has been dragged as perfectly as a Japanese Zen garden. Lentendre's steel-toed shoes are polished to a military-standard shine and his gray slacks have a neat crease. Most importantly, Bryant's first pitch pops Nakagawa's mitt, low and on the outside corner, with absolute precision. A couple seconds after the batter, Adam Klein, watches the pitch pass by, Lentendre motions a called strike. The game is on.*

*Bryant first appears on the field about an hour before his first pitch. He is in full uniform and sits down alone on the bullpen bench down the right field line. He is like the place kicker moments before attempting a game-winning field goal. Nobody says a word to him. He continues to sit for about 10 minutes, staring straight ahead until he knows it is time to warm up.*

He is six feet tall and 190 pounds. He looks like an athlete. He is competitive and focused. He is on the cover of the season's program. He is a local guy.

Bryant went to Durham High School, whose pitching mound is less than 10 miles away from the mound at Chico's Nettleton Stadium. Durham has about five thousand residents, which is about one-third of Chico State's enrollment. There are some sizable orchards in and around Durham, primarily producing almonds and walnuts.

Transitioning from high school to college ball has its challenges. "I came from such a small high school where not everybody was the best player, not everybody had the strongest arm," says Bryant. "The biggest adjustment was the speed of the players, the ability of the players, playing with people that may be seven or eight years older than me, and making the adjustment from being a starting pitcher to being a reliever." While Bryant started a few games as a sophomore, he joined the rotation on a full-time basis as a junior.

As with many players adjusting to college ball, the mental development is as important as the physical. "Just being in that atmosphere and learning from everybody else just helped me to learn my way through it," says Bryant. "One of the biggest things is just getting over that fact that everybody out there is doing the same thing, it's the same game you need to play, and once you have the confidence, you become a lot better player."

The University of California Davis (UC Davis) had shown interest in Bryant, but his choice was primarily between Chico and Butte Community College in Oroville, a two-year school with a good athletic reputation, about 10 miles due east of Durham. By choosing Chico, Bryant ultimately became the only senior on the team that spent all four years at the college. He has had two head coaches and three pitching coaches. Most Chico players are California community college transfers; it's the easiest way to reload with talent.

*His pre-game routine is similar to many college pitchers. He wanders into the outfield and simulates throwing without a ball. He then strolls back to the bullpen area to do his rubber band work, applying tension to his upper-body muscles in a very controlled manner. Bryant follows this with a series of stretching exercises with a teammate. A half-hour has elapsed and he has yet to pick up a baseball.*

*His first throwing involves long toss, in which he throws from center field back towards the right field foul line. For the next part of the routine, Bryant makes throws in which he takes one step before releasing the ball. It is then time for the bullpen.*

*In the final phases of his pre-game preparation, he makes a series of throws from about 50 feet without any stride. About three minutes later, he throws from about two feet in front of the pitching rubber. Lastly, he stands at the required distance from home plate, 60'6" and throws about 30 pitches. When completed, it is about ten minutes before the national anthem and Umpire Lentendre's signal to start play.*

*As Bryant faces Klein to start the game, this is a big series for both schools. Klein takes a ball and then another strike before hitting a solid line drive that Chico second baseman Robby Scott catches. The result is a small initial victory for Bryant and a moral victory for Klein.*

Like most teams, Chico has a few uniform combinations to choose from. The particular uniform that is worn is dictated by the day-of-the-week tradition rather than a captain's or pitcher's selection. On this Friday evening, Chico is wearing white uniforms with pinstripes. "Wildcats" is written in script on the front with a red number on the lower left chest. Bryant wears number 36.

Bryant is a Friday night pitcher. In the CCAA (California Collegiate Athletic Association), a team's ace usually pitches the Friday night game of a four-game series (a doubleheader is typically played on Saturday and a single game on Sunday). There certainly would not be an exception to the norm this Friday. Bryant has won all three of his previous starts and has a 1.50 earned run average. Opposing hitters have a combined average of just .200 against him. His good start to the season is fully expected, as Bryant was a Division II All-American the previous season, going 8–2 with a 2.41 ERA.

*The Golden Eagles' number two hitter, Jack Roche, hits an 0–1 pitch past Scott. Two batters into the game and both have hit the ball well. Perhaps tonight is going to be a challenge for Bryant.*

*Bryant then strikes out third baseman Jeff Carroll, who is hitting .438 coming into the game, and then gets designated hitter Kurt Crowell (.410) to hit an easy pop-up to the right of the mound to end the top part of the first inning.*

*Chico is 20 games into their regularly scheduled 56-game season. If things go well, the Wildcats will play more than 56 games given the possibility of the CCAA championships, the NCAA Division II West Regional and the NCAA championship finals.*

Although the CCAA is one of if not the best Division II baseball conference in the country, the colleges that are no longer members are noteworthy. The league's membership has usually been comprised of colleges in the California State University system, which has 23 campuses and over 400,000 aggregate students. Fresno State, Cal State Fullerton, Long Beach State, UC Irvine, UC Riverside and Pepperdine were all former CCAA members, and all of these schools were selected for the 2007 NCAA Division I regional baseball tournament. Irvine and Riverside are part of the separate UC system (which also includes UC Berkeley and UCLA among the 10-campus system) and Pepperdine is a private university.

While its opponent tonight, California State University L.A. (CSULA), is in first place in the CCAA with an 8–0 record (15-1-1 overall), Chico is ranked number one in the nation, based on *Collegiate Baseball*'s NCAA Division II poll. The CSULA Golden Eagles are ranked fifth. Chico has a 15–1 record, losing only to CSU San Bernardino two weekends earlier.

The loss to San Bernardino was frustrating to the Wildcats in that Chico led 5–3 going into the seventh and final inning. Per CCAA rules, the second game of a doubleheader is scheduled for seven innings, while the first game has the standard collegiate nine innings. After the first man was retired, San Bernardino had seven consecutive batters reach base against Chico's two best relievers, Marcus Martinez and Elliott Tyson. Six of those runners scored. Chico mounted a comeback in the bottom of the seventh but ultimately fell short, 9–7.

Being number one in a poll is a good indication of a team's season progress. Becoming number one is difficult; remaining first is even more difficult. That team is the hunted.

Besides the *Collegiate Baseball* poll, the National College Baseball Writers Association (NCBWA) compiles a national and regional poll and the NCAA publishes an eight-region poll.

Also, the Massey Ratings provide an interesting result, using a mathematical model to measure the past performance of college teams, combining Divisions I, II and III programs as well as ranking teams from each division separately. Kenneth Massey, an assistant professor of mathematics at Carson-Newman College (Jefferson City, Tennessee), developed ratings for college football that are used as a component of the Bowl Championship Series (BCS) process.

Massey's baseball ratings suggest that perhaps a dozen or so Division II programs are within the top 100 baseball programs for any college division. This is impressive considering there are about 290 Division I programs. Massey concedes the data for Division I versus Division II programs is rather limited and the data used would not account for a "mismatch game" (for example, a game in which the Division II program is throwing its best pitcher against a Division I pitcher who is lower in the depth chart).

*Kyle Owsley takes the mound for the Golden Eagles in the bottom of the first inning. Things do not start well for him as he hits right fielder Danny Pignataro with the first pitch of the game. Two pitches later Robby Scott lays down a sacrifice bunt for the first out, and Owsley is immediately in danger of giving up a run.*

Chico shortstop Edgar Sedano is the number three hitter. Sedona's prior season average of .160 (4-for-25) must be put into context. He hit that for Long Beach State, a highly respected Division I team that has been to the College World Series four times. By contrast, prior to his attending Long Beach, he hit over .330 for both seasons at East Los Angeles Junior College where he was an all-conference player.

Long Beach State used Sedano as a back-up third baseman and a designated hitter, but didn't use him much. Sedano was looking to spend his senior year as a starting player and that was not likely with Long Beach. Since there is no waiting period while transferring from a Division I to a Division II program, Sedano had his chance immediately at Chico. Coming into this at-bat, he was hitting .364 for the Wildcats.

In Division I-A football and Division I basketball, a transfer must sit out a year before playing for the new college. That rule had not existed for college baseball, but after August 2008, it probably will. The rule is designed to prevent players from jumping programs on a whim. However, there is not a one-year wait period for football players transferring to a Division I-AA (Football Championship Subdivision) program or lower, or for any athlete transferring to a Division II or III program.

*Sedano takes ball one. The next pitch he drills into left field. Tommy Horning, the Golden Eagles' left fielder, charges the ball and throws accurately to home, where catcher Henry Contreras tags Pignataro for the second out. Up next, designated hitter Daniel Code strikes out looking and Chico fails to score. There is a brief sense of deflation from the Chico fans. One gets the feeling that the oh-so-close run that didn't score might have been helpful later.*

*As CSULA pitcher Owsley runs back to the third-base dugout, a familiar person jogs across his path. That person is Dave Taylor, the Chico third base coach and head coach of the Wildcats. Last season, Taylor was the head coach of Cal State L.A., Owsley's coach.\* Also, Owsley's pitching coach from last season, Alex Carbajal, is in the Chico dugout.*

*Bryant's second inning is a pitcher's dream: seven pitches, five for strikes, three consecutive outs. For the first seven hitters, only one has received as many as two balls.*

This control is very characteristic of Bryant. Coming into this game he had 17 strikeouts and four walks in 18 total innings. In his junior season, his strikeout-to-walk ratio was a similar 4.45 to 1.

---

\* *For a complete description of coach Dave Taylor's route to the Chico head coaching job, refer to Chapter 4, Lewis-Clark State College and a discussion of coaching.*

Bryant likes to throw fastballs away to both right-handed and left-handed hitters to determine what they can do with that pitch. Once he gets ahead in the count he likes to throw his off-speed stuff, a slider to right-handed hitters and a change-up to left-handers. If he sees something that the hitters are doing, he may go with a fastball in, just to set up the next pitch. Depending on the type of hitter, the pitch he has just thrown, and the pitches he has thrown in previous at-bats, these factors will dictate the pitch a hitter will see next. Bryant's usual pattern is to stay on the outside part of the plate with fastballs while he mixes in a slider or change-up.

*In the bottom of the second, first baseman Aaron Demuth leads off with a pop-up to shallow center for a routine out. Carl Fairburn, the right fielder, lays down a bunt with a 1–1 count and beats it out for a hit. When Lorin Nakagawa hits a 1–1 pitch for a ground ball to the shortstop, it looks like it might be an inning-ending double play. However, Felipe Gallo bobbles the ball and both runners are safe. The Wildcat third baseman, Jesus Luna, then hits the first pitch up the middle past Gallo, who has no chance to immediately redeem himself, and Fairburn comes around to score.*

*After center fielder Greg Finazzo pops up to the second baseman, resulting in the infield fly rule, Pignataro the lead-off hitter, shows his unusual offensive weapon for the evening and gets hit by a pitch for the second at-bat in a row. This loads the bases, but there are two outs. Robby Scott, who is hitting .372 coming into the game, hits the first pitch to second baseman Jack Roche, who throws to shortstop Gallo for the inning-ending force out. Chico takes a 1–0 lead, but for the second straight inning the fans are teased by what might have been.*

*In the top of the third inning, Bryant hopes to have an inning similar to the second. The first two batters are Felipe Gallo and Tommy Horning. These two make an interesting tandem at the bottom of the batting order. They are 5'7" and 5'8", respectively, and both are very capable of getting on base. After Bryant gets ahead 0–2, Gallo takes three straight balls. It is Bryant's first three-ball count. Gallo then grounds out to third baseman Luna for the first out.*

*Horning grounds a 1–2 pitch to second baseman Robby Scott, but Scott boots the ball for his fourth error of the season. Bryant is aware that Horning is a base-stealing threat and throws over to first after falling behind lead-off hitter Klein 2–1. On the next pitch, a swinging strike, Horning takes off but Nakagawa makes a strong throw to Scott covering the bag. A portion of the ball extends above Scott's glove, a "snow cone," but the ball does not fall out. The Chico defense now has two outs, and one pitch later Klein swings and misses for the third out. For the first three innings Bryant has allowed but one hit and no walks. He is on his game.*

*The bottom of the third is uneventful for Chico. After Edgar Sedano strikes out looking, designated hitter Daniel Code works an eight-pitch walk. When Aaron Demuth comes up for the second time, it is a marked contrast to the CSULA's pair of Gallo and Horning. Code and Demuth are back-to-back line-backers. Code is 6'3", 228 pounds and Demuth is 6'5", 245 pounds. Although Code and Demuth are imposing athletes, they cannot be football players at Chico.*

Of the 23 California State University campuses, only six have football programs. Chico State is not one of them. Only two of these six schools rou-tinely play against each other — Fresno State and San Jose State in the West-ern Athletic Conference (WAC). San Diego State is the only other Division I football program and it competes in the Mountain West Conference. In recent years, only Fresno State has had an impact on the national football scene.

Cal Poly San Luis Obispo competes in the Great West Conference for football (as a Football Championship Subdivision program) and in the Big West Conference for baseball and other sports. Sacramento State's football team participates in the Division I-AA Big Sky Conference, but since it is the only Big Sky member with a baseball team, it plays in the WAC solely for that sport, effectively taking Boise State's place for baseball since the Broncos do not have a baseball program. The sixth and final California State University with a football program is Humboldt State, in the northern coastal part of California. It is an independent Division II football team that will rejoin the Great Northwest Athletic Conference in 2008 for football. Humboldt does not have a baseball program and otherwise is a member of the CCAA.

Largely due to budget constraints and mediocre attendance, Chico State dropped its football program in 1997. It was a decade of football decline among California State Universities. Long Beach State's football program was discontinued in 1991; Cal State Fullerton's program ceased in 1992. CSULA was apparently well ahead of the trend when its football program was dropped in 1977. For many state universities, the football fields have been converted to soccer fields, creating a huge excess of available seating.

*Demuth goes through a hitting ritual almost every pitch. He taps his cleats with his bat to loosen dirt that is not there. He removes his helmet and wipes his brow with his forearm to remove perspiration that is not likely there. In this at-bat, he hits a routine grounder to third that forces Code at second. The next bat-ter, Carl Fairburn, flies out to center field with the first pitch to end the inning.*

*In the top of the fourth, Bryant is facing the heart of the order. CSULA sec-ond baseman Jack Roche gets a bloop hit to shallow center field. Jeff Carroll grounds out to Luna at third to put Roche into scoring position. However, des-ignated hitter Kurt Crowell strikes out looking on a good off-speed pitch and first baseman Mike Diaz strikes out swinging to end any threat.*

*The bottom of the fourth is equally as routine, the only item of note being that Danny Pignataro did not get hit for a third time. He instead flied to center field to strand the number nine hitter, Greg Finazzo, who had singled and stolen second.*

*In the top of the fifth, center fielder Fernando Franco pops up meekly to first base and catcher Henry Contreras flies out to right. Felipe Gallo, with his small strike zone, takes three straight balls from Bryant. Bryant works the count to 3–2 and then walks Gallo. Bryant is starting to miss up in the strike zone. Horning, the number nine hitter, takes a strike before taking a very high ball. After catcher Lorin Nakagawa has to reach up quickly for the pitch, he jogs out to the mound.*

In one sense, Lorin Nakagawa is a typical player on the Chico State roster. He is a transfer from a California junior college, in this case Porterville College. Porterville is in the central part of the state, near Sequoia National Park. What is unusual about Nakagawa's path to Chico is that he graduated from Moanalua High School in Honolulu. A high school teammate, a year ahead of Nakagawa, played on Porterville's baseball team and got the junior college interested in Nakagawa and visa versa.

*Nakagawa recalled, "I told him (Bryant) to take a deep breath, remember your mechanics, stay back, and hit my mitt." It is seemingly simple advice, but often the difference between effective and ineffective pitching is a matter of relaxation and focus. Besides mechanics, Nakagawa is of the opinion that by "just establishing a presence on the mound," showing poise and confidence, a pitcher can still make a mistake and get away with it. Nakagawa returns to home plate and Horning fouls off the next pitch. With a 1–2 count, he swings and misses to end the inning. Although Bryant shows a small trace of vulnerability in the fifth, he continues a very good outing.*

*In the bottom of the fifth, the Wildcats' two, three, and four hitters (Scott, Sedano, and Code) go down in order, although Code's out is a well-hit ball to deep center.*

Just beyond the center field fence where Fernando Franco caught Code's deep drive are several tall Valley Oaks. The trees had yet to blossom a few weeks before the start of spring, but in the darkness of the night the long, bare branches were dramatically silhouetted by the Nettleton Stadium lights. A certified landscape lighting specialist could not have created a more impressive view.

This is not the only place one can see trees. As one drives into town from Highway 32, after crossing the Sacramento River, there is Chico's welcoming sign indicating it is the "City of Trees." The surrounding campus is filled with Valley Oaks and other varieties. A few miles away are the forest of trees in Bidwell Park, a city-owned park that is 11 miles long and 3,700 acres big. It is one of the largest municipal parks in the United States. Big Chico Creek flows not only through the park but snakes its way through the Chico campus as well.

The Chico campus is a blend of the old and new. Kendall Hall, built in the early 1930s with its rotunda and Romanesque style, is the centerpiece of the central part of the campus. Along with Trinity Hall and Laxson Auditorium, these buildings have the old-brick and ivy look that is very reminiscent of an East Coast school. Close behind these buildings is Big Chico Creek, which not only creates a natural separation for a small amphitheater but cuts through the rest of the campus. The other buildings on the 120 acres of college property have contrasting brick-style architecture from the 1950s and each decade afterwards. Aesthetically, Chico is at or near the top of the California State University system campuses.

*Bryant takes the mound in the sixth with a slim 1–0 lead. Adam Klein, the Golden Eagles' lead-off hitter, swings with a 1–1 count and hits the ball to deep right-center field. It carries to the fence and Klein swiftly reaches third base with a triple. The one-run lead looks very precarious. Jack Roche comes up next, having gone 2-for-2 prior to this at-bat. Bryant quickly gets ahead 0–2 and, with a 1–2 count, Roche grounds to Sedano at shortstop. With the infield playing back and Klein running on contact, he scores easily as Sedano's only play is to throw Roche out at first. The next hitter, Jeff Carroll, works a 3–1 count before fouling off three consecutive pitches. He swings and misses the next pitch. Similarly, Kurt Crowell gets to a 3–1 count and, like Carroll, fouls off the next pitch and then strikes out swinging. Although Bryant has only given up one run, three hits and a walk through six innings, Kyle Owsley is pitching a good game as well. As the cliché goes, "It's anyone's ballgame."*

Not much is usually said to Bryant once the game starts. Like his pre-game demeanor, he likes to get into a zone and be left alone. He generally just follows the game plan that the coaches have determined.

The pitching/defensive game plan is based on the opposing hitters' skills and tendencies. Chico keeps an 8½ × 11 sheet for each opposing player that has batted against Chico. The page indicates what type of stance and swing the player has along with bunting and base-running histories. Each type of pitch is charted for each at-bat, and the results of hit balls are memorialized on one of two playing field diagrams, one for right-handed pitchers and the other for left-handed pitchers.

It is useful knowledge that also has its limitations. In a league with a high percentage of community college transfers, the first game of a series may be the first time a coaching staff has the opportunity to evaluate an opposing hitter. This is not the major leagues, where teams have advance scouts observing their next opponent.

Head coach Taylor determines the pitch selection and pitching coach Alex Carbajal relays it first to Lorin Nakagawa and then to the two middle infielders. He flashes his fingers in a sequence of three to communicate a code for a particular pitch. The catcher, shortstop and second baseman each have a plastic-covered wristband that contains the card for the type and location of dozens of pitch possibilities. The process is similar to that used by many quarterbacks.

"The coaches are well prepared for the game, know all the hitters, and they know what approach they are going to take with them," says Bryant. "The coaches are out there watching BP (batting practice), watching what each hitter does. When the hitter steps into the box, I can see his approach too. I kind of think about things in my head as well, along with the coaches.

"There will be occasions when I shake it (a sign) off. The coaches always say make sure you're committed to the pitch and throw the pitch that you're 100 percent committed to. So, if they throw a pitch down that I'm not committed to, I'm going to shake it off and throw the one that I'm committed to." Most of the time Bryant just tries to do the best he can with the pitch selected.

Knowing early on that he wanted to coach, Taylor absorbed everything he could as a catcher, from his seasons with the University of Arizona through minor league ball. He listened closely to what the pitching coaches said regarding mechanics and situational pitching. When it comes to pitching, he feels his biggest strength is calling a game, determining the pitches to call in different situations against different hitters.

Before the game, Carbajal will relay to Taylor how the pitcher looks in the bullpen. He may mention something like, "The fastball is really good today; the slider is a little flat, let's stay away from it; the change-up is dirty." Taylor will occasionally ask for Carbajal's opinion as to a pitch selection during the game. Although calling the pitches from the bench relieves some anxiety from the pitcher, Carbajal still wants pitchers to think along and understand why certain pitches are being called.

Carbajal is 29, and not only can he easily pass for one of the pitchers, he knows how they think. He was an outstanding pitcher for Chico when the school won the national championship in 1999 and was the western regional champions the following season. He played in the minor leagues for the Tampa Bay and Boston organizations and was the pitching coach for the Chico Outlaws in the independent Golden State League.

There is a balance between selecting a pitch based on the pitcher's strength as opposed to the batter's weakness. The tendency is to first go with what the pitcher is most capable of throwing well and then factor in a hitter's flaws.

The "brain" or pitching code cards are changed every few innings and even include pitch-out and pick-off moves to first (of which there are four, varying as to the time and types of moves), second (five types) and third (two types).

*In the bottom of the sixth, Aaron Demuth leads off with an opposite-field single to right, but two fielder's choices sandwiched around a caught stealing ends any threat.*

*Bryant begins the seventh the way he ended the sixth, with a strikeout. Fernando Franco follows with a fly out to right field. The Golden Eagles' catcher, Henry Contreras, works the count to 3–1. There are two outs and nobody on base, but Bryant has thrown eight balls out of the strike zone to three batters in this inning. Pitching coach Carbajal notices that he is turning his hips too early, which causes his fastball to rise. It is a refinement that will be the topic of discussion after Bryant is finished for the evening. Contreras hits the next pitch for a double to right field. Felipe Gallo gets behind 1–2 before tapping a soft grounder towards third. Luna, the third baseman, has little chance to get the quick Gallo and the latter beats it out for a single. A two-out rally is in full effect. The ninth hitter, Horning, tries to surprise the Wildcats with a bunt on the first pitch. Bryant, however, is quick off the mound to field the ball and throws out Horning. With the Chico bullpen warming up, one gets the feeling the 111th pitch may be Bryant's last.*

*Back in the fourth inning, when Finazzo stole second base after his single, it was the last time that Chico State had a runner advance past first. The Wildcats were putting the ball in play and getting some hard-hit outs, but Oswald still had allowed but one run. Finazzo hits one into the right-center field gap and sprints safely to third base. The crowd, which had been subdued by some "could-have-been" plays, erupts. A small but boisterous group of students seated high behind the Chico dugout begin a chant of "beat L.A." and stomp on the aluminum bleachers. CSULA head coach Pat Shine comes out and replaces Oswald with a tall (6'6") right-hander, John Mitchell.*

*Pignataro falls behind Mitchell 0–2 before working the count full. He then hits the ball sharply to short and Gallo throws home well ahead of Finazzo. It's a rundown. The catcher Contreras runs Finazzo back towards third and then tosses the ball to Carroll, who applies the tag. It's one out and more frustration for the Wildcats. The only positive to come from the play is that Pignataro advances to second during the rundown. Mitchell then falls behind Scott 3–1 before Scott hits a sold single up the middle, scoring Pignataro. Sedano then hits the first pitch into the right-center field gap for a double, and the score is now suddenly 3–1. The crowd is back cheering, delighted both in the unfolding rally and the reversal of game-long frustration.*

*After the relay throw makes its way back to Gallo at shortstop and the noise subsides, he suddenly sprints to second base and applies a tag on Sedano — the hidden ball trick. Sedano appears to be on the bag but Gallo is emphatic that he has the out. James Lamb, the umpire standing near second base, had returned from the outfield (going out on the double), as the other base umpire, Eric Martinez, and Scott Lentendre were settling into their positions. Lentendre sees the play unfold and concludes that Sedano is safe, but it isn't necessarily his call to make. Lamb calls Sedano safe. CSULA head coach Pat Shrine joins Gallo in an appeal to Lamb, Martinez, and finally to Lentendre, but to no avail. To Lentendre, this is the first moment of controversy in an otherwise peaceful game for the umpires.*

To a pitcher, the impact of the home plate umpire may not be as great as his defense or the opposing batter, but it is significant nonetheless.

Lentendre lives in Weed, about 50 miles south of the Oregon border, in the foothills of Mount Shasta. He played baseball through junior college, ending his playing career at the College of the Siskiyous. He started umpiring at the Little League level, when he was but a few years older than the players, working his way up to work a regional Little League playoff at just 16 years old.

Like most of those aspiring to umpire professionally, Lentendre attended a professional umpiring school — the Jim Evans Academy in Florida. He started his career in the Western Baseball League, a minor league made up of independent teams whose rosters contained many ex-minor league players hoping to get one more chance to ascend in their baseball careers. He worked his way up to the AAA level through the 2004 season before realizing the chances were not in his favor to attain one of the infrequently available major league jobs. Instead, he decided that a career change to operate the bowling alley in Weed was a better long-term choice. However, Lentendre calls some CCAA, West Coast Conference (WCC) and junior college games each season to continue doing something he still enjoys.

Lentendre sees pitches from the "slot," the space between the catcher's shoulder and the batter's body. He tries to set the bottom of his chin at the same level as the top of the catcher's head. Umpires use various stances to consistently attain this position: the tallest go to one knee, some use a "scissors" style (the front leg far in front of the back one), and many, like Lentendre, use a squat technique.

According to Lentendre, the expectation in college baseball is for umpires to call the "rule book" strike. This is a pitch that travels over any part of the plate between the bottom of the batter's elbows (which is generally the equivalent to the midpoint between the waist and the armpits) and the bottom of the knees. This means the high strike will be called much more frequently at the college level compared to the major leagues. It also means calling a pitch one ball-width off the outside or inside corners since, from a fairness perspective, the batters use of metal bats enables them to solidly hit such pitches.

"My theory is the more strikes I can call, without being ridiculous, the better flow the game will have," says Lentendre. "If batters know you're going to call strikes and pitchers are around the plate, pitchers are happy, pitching coaches are happy, catchers are happy, and batters will adjust. Every pitch is a strike until something makes it a ball."

If umpires have certain tendencies in calling balls and strikes or when they simply miss a pitch, it is not something pitching coach Carbajal wants the pitcher to focus on. It is not a topic he brings up in pre-game or in-game conversations. If a pitcher feels an umpire missed a call, he does not want his pitcher to indicate, by way of a gesture or body language, his displeasure. Carbajal feels umpires respect this and his pitcher may get the next close call.

Carbajal applies a somewhat similar approach to pitches that miss the mark. "If you miss a fastball up in the zone and you were supposed to hit it down and away, and, for whatever reason it sails up, make it look like it was part of your plan, like you were setting him (the batter) up. Don't let the hitter know, or anybody know, that you are trying to find your release point."

In determining those pitches that are strikes, according to Lentendre, "A good umpire has timing. Timing is what you do with your eyes, tracking the pitch with your eyes from the pitcher's hand, through your zone, which is up-down and across the plate, and then where the catcher catches it. Once I've seen all of that and I follow the ball all that way to the glove, my mind then decides that pitch is a strike."

How the catcher receives the ball influences the ultimate call. College catchers, who are still developing their "presentation" skills, or ability to frame a pitch, provide occasional challenges for umpires. When a borderline low strike that continues to drop is caught by the catcher with his glove hitting the ground, this technical strike will likely be called a ball.

Neither the many variations of pitching deliveries nor the disparate size of batters present challenges for Lentendre to call pitches. He thinks the most difficult pitch to call is one in which the batter crowds the plate and the catcher sets up inside. The slot is all but gone, making it difficult to see exactly where the ball is caught.

Very few of Lentendre's ball/strike calls in this game result in dissent. With two runs in and Sedano on second, the seventh-inning rally ends with Code's ground out to third and Demuth's three-pitch strikeout. It's the familiar recipe to Chico observers: Bryant pitches very well, leaves with the lead, and the bullpen will shut down opposing hitters for the win.

The 3–1 lead is handed over to Jason Gillard, a sidearm reliever. Gillard will handle the eighth, and Marcus Martinez will presumably pitch in the ninth for the save. It's a nice plan that has worked many times. Adam Klein leads off the inning with a single to left. Roche likewise follows with a single to left. Carroll then hits a fly to right-center that is deep enough for Klein to tag and go to third. Then, as is apt to happen during a game at Chico, a southbound train travels perhaps only 100 feet behind the right field fence. The elevated tracks make the top of the cars visible at field level, requiring the batter some powers of concentration to ignore box cars that are often white, green or orange. As soon as the train passes, Crowell takes a called third strike, and for an instant everything is looking much better for Chico. A second later, Roche is running on the pitch and Nakagawa lets loose with a throw that goes into center field. Klein scores easily and Roche continues to third. Mike Diaz, who has struck out in his previous two at-bats, singles to right and ties the game. Franco ends the inning by grounding into a fielder's choice, but the damage is done. Tonight, the recipe is flawed.

Carl Fairburn, despite getting behind 0–2, leads off the bottom of the eighth with a double down the left field line. Nakagawa hits a line drive to the shortstop, but that doesn't damper hopes when Matt Bitker comes up to pinch hit. Bitker looks every bit of the 250 pounds he is listed in the program. He's from Paradise, an aptly named town up a ridge at about 2,000 feet, only 15 miles or so east of Chico. An occasional starter at first, Bitker has four home runs in just 18 at-bats. He typically swings hard, Adam Dunn or Vladimir Guerrero hard. Tonight he swings hard but misses three straight pitches. After Finazzo follows, getting hit on the second pitch, Mitchell is lifted for Arturo Reyes. Reyes is 5'7", but he looks shorter than that, having replaced the 6'6" Mitchell. Pignataro comes up for his fifth at-bat and flies out to Franco, giving the center fielder his fifth putout. Fairburn is stranded at second and the score remains tied after eight.

For Chico fans, there is an "oh-no" start to the top of the ninth. Contreras, who doubled in the seventh, doubles again. It comes as little surprise that Gallo sacrifices Contreras to third. Brian Hernandez, one of the few freshmen on the team, comes up as a pinch-hitter. He falls behind 1–2 and looks slightly overmatched before hitting a chopper to a drawn-in infield, beyond the reach of replacement third baseman Trevor Moore. For Chico, the game has now reached a new level of frustration as the Golden Eagles have taken a precious one-run *lead. Jason Maes, a 6'4" left-hander, comes in for Gillard for a lefty-lefty match-up against Adam Klein. Klein strikes out for the second out and Marcus Martinez is brought in to face the predominantly right-handed hitting lineup. It is not a typical save situation, but Coach Taylor is willing to do what it takes to give the Wildcats the best chance to win this first game. It may impact Martinez's availability the rest of the series.*

Martinez's arrival at Chico the previous season was a result of his pitching coach at Cuesta College (San Luis Obispo) being good friends with the former Wildcat pitching coach, Jason Kelly. Martinez was a third-team All-American the prior season based on his 12 saves, 2–0 record and 1.88 ERA in 20 appearances. Unlike most college pitchers, he became a reliever in high school (in Morro Bay, on the coast in central California). Unlike most college pitchers, he is a father.

Coming into this game he had five saves in five opportunities and had yet to give up a run.

Martinez' physical limit is usually three games in a four-game series. His maximum usage is usually two innings (three, if he has had sufficient rest). Last year against CSULA, he pitched on Friday night as well as both games in Saturday's doubleheader. The doubleheader is actually the easiest multi-use challenge for him since he usually still feels warm for the second game if he pitches in the first.

*Jack Roche lays a bunt down for a hit, but the inning ends as Martinez strikes out Jeff Carroll. The Wildcats are down by one, but the middle of the batter order will get a chance to hit in the bottom of the ninth.*

*Scott leads off the ninth with a pop-up to third baseman Carroll. Edgar Sedano follows with a solid single to right for his third hit of the night. Hope flows back into the Chico crowd. Reyes is concerned about Sedano stealing his way into scoring position and throws over to first twice during Code's at-bat. Code looks at a called third strike; suddenly and improbably the number one-ranked Division II team in the country is one out away from losing. What suspense is left evaporates quickly as Demuth strikes out swinging to end the game.*

Chico's loss, as frustrating as it was for the Wildcats, is not something they could dwell on for long. They had to be back at Nettleton Stadium in less than twelve hours to play a doubleheader. They would then return early Sunday morning to close out the series.

*If Daniel Code and Aaron Demuth look like a couple of linebackers, then Sunday's starter, Chris Bodishbaugh, looks like a quarterback. This may be because he was one. Only his number, 25, is un-quarterback-like. As the national anthem plays, the 6'3" Bodishbaugh stands next to his catcher, Nakagawa, on the grass between the mound and second base. He towers over him. The infielders — Demuth, Scott, Sedano and Luna — gather in shallow center, four astride. Lastly, the trio of outfielders, Fairburn, Finazzo and Casey Smyth, stand together in center field. It is an alignment followed by many college teams prior to the start of the game.*

Bodishbaugh was put in the unusual role of stopper in this series, as in stop the losing. The unthinkable had happened, as Chico was swept in Saturday's doubleheader, 8–3 and 7–1. After Friday night's difficult loss, things had gone from bad to worse. By late Saturday afternoon, everyone knew the Wildcats were free-falling out of the nation's number one ranking.

In the first game of the doubleheader, Chico starter Billy Spottiswood had a 28-pitch first inning that likely disrupted his rhythm and confidence. A starter is realistically hoping for a 12- to 15-pitch inning, allowing him to go deep into the game. Typically a very effective pitcher, Spottiswood struggled in this game. His variety of pitches is more than the pitch cards can accommodate. Daniel Code's first-inning home run was one of the few satisfying moments for the Wildcats.

Kyle Woodruff started Saturday's second game. His walk of lead-off hitter Adam Klein probably caused the Chico fans to mutter a collective expletive. Indeed, Klein came around to score as he would two more times that game. Other than Demuth's solo home run in the fourth, the Chico offense languished in the afternoon sun. The Wildcats managed just three hits in the seven-inning game.

The pitching staff on Saturday provided Coach Carbajal plenty to analyze. Every pitch is recorded from a center-field camera. Many mechanical flaws that aren't picked up in real time can be noticed in video. He reviews the video the night of the game and talks to the pitchers the next day.

*Bodishbaugh starts the game walking Klein on five pitches. Even the most optimistic Chico fan is immediately concerned. However, Kyle Williams, starting at second base for the Golden Eagles instead of Jack Roche, grounds into a double play. After Jeff Carroll's infield hit, Kurt Crowell hits a foul pop-up to Nakagawa. Perhaps the negative vibe has been purged.*

Bodishbaugh's mannerisms are more like a country boy from the Midwest rather than the outskirts of suburbia. He was raised in Oakley in the eastern part of the San Francisco Bay Area.

He did not view the fourth starting role as a "low value" assignment.

Given that the bullpen may be tired by Sunday, he can help the team significantly by going deep into the game. That, plus the fact that every win counts the same, gave him sufficient motivation for each start.

*Sunday was a perfect day for baseball (temperature in the high 70s), particularly for mid–March. The morning chill had disappeared. As the game was in its earliest moments, at least a few fans observed what a great setting they had to enjoy. Nettleton Stadium is not only a very good Division II college baseball venue, but a very good college baseball venue in comparison to all levels.*

While some schools like the University of Utah (using Franklin Covey Field for the Los Angeles Angels of Anaheim's Triple-A affiliate in Salt Lake City) and the University of New Mexico (using Isotopes Park for the Florida Marlins' Triple-A affiliate in Albuquerque) play in minor league parks, these are usually off-campus facilities. In the CCAA, Cal State San Bernardino plays at Arrowhead Credit Union Park, the home of the Inland Empire 66ers, a Class A California League affiliate of the Los Angeles Dodgers.

Nettleton was built primarily through the funding provided by Steve Nettleton, a one-time supermarket owner and the founder of the Chico Heat baseball club. The Heat used the stadium from their opening day in 1997 through 2002, when the Western Baseball League folded. Besides the Wildcats, it is presently the home to the Chico Outlaws.

The Outlaws received some notoriety in the summer of 2006 when they played host to Jose Canseco and the San Diego Surf Dawgs. Before a record crowd of 4,500, Canseco began his brief comeback, going 0-for-3.

The stands are comprised of three separate symmetrical grandstands, each about three stories tall, with bench-style seating. The grandstand behind home plate has backrests attached to the benches. The outside of the structures have a three-color combination comprised on beige, dark beige and terra cotta complementing a series of decorative arches affixed to the exterior. Within the buildings are locker rooms, offices, rest rooms, and snack bars. Although the stucco is showing a few signs of wear, it is nonetheless an overall impressive facility, particularly for those who turn into the adjoining parking lot for the first time.

Esken Hall, which is next to Mechoopda and Konkow halls, is a dormitory that is slightly more than a foul ball away. More than a few of the students are awakened by the weekend batting practice music that starts about three hours before game time.

*With the help of a double play, Chico sends but three players to bat in a short-lived bottom of the first. Manny Hernandez, a left-hander who has not given up an earned run in the 15⅓ innings he has pitched coming into this game, gets the start for CSULA. As quickly as the bottom of the first goes, Bodishbaugh has a pitcher's wish, a one-two-three, six-pitch inning in the second.*

Of course, things usually don't go as smoothly as a six-pitch inning. This is where the mental side of pitching is important. Coach Carbajal often reminds his pitchers to "release things" when bad outcomes occur, and he wants them to realize that they do not have to make perfect pitches to be successful.

"In college ball you are going to have jam shots that fall in, that's just part of the game; you are going to have an umpire who is going to squeeze you, that's just part of the game," Carbajal says. "At the same time, you throw a great pitch and it is hit really well or you'll hang a slider and your outfielder makes a diving play. You don't deserve that but it evens itself out."

He likes pitchers to remember the feeling of a good pitch and return to it when the need arises.

*In the bottom of the second, Code hits the first pitch for a routine out in center and Demuth follows with a grounder that Gallo dives for and stops, but the shortstop cannot get the throw off quickly enough to get the out. Chico hadn't gotten many close plays to go its way in this series, so perhaps this is a positive sign. However, the "maybe this will be our inning feeling" dissipates with a 1–1 count on Fairburn. Hernandez, who showed a good pick-off move in the first, freezes Demuth leading off the bag and, with a strong throw, picks him off.*

*Fairburn hits the next pitch for a single to left and Nakagawa follows with a single to right. Luna walks on five pitches, and a two-out rally is in full blossom. Smyth, who had gone 1-for-5 in the doubleheader, is up as the number nine hitter. He is the only hometown player on the team, having gone to Chico High School, which is but a few hundred yards from the batter's box in which he stands. He strikes out on three pitches.*

*In the top of the third, Bodishbaugh faces the diminutive duo, Gallo and Horning, for the first time. Gallo walks on five pitches, the last three missing high before the fourth ball flies over Nakagawa's mitt. He falls behind Horning 2–0 and Nakagawa goes out for a talk. He thinks Bodishbaugh does not look balanced or fluid. He tells him "to trust his stuff, that he is a better pitch than they are hitters and to just hit his mitt." The next pitch is a strike. The count goes 3–1 before a called strike and then three consecutive fouls. However, he cannot put Horning away and walks him on the ninth pitch of the at-bat. After Klein sacrifices the runners to second and third, respectively, second baseman Kyle Williams, receiving his first start of the series, gets hit by a pitch.*

*The number three hitter, Carroll, is up. He has had mixed results in this series, stroking four hits in 14 at-bats with four strikeouts. This time he hits a ball to the right-center field gap for a double. Smyth chases the ball down and relays the throw to second baseman Scott, who, in turn, makes a strong throw to Nakagawa. Horning slides but misses the plate as Nakagawa applies the tag. Not only does Chico record the second out, the Wildcats also allow only one run to score on a bases-loaded double. With runners on second and third, Bodishbaugh strikes out Crowell swinging to end the threat.*

Bodishbaugh did not take the typical path to pitching in college. After graduating from high school, he earned a scholarship to San Jose State as a quarterback. After red-shirting his freshman year, he took part in football's spring practice, and his future looked promising. But baseball was still on his mind.

Following his freshman year he decided to play on a summer team that was coached by Tony Dress, who also coached at Los Medanos Junior College (Dress, a Chico grad, eventually took the head coaching job at San Francisco State, a league opponent of the Wildcats). Despite not having pitched in a game for more than a year, he pitched nine innings and struck out 14 in his first summer outing. Baseball looked good again.

Bodishbaugh decided not only to transfer to Los Medanos for his sophomore year, he also quarterbacked the junior college team. That proved to be his final season of football; he concluded that baseball was his sport. It took him about a month to "lengthen his arm out" and adjust from football's short motion to baseball's longer motion. A transition from quarterback to catcher is more natural than becoming a pitcher given the quick, short release of the former.

*The bottom of the third is uneventful but for one play: the pickoff. Finazzo reaches first when first baseman Diaz drops a routine throw on a ground ball. He is not there for long; after Scott is retired on a pop fly to right and Sedano is up, Finazzo is caught leaning the wrong way, and Hernandez has his second victim. As the pick-off throw is made, Finazzo has little choice but to break for second, where Gallo tags him out easily after a throw from Diaz. Sedano's scorched single is followed by Code's foul pop-up to the catcher. The Wildcats don't make the Golden Eagles pay for their initial error.*

*Bodishbaugh throws an off-speed pitch high in the strike zone to begin the fourth. Scott Lentendre, umpiring behind the plate as he did Friday night, calls the strike. Immediately head coach Pat Shine yells out, "Come on, Scott. You're better than that." The disagreement is short-lived as is the inning. Nine pitches, six strikes later, Bodishbaugh has retired the side.*

Coach Taylor views most junior college transfers, like Bodishbaugh, as pitchers that need fine-tuning, not major overhauling. But that fine-tuning he leaves for his pitching coach, Carbajal. Taylor was a pitching coach for his predecessor at Chico, Lindsay Meggs (who left for Indiana State). Meggs gave Taylor the responsibility for the pitching staff to "mold them, groom them and do your thing with them."

"I think that is how you have to do it," said Taylor. "If you want a consistent approach with the guys, to be a head coach and tinker with those guys, you can, but you can't have two guys really involved with that. They got to be able to listen to one guy and do the things that person is asking them to do."

Carbajal doesn't believe in tinkering with a pitcher's mechanics just to fit a predetermined mold. He does, however, believe in certain fundamentals.

"The main themes are there as far as getting to that balanced position. It doesn't matter who you are; if you don't stay on that back leg, you have no power and cannot get on top of the ball. Next, I've learned from a lot of big league coaches who worked with me, is 'getting your head into the catcher's glove', meaning once you get to that balanced position and go for that power, if you're veering off with your head at all, it's not going to work. You have to 'bury your head into the catcher's glove.'"

*The bottom of the fourth is uneventful but for one play: the pickoff. With one out, Fairburn singles. As he takes his lead, Hernandez appears to have his third base runner stuck in concrete as he throws over to first, and Fairburn is easily thrown out while futilely trying to reach second. Lentendre indicates the runner is safe, which incites vocal displeasure from the CSULA fans. Perhaps many think he has overruled the base umpire on the tag out at second, but he actually called a balk.*

*As Lentendre sees it, Hernandez' initial motion was so much in the direction of home plate that he almost fell forward as he tried to redirect his pick-off throw to first base. Once a pitcher starts his motion to home plate, he must continue it or be subject to a balk call. Predictably, Shine comes out to discuss the call, but his disagreement is short-lived. Although Nakagawa follows with the base hit, Fairburn is unable to score. A dreaded double play on a hit-and-run ends the threat and the inning.*

*Bodishbaugh can't be thrilled to face Gallo and Horning, the two with the small strike zone, to start the fifth inning. Gallo beats out a grounder to short and becomes Bodishbaugh's preoccupation. The former survives two pick-off throws and a pitch-out. Horning is the beneficiary of the distraction as he walks. After Klein and Williams are quickly retired, it's Carroll's turn in the batting order, and his appearance prompts a conference between Bodishbaugh, Nakagawa and Coach Taylor. Carroll walks to load the bases. However, in one of those*

*potential game-changing moments, Bodishbaugh comes back from a 2–0 count
and gets Crowell to ground out to keep it a one-run game.*

*Smyth's lead-off single in the bottom of the inning ends quietly when he is
stranded on third after Sedano strikes out swinging with two outs.*

*Bodishbaugh, who is fighting some arm discomfort, does not come out for
the sixth inning and is replaced by Elliott Tyson. He throws eight pitches, all of
them strikes, to quickly retire CSULA's five, six and seven hitters. The last pitch
results in Tyson bare-handing a hard-hit bouncer right back to him.*

Tyson is laid-back, a free spirit. The right-hander is from Southern California (Anaheim) who has a deceptive motion in which he hides the ball
well. He made 33 appearances the prior season to set a Chico record. At Santa
Ana Junior College he fell into the closer role. In his very first outing, he
entered the game with the bases loaded and a two-run lead. He got out of the
inning unscathed and was hooked on the challenge of never knowing when
he would be used.

He is one of 12 pitchers on the staff. Coach Taylor typically has 11 to 13
pitchers on the spring roster after having 18 to 20 in the fall. He builds the
staff around four "weekend guys," the consistent starters. Next, he has two
"starter-stuff guys" that can be used as set-up pitchers in the late innings. He
likes to carry one or two "lefty match-up guys" that can be put into the game
late to get a key out against a left-handed hitter. He relies on two pitchers to
close games. That leaves the 11th and 12th pitchers as "long guys" to be used
for those infrequent games that get lopsided against Chico.

Tyson, along with Marcus Martinez, is one of the two key relievers. He
has been used three consecutive days in the past as well as during both ends
of a doubleheader. Although his velocity may decrease by Sunday in a four-
game weekend series, he usually maintains good control and ball movement.

*With Tyson's superb inning, the feeling is that the Golden Eagles' offense
might be held in check. All Chico needs to do is to put a rally together, but other
than the seventh inning of game one, they have not put multiple hits together
to score runs. Code's lead-off double past a diving Carroll and subsequent tag-
up on Demuth's fly out to right field seems to be the start of at least something.
However, David Chacon makes his first appearance in the series by relieving Hernandez, and strikes out Nakagawa and Luna. Another opportunity dissipates.*

*In the seventh, Tyson claims success by retiring Gallo and Horning for the
first time in the game. When Klein singles and steals second, Chico has an uneasy
feeling about a Golden Eagle runner in scoring position. With a 1–1 count on
Williams, Tyson calls Nakagawa out to the mound. It is simply a case of the latter flashing the signs too quickly for Tyson. He then strikes Williams out.*

*For the second time, Smyth leads off with a single, Finazzo sacrifices him to second, and Scott hits a grounder to second. This time Scott isn't retired at first as the second baseman, Williams, throws to third to retire Smyth running on the play. Manny Urresti comes in to relieve and nearly catches Scott leaning the wrong way with his lead off of first base. However, the Wildcats escape having a third runner picked off. Instead, Sedano grounds out to end the inning.*

*Tyson has another good inning, getting through the heart of the order with only a single to Crowell. It did not necessarily have this feel at the beginning, but the game has developed into a tense pitcher's duel. One mistake, one fortuitous break might make the difference.*

Tyson lives by the slider, thrown at different speeds. Unlike most starters, who may throw a variety of different pitches when hitters come up for the second or third at-bats, Tyson complements his slider with a two-seam fastball and a change-up that he generally only throws to left-handed batters.

*The bottom of the eighth is uneventful but for one play: the pickoff. After Demuth's one-out single, Shane Farmer comes in as a pinch-runner. With Fairburn up, Urresti is determined to keep him from advancing. He throws a pitchout on the second pitch and then throws over to first with the count 1–2. He throws over a second time, and Farmer is too late diving back to first. He is out, and on the next pitch, Fairburn flies out to keep it a 1–0 game going into the ninth.*

*Tyson completes a masterful relief appearance by retiring Contreras, Gallo and Horning on eight combined pitches. Bodishbaugh and Tyson have held the Golden Eagles to but one run and caused CSULA to fail to score seven runners who were in scoring position. The last time Chico lost a 1–0 game was about two years earlier at Sonoma State when then-reliever Nick Bryant took the loss. They still have three outs to prevent that from happening.*

*As he did on Friday night, Arturo Reyes comes in with a one-run lead to try to earn the save. This afternoon there is no bottom-of-the-ninth drama for the Wildcats. Reyes needs just nine pitches to retire the side and have CSULA accomplish the unthinkable: a sweep of Chico.*

Through the ups and downs of the season, Coach Carbajal may tinker with his pitchers' psyches as much as their mechanics. "My family worked with horses my whole life. My dad was a horse trainer. I'd hear him talk about different horses and I relayed it a lot to baseball. Every horse has a different personality, and I kind of think of my pitchers as horses as well. You have to find a way to identify what their strengths and weakness are and work with them. If a guy gets distracted a lot, you have to kind of put blinkers on him and make sure you get him focused again. If a guy is a big-time competitor, you have to slow him up sometimes."

*As the Chico fans walk out of Nettleton Stadium to enjoy what is left of their Sunday afternoon, they are comforted by one thought: fortunately, there is plenty of season remaining.*

## #5 CAL STATE L.A. GOLDEN EAGLES VS. #1 CHICO STATE WILDCATS
### MARCH 9, 2007 AT CHICO, CALIFORNIA
### NETTLETON STADIUM

### Cal State L.A. (16-1-1, 9–0 CCAA)

| Player | AB | R | H | RBI |
|---|---|---|---|---|
| Klein, Adam rf | 5 | 2 | 2 | 0 |
| Roche, Jack 2b | 5 | 1 | 4 | 1 |
| Carroll, Jeff 3b | 5 | 0 | 0 | 0 |
| Crowell, Kurt dh | 4 | 0 | 0 | 0 |
| Diaz, Mike 1b | 4 | 0 | 1 | 1 |
| Hale, Darrick pr | 0 | 0 | 0 | 0 |
| Winkelman, Matt 1b | 0 | 0 | 0 | 0 |
| Franco, Fernando cf | 4 | 0 | 0 | 0 |
| Contreras, Henry c | 4 | 1 | 2 | 0 |
| Gallo, Felipe ss | 2 | 0 | 1 | 0 |
| Horning, Tommy lf | 3 | 0 | 0 | 0 |
| Hernandez, Brian ph/lf | 1 | 0 | 1 | 1 |
| Owsley, Kyle p | 0 | 0 | 0 | 0 |
| Mitchell, John p | 0 | 0 | 0 | 0 |
| Reyes, Arturo p | 0 | 0 | 0 | 0 |
| Totals | 37 | 4 | 11 | 3 |

### Chico State (19–2, 7–2 CCAA)

| Player | AB | R | H | RBI |
|---|---|---|---|---|
| Pignataro, Danny lf | 3 | 1 | 0 | 0 |
| Scott, Robby 2b | 4 | 1 | 1 | 1 |
| Sedano, Edgar ss | 5 | 0 | 3 | 1 |
| Code, Daniel dh | 4 | 0 | 0 | 0 |
| Demuth, Aaron 1b | 5 | 0 | 1 | 0 |
| Fairburn, Carl rf | 4 | 1 | 2 | 0 |
| Nakagawa, Lorin c | 4 | 0 | 0 | 0 |
| Luna, Jesus 3b | 3 | 0 | 1 | 1 |
| Bitker, Matt ph | 1 | 0 | 0 | 0 |
| Moore, Trevor 3b | 0 | 0 | 0 | 0 |
| Finazzo, Greg cf | 3 | 0 | 2 | 0 |
| Bryant, Nick p | 0 | 0 | 0 | 0 |
| Gillard, Jason p | 0 | 0 | 0 | 0 |
| Maes, Jason p | 0 | 0 | 0 | 0 |
| Martinez, Marcus p | 0 | 0 | 0 | 0 |
| Totals | 36 | 3 | 10 | 3 |

### Score by Innings

| | | | | | | | | | | | R | H | E |
|---|---|---|---|---|---|---|---|---|---|---|---|---|---|
| Cal State L.A. | 0 | 0 | 0 | 0 | 0 | 1 | 0 | 2 | 1 | - | 4 | 11 | 2 |
| Chico State | 0 | 1 | 0 | 0 | 0 | 0 | 2 | 0 | 0 | - | 3 | 10 | 2 |

2B — Contreras 2 (2); Sedano (2); Fairburn (5). 3B — Klein (1); Finazzo (1).

| Cal State L.A. | IP | H | R | ER | BB | SO |
|---|---|---|---|---|---|---|
| Owsley, Kyle | 6 | 6 | 2 | 1 | 1 | 3 |
| Mitchell, John | 1⅔ | 3 | 1 | 1 | 0 | 2 |
| Reyes, Arturo | 1⅓ | 1 | 0 | 0 | 0 | 2 |

| Chico State | IP | H | R | ER | BB | SO |
|---|---|---|---|---|---|---|
| Bryant, Nick | 7 | 5 | 1 | 1 | 1 | 9 |
| Gillard, Jason | 1⅓ | 5 | 3 | 3 | 0 | 1 |
| Maes, Jason | ⅓ | 0 | 0 | 0 | 0 | 1 |
| Martinez, Marcus | ⅓ | 1 | 0 | 0 | 0 | 1 |

Win — Reyes (2–0). Loss — Gillard (2–1). Save — None.

Start: 6:00. Time: 3:40. Attendance: 633

## #5 Cal State L.A. Golden Eagles vs.
## #1 Chico State Wildcats
## March 11, 2007 at Chico, California
## Nettleton Stadium

### Cal State L.A. (19-1-1, 12–0 CCAA)        Chico State (19–5, 7–5 CCAA)

| Player | AB | R | H | RBI | Player | AB | R | H | RBI |
|---|---|---|---|---|---|---|---|---|---|
| Klein, Adam rf | 3 | 0 | 1 | 0 | Finazzo, Greg cf | 2 | 0 | 0 | 0 |
| Williams, Kyle 2b | 3 | 0 | 0 | 0 | Scott, Robby 2b | 4 | 0 | 1 | 0 |
| Carroll, Jeff 3b | 3 | 0 | 2 | 1 | Sedano, Edgar ss | 4 | 0 | 1 | 0 |
| Crowell, Kurt dh | 4 | 0 | 1 | 0 | Code, Daniel dh | 4 | 0 | 1 | 0 |
| Diaz, Mike 1b | 4 | 0 | 0 | 0 | Demuth, Aaron 1b/dh | 4 | 0 | 2 | 0 |
| Franco, Fernando cf | 4 | 0 | 0 | 0 | Farmer, Shane pr | 0 | 0 | 0 | 0 |
| Contreras, Henry c | 4 | 0 | 0 | 0 | Cauley, Shane 1b | 0 | 0 | 0 | 0 |
| Gallo, Felipe ss | 3 | 1 | 1 | 0 | Fairburn, Carl rf | 3 | 0 | 2 | 0 |
| Horning, Tommy lf | 2 | 0 | 0 | 0 | Nakagawa, Lorin c | 4 | 0 | 2 | 0 |
| Hernandez, Manny p | 0 | 0 | 0 | 0 | Luna, Jesus 3b | 2 | 0 | 0 | 0 |
| Chacon, David p | 0 | 0 | 0 | 0 | Bitker, Matt ph | 1 | 0 | 0 | 0 |
| Urresti, Manny p | 0 | 0 | 0 | 0 | Smyth, Casey lf | 4 | 0 | 2 | 0 |
| Reyes, Arturo p | 0 | 0 | 0 | 0 | Bodishbaugh, Chris p | 0 | 0 | 0 | 0 |
| | | | | | Tyson, Elliott p | 0 | 0 | 0 | 0 |
| Totals | 30 | 1 | 5 | 1 | Totals | 32 | 0 | 11 | 0 |

### Score by Innings

| | | | | | | | | | | | R | H | E |
|---|---|---|---|---|---|---|---|---|---|---|---|---|---|
| Cal State L.A. | 0 | 0 | 1 | 0 | 0 | 0 | 0 | 0 | 0 | - | 1 | 5 | 1 |
| Chico State | 0 | 0 | 0 | 0 | 0 | 0 | 0 | 0 | 0 | - | 0 | 11 | 0 |

2B — Carroll; Code.

| Cal State L.A. | IP | H | R | ER | BB | SO |
|---|---|---|---|---|---|---|
| Hernandez, Manny | 5⅓ | 9 | 0 | 0 | 2 | 2 |
| Chacon, David | 1⅓ | 1 | 0 | 0 | 0 | 2 |
| Urresti, Manny | 1⅓ | 1 | 0 | 0 | 0 | 0 |
| Reyes, Arturo | 1 | 0 | 0 | 0 | 0 | 1 |
| *Chico State* | IP | H | R | ER | BB | SO |
| Bodishbaugh, Chris | 5 | 3 | 1 | 1 | 5 | 2 |
| Tyson, Elliott | 4 | 2 | 0 | 0 | 0 | 2 |

Win — Hernandez (2–0). Loss — Bodishbaugh (2–1). Save — Reyes (3).

Start: 12:00. Time: 3:05. Attendance: 682

# 6

# San Jacinto Community College Gators

San Jacinto Community College Gators *vs.*
Laredo Palominos
March 17–18, 2007
HITTING
Solid Contact

*As San Jacinto warmed up for the doubleheader against Laredo, they likely were not thinking that spring break wasn't much of a break.*

They played a doubleheader on Saturday against Galveston and were scheduled to play two more games on Monday against Angelina College, but it was rained out. They played a doubleheader on Thursday against South Suburban of the Chicago area. They played a late-scheduled Friday night home game against a visiting St. Louis Community College. The weekend schedule had three conference home games against Laredo Community College.

There were torrential thundershowers hitting the Houston area on Monday and Tuesday. The left field foul pole had been blown down. If the rains had continued throughout the week, there was some thought of moving the series to Laredo and then playing the Palominos back in Houston when they were scheduled for a rematch in late April. The weather turned for the better, however, as the week progressed and the Laredo series was assured as scheduled.

On Saturday, the teams play a doubleheader. The first game is scheduled for seven innings and the second, nine. If the first game exceeds seven innings, then the second game is adjusted to seven.

The season began well enough for the Gators. They won 10 of their first 13 games before the team hit a collective slump. They lost eight of the next 12 games heading into spring break. It had been a joint effort of sub-par hitting and pitching.

San Jacinto is a junior college ("juco") located in Houston, Texas. It is comprised of three separate campuses, two in Houston and one in nearby Pasadena. The men's basketball team and the women's volleyball team, the Ravens, are part of the central campus in Pasadena. The softball team and the men's soccer team, the Coyotes, are part of the south campus. The baseball team and the women's basketball team, the Gators, are part of the north campus in northeastern Houston.

If Chico, California, proclaims itself as the "City of Trees," then this part of Houston is the "Section of Forests." The nearby apartment complexes drive home the point: The Oaks of Woodforest, Woodforest North, Forest Creek, Rollingwood Oaktree, Wood Bayou, Pine Creek, Deer Wood Pines and the Willows of Woodforest.

In the 20-minute drive from Houston's airport (George Bush Intercontinental), one will see lots of trees. The closer one travels to San Jacinto, one can readily spot Baptist churches, donut shops, 99-cent stores, and, of course, trees.

"Jacinto" is most frequently pronounced with a j-sound, as in "jersey." However, the more Latino roots one has, the more likely the word is pronounced with an h-sound, as in "jalapeño." To the locals, the community college is simply known as "San Jac" (with a "j" sound). The shortened name, in script lettering, is on the front of their jerseys.

When approaching John Ray Harrison Field, an impressive football stadium is in the background. It is not part of the San Jacinto campus; the college does not have a football team. It is the home to the North Shore Mustangs, the 2003 Texas high school state champions. Most of the San Jacinto campus buildings are of 1970s vintage and not particularly interesting. However, two exceptions are the new fine arts center and the interactive learning center on the opposite side of the campus from the baseball field.

Harrison Field is a nice juco facility that was renovated in 1993 and upgraded in 2002. In right field, the scoreboard includes a message board. While a 30-foot-high green backdrop is in straight-away center field, there are dozens of trees just beyond the perimeter of the outfield fence. The entrance has a smaller-scale minor league park feel to it. Two sets of bleachers provide a close-up view to the game, and while its seating capacity is perhaps a couple of hundred, it is sufficient for the typical junior college game. Immediate family, girlfriends and the occasional scout are usually the only ones in attendance.

San Jac plays in the National Junior College Athletic Association (NCJAA) Region XIV South Conference that includes Alvin, Blinn (Brenham), Galveston, Laredo and Wharton.

*Hank Williamson begins Saturday's doubleheader by falling behind Laredo's lead-off hitter, Humberto Miranda, 3–1. The former is 6'5" and north of 200 pounds. On two of the pitches, borderline low strikes, he appears to get squeezed by the home plate umpire. After the second close pitch, Jimmy Durham, the Gators' assistant coach, calls out, "Raise it up a quarter of an inch." His voice is not loud enough to reach the home plate area, but it gets a quick laugh from the dugout. Williamson yields the walk. James Green follows with a bloop hit, barely reaching the right field grass.*

*After Cody Pifer successfully sacrifices, Carson Vitale comes up. Before he strikes out, Williamson watches a passed ball score Miranda and a wild pitch score Green. Despite allowing just a soft single, the Gators are down, 2–0.*

Williamson's arrival at San Jac is different than most. He spent his freshman year at St. Edwards College, a strong Division II program in Austin, Texas. He then transferred to Rice University, a beautiful campus of bricks and trees less than 20 miles southwest of San Jacinto. He did not pitch for the Owls and decided to attend San Jac.

The reasons players attend a junior college are varied. For some, it is strictly a financial decision. The tuition for community college is significantly lower than even an in-state, four-year public college. For somebody who is receiving a partial baseball scholarship at a university, the financial burdens can still be substantial. Since the prerequisite courses are often similar in a junior college versus a four-year school, many juco enrollees, particularly commuting students, do not feel they are missing much for the first two years. The diploma only indicates where one graduated, not how one earned it.

For some students, junior college is their best baseball option. Those players who are drafted out of high school, but not in a round high enough for their financial liking, can be redrafted after each junior college season. In four-year colleges, a player cannot be drafted until he has finished his junior year or has turned age 21.

Some players decide that they may have a better chance to play in their freshman year if they go to a junior college. Other players may have been passed over, rightly or wrongly, by four-year schools due to baseball skills and/or high school grades, and a junior college may provide the only realistic chance to play at a competitive level for the time being. According to assistant coach Durham, "They're in junior college for a reason. Some of them choose to because of the draft, but some of them don't consistently do things that would keep them at the Division I level."

*After Laredo scores two in the top of the inning, Tanner Hines leads off the bottom of the first just as Laredo did — with a walk. Hines is lean, 140 pounds lean. It is completely expected when he steals second. After Kris Miller flies to deep center against Laredo's left-handed starter, Anthony Garcia, the designated hitter, Brandon Belt, is up to bat. He is also lean, but his 195 pounds are distributed over a 6'5" frame. Belt, appropriately named, singles to center, driving in Hines and taking second base on an error.*

*As soon as Hines returns to the dugout, head coach Tom Arrington immediately asks him what catcher's signs he picked up while standing on second base. It is information that could come in handy later in the game. Arrington is of the opinion that most junior college teams are usually not diligent in terms of changing the pitch selection signs with runners on second base or from inning to inning.*

*After Eric Fry walks and Jeremy Barfield flies out, Taylor Hammack singles and drives in Belt. The Gators have matched the two runs they spotted Laredo in the top of the inning. Trey Sperring walks on four pitches and the bases are loaded. While Garcia gets a visit on the mound, Coach Arrington mentions to the next hitter, Killan Kinart, not to swing at the first pitch. He doesn't. However, he sees three straight strikes and is out looking.*

Head coach Tom Arrington may be an expatriate, but he seems very much at home in Houston. He grew up in the town of Mill Valley, Marin County, in the San Francisco Bay Area. He was an all-conference pitcher at College of Marin, a community college in Kentfield, before becoming an all-conference pitcher at Texas A&M.

His professional playing career began with the Salt Lake City Trappers and meandered to the point where he was slated to be the Opening Day starter for the Texas Rangers as a replacement player in 1994. The strike was settled just before regular season was to begin, and he instead was sent to their Class AAA team, the Oklahoma City 89ers. That assignment evolved into a season in Guadalajara, Mexico, which he foresaw as an enjoyable ending to the playing portion of his career.

He returned to the Bay Area as an assistant and then as a head coach at College of Marin. When the pitching coach position opened up at San Jac for the 2000 season, he welcomed the opportunity to work under head coach Chris Rupp. A year later, Rupp joined Rice coach Wayne Graham, who was a legend (five national titles) in his 11-year tenure at San Jac. Arrington accepted the high expectations. Not only have there been frequent NJCAA World Series appearances, but the teams are usually loaded with talent.

This squad has 14 players who were selected in the major league draft. Even though San Jac is a junior college, it is natural to hypothesize how the team would fare against a good four-year college program. "I would have to say that our pitching would match up with just about any Division I (school) in the country," says Arrington. "The maturity and strength issues with position players is superior at a university because there is just more years of development. We are definitely dealing with those elite players (at San Jac)

112    Nine College Nines

and we could match up strongly with a lot of Division I's." He makes the observation very matter of factly without a hint of boasting.

Arrington is part of an effective coaching staff that includes Durham, who was an assistant at New Mexico Junior College, the 2005 NJCAA national champions and an experienced high school coach; D.J. Wilson, a former Gator with 10 coaching seasons at San Jac; and Kory Koehler, a catcher on the 2000 squad in his sixth season as a Gator assistant.

As engaged as Arrington is during games, he has both a calm and a sense of humor about him. Perhaps with the success he has had, it is hard to be stressed.

*Williamson looks to have a shut-down inning to keep the momentum the Gators' offense provided in the prior half-inning. He begins with a strikeout of Jose Salmon. Although Wes Callihan is hit by a pitch, Williamson gets consecutive ground ball outs from Brad Aitken and Wes Schneidner.*

*Kevin Kelso leads off the bottom of the second with a base hit. Tanner Hines shows another lead-off hitter skill with a sacrifice bunt. Kris Miller then hits an almost duplicate of Kelso's soft single to left and the latter advances to third. Belt, whose solid single in the first drove in a run, hits a soft grounder to first, which easily scores Kelso. Nothing in the inning is hit terribly hard, but it results in a run. The Gators take the lead.*

Tanner Hines is a polite freshman, listed at a mere 140 pounds, but he is an effective lead-off hitter. He is from Lufkin, which is about 120 miles northeast of Houston. In high school, he typically batted first or second in the order. He was a late-round (44th) selection of the Pittsburgh Pirates in the 2006 major league draft. He considers his job is to be very selective, work the count, make contact, and be a tough out. In the first inning, he wants his teammates, either in the on-deck circle or in the dugout, to get a good look at what the pitcher is throwing.

Since arriving at San Jac, Hines has had to make an adjustment to facing consistently better pitchers than what he saw in high school. "At the high school level, you'd run across a good pitcher every once in awhile, but mainly the biggest difference would be the strike zone. College pitchers are always around the strike zone and more hit their spots than high school pitching. In high school pitching, a strike to them would be right down the middle; for a college player, they work in and out, up and down, and their off-speed is always usually around the plate."

Pitch selection is Hines' biggest challenge. In batting practice or hitting off a tee, he usually sees a nice strike. Not so in a game. "If you get a good pitch to hit, usually the odds are going to be more in your favor than if you chase a pitch," said Hines. He looks for a certain type of pitch more than a particular location for a pitch. He anticipates the pitch type based on the count and the pitcher's tendencies.

Tanner's thinking on this topic is generally consistent with that of his head coach. "Probably a dilemma that's picked apart for years and years is whether you look for a certain pitch or whether you look for location," says Arrington. "Here, we don't promote either one of those. We promote the fact that certain pitchers are going to have tendencies and, if we can pick that tendency up, then we'll sit on a pitch. Other pitchers don't have tendencies so you're going to have to get a ball in your zone, something you can handle, and kind of zone hit on the guy. The best hitters in the big leagues can do both."

*After an uneventful third inning and top of the fourth, the Gators get a two-out Kris Miller double that hits the bottom of the wall in left field. Belt follows and gets ahead in the count 3–0. He then sees a pitch he thinks he can drive, but the result is a weak ground ball to the second baseman for the third out.*

*In the top of the fifth, Williamson starts out with a strikeout, but he walks the number nine and number one hitters, respectively. These are the first walks he has given up since the lead-off batter of the game. James Green then hits what could be an inning-ending double play. First baseman Taylor Hammack fields the ball and throws to get the force at second. Williamson is a little late covering first base, and Hines' relay throw sails past the bag towards the fence adjoining Laredo's dugout. One run scores and Green winds up on second base. Green, who not only has shown speed on the bases but also is very animated with his leads, steals third. He comes home on a Cody Pifer single and Laredo takes a 4–3 lead.*

*San Jac had an answer when Laredo scored in the first. Could they do it again in the fifth? Eric Fry leads off with a single and Jeremy Barfield follows with his third fly ball out of the game. With Hammack up, Fry runs on the first pitch and steals second. After Hammack walks, Trey Sperring doubles, scoring Fry and advancing Hammack to third. Garcia's pitching day is over, and Matt Brown comes in for the Palominos.*

*While the pitching change takes place, Coach Arrington and D.J. Wilson confer and the former decides he does not want to attempt a safety squeeze. He pinch-hits Quentin Luquette for Kinart, providing a left-handed hitter to face the right-handed Brown. Luquette flies to right to score Hammack with the go-ahead run. The lead is significant because, in a seven-inning game, Laredo has just two innings remaining.*

Wilson grew up in Austin, and attended San Jac and the University of Houston. The 31-year-old coaches third base, and at times one can spot a stopwatch in his back pocket. The watch serves one purpose: to calculate the time it takes from the pitcher's first motion to the plate until the pitch hits the catcher's glove. If it is over 1.3 seconds, the Gators feel they have a chance to successfully steal bases. Time is on their side.

From his coaching box, he is seeking any little edge he can get throughout a game. Most of the time the hitter is free to use his own judgment. In selected situations, the strategy is generally predetermined based on the opposing pitcher and catcher.

If a pitcher is in a groove, Wilson may give signs to the hitter every pitch just to slow down the pace ever so slightly. If a hitter does not look down at Wilson because the former knows that nothing is going on, Wilson may yell, "Hey!" to get the batter's attention. He will then go through a series of meaningless signs just to get the pitcher and defense thinking and perhaps distract them.

Besides coaching third base, Wilson works a lot with the hitters. While most mechanical adjustments are done in the fall, during the season either the batting cages or that pre-game ritual known as batting practice ("BP") is used to fine-tune a player's swing. For example, a coach may purposely throw pitches outside to force a player to work on opposite-field hitting.

Batting practice pitches are thrown from a distance of about 50 feet, which makes the coach's seemingly effortless pitch to the plate equate to slightly over 80 miles per hour. Wilson indicates that BP can help to get a player ready for a game by allowing a hitter to get loose with the bat or work on bat control. San Jac usually has one group running the bases while the other group is hitting.

The first round for the batter consists of four bunts: one but down each line, a drag bunt and a push bunt. In the second round, the batter will be simulating a hit-and-run situation and thinking of hitting to the opposite field. After this, the batters will hit for four rounds, seeing four pitches each round. One of these rounds may be a two-strike round in which the hitter pretends he has only one strike to work with and must focus on making good contact. For some hitters, they may work on a current weakness by seeing, for example, mostly curveballs or inside fastballs.

Even with the goal of a consistent swing, game adjustments might be necessary. For example, a pitcher with a lot of sink on his ball will tend to get a lot of ground ball outs. "You can make adjustments, they are fine adjustments and, sure, big league guys make the adjustments a lot faster," says Wilson. "Usually that's why once the lineup comes through a second time, they start getting to a pitcher because you kind of get a feel for what the guy's ball is trying to do and how he's going to pitch you and you can make adjustments." The adjustment may be more of a tweak to get to a more fundamentally sound swing rather than doing something out of the ordinary.

*Matthew Coburn comes out to pitch the sixth inning for San Jac. He strikes out three of the four batters he faces.*

*Although the Gators get three batters on base in the bottom of the sixth, they do not score. That leaves Laredo with three outs to try to tie the score. Coburn retires the number eight and nine hitters on a fly out and strikeout, respectively. Humberto Miranda, who has two previous walks, get his third walk to become the potential tying run. That leaves James Green as the next batter. He has proven to be a pesky hitter and even more of a pesky runner once on base. He sees seven pitches, working the count to 3–2. On the next pitch he hits a fly to right-center and Luquette, who remained in the game for defensive purposes, makes a good running catch. It's the third out and the end of the game.*

*Laredo comes into Sunday's series finale frustrated. In Saturday's double-header the Palominos lost both a close game (4–3) and a blowout (11–1).*

Every time they play, San Jacinto's opponents view the game as an opportunity to beat one of the best. It's like playing Duke in basketball or USC in football. A win is special.

If visiting teams needed any reminder as to how formidable their opponent is, they need only to look at the outfield fence. In right field, there is a sign that shows the five national championships: 1985, 1986, 1987, 1989 and 1990. In left field, there is a sign that shows the 18 JUCO World Series appearances.

The Junior College World Series is played each year in Grand Junction, Colorado. While the very first championship was played in Miami, Oklahoma, in 1958, the next year it moved to Grand Junction where it has remained ever since. The games are played at Suplizio Field, which is also the home field for Division II power Mesa State College. The games are embraced by the local community, as the games in the preliminary rounds routinely draw four thousand fans. The championship game can attract in excess of 11,000.

The JUCO World Series has alumni who have gone on to successful major league careers. Kirby Puckett (1982, Triton College, River Grove, Illinois) still holds the individual batting average record at .688. Travis Hafner (1996, Cowley County Community College, Arkansas City, Kansas) and Adam LaRoche (2000, Seminole State College, Oklahoma) were both tournament MVPs.

San Jac routinely sends players to highly regarded four-year colleges and professional baseball. The most distinguished former players are Roger Clemens (1981) and Andy Pettitte (1991).

Coming into the season, San Jac was ranked fourth in the nation in the NJCAA poll. Given their recent slump, the Gators were struggling for a top-20 spot. The NCJAA poll has community colleges from states one would expect: Florida, Texas and Arizona. There is one state — California — that is a glaring omission.

Ironically, the NJCAA was formed in Fresno, California, in 1938 and all the charter members were California schools. Prior to World War II, the organization primarily sponsored a national track and field competition. After the war, the organization expanded to include all sports and divide the junior colleges throughout the United States into separate districts.

With the California schools comprising the significant membership and the athletic power of the NJCAA in the late forties, it seemed nonsensical to California school administrators for two California schools to travel outside the state to compete for a national championship. Then, the California Junior College Association was formed in 1947 to administer junior college athletics in California. By 1951 this governing body decided that its concern about travel costs, undistinguished national championships, and perceived undemocratic processes of the NJCAA was significant enough to mandate that California schools could not participate in national events. Thus, today approximately 90 California junior college baseball programs are not part of the NJCAA, its rankings or national championship process. The California schools are included, however, in the PG CrossChecker.com junior college rankings.

San Jac and other NCJAA members differ from the California schools by offering scholarships. The Gators' conference permits 18 full scholarships, which can be divided among a maximum of 24 players. A scholarship includes books, tuition, fees, meals in the school cafeteria and a stipend for apartment living.

*San Jac is wearing white uniforms with green lettering and numbering. With their white shoes, the look is similar to the Oakland A's. Brandon Belt, the Gators' number three hitter, is the starter. He gets Humberto Miranda to start the game on a three-pitch strikeout. James Green comes up in his familiar number two spot in the batting order. In yesterday's doubleheader, he was on base in seven of his eight plate appearances. Once on, he stole five bases and advanced five other times on either a passed ball, wild pitch or a balk. He is an incredible distraction. To opposing pitchers he is annoying. Rickey Henderson annoying. Ichiro Suzuki annoying. Nobody is surprised when Belt walks him. What is a surprise is that Belt picks him off, but his throw gets by Hammack. Instead of having two outs and nobody on base, Green is in scoring position with only one out.*

*After a Jose Salmon foul pop-up for the second out, the Gators are two-thirds of the way out of the inning. Carson Vitale then singles to right-center and Barfield's throw to the plate is too late to get the speedy Green. On the throw,*

*Salmon breaks for second. It looks like Salmon will be nailed at second, but Kil-lan Kinart's throw sails high. After Ethan Wagner walks, Brad Aitken singles and, just like yesterday, the Palominos have jumped out to a 2–0 lead in their first at-bat. Unlike yesterday, the Gators do not have an immediate answer as they do not score in the bottom of the inning against Trevor Lishanko.*

Belt is an unusual, but not rare, two-way player. He was a teammate of Tanner Hines at Hudson High School in Lufkin. He earned all-state and All-American honors and, as a coveted left-hander, he was selected by the Boston Red Sox in the 11th round of the 2006 draft. He had originally committed to play for the University of Texas during the early signing period prior to his senior season. When an anticipated early-round major league draft selection did not materialize, he opted to go to San Jac to keep his baseball options open.

Belt's third spot in the batting order is an acknowledgment of his hitting skills and his adjustment to college pitching. Compared to his relatively small high school experience, the fastballs come in harder and the breaking balls are sharper. Not surprisingly, he maintains a rather simple approach to hitting: "Just see the ball, throw my hands out and hit it." He is occasionally challenged by trying to do too much with a pitch instead of just "see the ball and react to it."

The reason many potential two-way players are scarce is they typically devote so much time to working on pitching that it leaves little time to effectively practice hitting. Most often a pitcher will take himself out of the hitting equation once he realizes the challenges. Belt is not one of those.

*San Jac does have an answer in the second inning, but it seems unlikely at first. After Eric Fry grounds out to first, Jeremy Barfield hits a very high foul ball that Vitale tracks towards the backstop. He completely misses the ball before it hits the base of the wall. The Palominos are likely thinking this is not the type of hitter one wants to give a second chance. Sure enough, two pitches later, Barfield hits a double. After the second out is recorded and Trey Sperring walks, Kinart rips the first pitch just foul down the third base line. He then hits a double, scoring Barfield and sending Sperring to third.*

*With the number nine batter, Kevin Kelso, at the plate, Lishanko appears to begin over-throwing and gives up the walk to load the bases. Before Tanner Hines steps into the batter's box, Arrington calls him aside and says, "I don't care if he goes 3–2, I want it perfect (before you swing)." It isn't perfect and Hines walks on five pitches to force in Sperring. Lishanko falls behind Miller 2–0. Looking for a pitch to drive, Miller elicits a dugout full of groans as his check swing accidentally puts the ball into play with a weak grounder to first. The Gators settle with tying the score.*

Barfield is a natural power hitter, and he looks the part. One of his swings at each at-bat usually gets an audible "wow." He is 6'5" and 230 pounds. He is confident and articulate. He led the greater Houston area in RBIs while playing for Klein High School in Spring, Texas (25 miles due north of downtown Houston). His father, Jesse, had a 12-year major league career with the Toronto Blue Jays and New York Yankees and his brother, Josh, is a second baseman for the Cleveland Indians. With his high school success and proven family skills, the New York Mets selected him in the ninth round.

As feared of a hitter as he was in high school, he realizes it is not that easy as one moves up. "For the most part, you see a lot better pitching. The guys are older and more mature, have more confidence, and so they pitch different ways. They also throw inside more and are not afraid to throw a good fastball." Barfield didn't see many inside pitches in high school, and it is one of his biggest challenges at the college level. He is focused on being a better two-strike hitter, looking to make solid contact rather than swinging for the fences as he may have done in high school.

Like other freshmen, until the season progresses further, almost all of the pitchers he sees are tosses he is seeing for the first time. Despite the challenges, the coaching staff respects his hitting enough to bat him fifth in the order.

*Belt loads the bases in the third but gets out of it unscathed. The break between innings apparently did not help to get Lishanko back into a grove. He walks both Belt and Fry to start the inning. After his sixth walk of the game, Jake Wilson is brought in. He gets Barfield to strikeout, but Hammack waits on an off-speed pitch and strokes an opposite-field hit to drive Belt in for the go-ahead run.*

Hammack had been working recently in the batting cages beyond right field, trying to keep his head back and not have a lot of motion in his front side. He attended Angleton High School, about an hour's drive south towards the Gulf Coast. After successful sophomore and junior seasons on the mound, a shoulder injury curtailed his pitching in his senior year. Just like Brandon Belt, Hammack originally signed a letter of intent to attend the University of Texas before the start of his senior season of high school. The San Francisco Giants selected him in the 46th round.

With a strong pitching staff available for the season, it is not imperative to rush the left-handed Hammack back to the mound to have him throw his 90-mile-per-hour fastball and effective slider. With his 6'4" and 215-pound linebacker-like frame, he is valuable to the team playing first base and batting sixth. According to Hammack, his priorities at-bat include "hitting outside pitches and staying within myself, not trying to do too much or trying to hit home runs all the time, and using the whole field."

*With a lot of action in the first three innings, the fourth was quiet. In the top of the fifth, to nobody's surprise, James Green walks, advances to second on a sacrifice bunt, and reaches third on a steal. Coach Arrington decides to bring the infield in. Vitale hits a 3–2 pitch right to Hines at short. Green is part way down the line, and Hines decides to run right at him to force the runner to commit. Green breaks for the plate, but Hines uses his running start and favorable angle to pursue him like safety chasing a wide receiver. With Green three strides from home, Hines lunges at him and barely tags him out. Belt then records a strikeout to end the inning.*

*With enthusiasm carrying over from the defense, Fry leads off the bottom of the fifth with a drive that hits the bottom of the left field fence. A strikeout, walk and fielder's choice leaves Fry on third and Sperring on first with two outs. With the count 2–1 to Kinart, Sperring takes off for second while Fry has a big lead. Fry comes into score before Sperring is tagged out at second. The Gators have their fourth run.*

Fry is a sophomore and one of the leaders on the team as well as one of the comedians. He is one of three non–Texans on the squad, arriving from Lake Charles, Louisiana. Coming out of Barbe High School, Fry was selected in the 29th round by the Detroit Tigers. After his freshman year at San Jac, in which he was selected for the NJCAA World Series all-tournament team, the Texas Rangers selected him in the 33rd round.

The center fielder has adjusted to his second year of juco baseball. "Last year I was a dumb hitter. This year I'm a smarter hitter, swinging at more strikes than balls." His focus this year is to not lunge for the ball and try not to pull pitches.

*In the top of the sixth, the Palominos have the bottom of the order. After Aiken flied out to left, Callihan doubles and Schneider singles. Belt is concerned about a steal and throws over to first. He throws over again and Schneider is picked off. After a brief run-down, Callihan breaks for home and the throw is too late. The run scores and the potential tying run is standing on second. Probably a bit distracted, Belt walks the number nine batter, Roman. It is his last pitch of the day.*

*Arrington brings in Garrett Clyde to face the pinch-hitter, Kike Granados. He gets the strikeout. James Green is up and, what else, he walks on four pitches to load the bases. At least he cannot steal. With the game in the balance, Clyde gets Jose Salmon to pop out to Tanner Hines at short to end the inning.*

*Jake Wilson has largely been effective for Laredo since entering the game in the third. Although San Jac has had a runner on base every inning, Wilson has kept the damage to only one earned run. In the sixth he gives up a harmless two-out single, and in the seventh, he strikes out three. For the Gators, Clyde is very effective, having a one-two-three seventh and eighth innings.*

*When Sperring hits a one-out single, Arrington plays for one run with the bottom of the order coming up. Kinart executes a sacrifice bunt and Kevin Kelso follows with a single up the middle. The strategy works perfectly as Sperring scores and San Jac increases its lead to 5–3 going into the ninth.*

Clutch hitting, or hitting in general, is based on basics. "We try to get back to the basic attributes," says Coach Arrington. "The fewest amount of head movement, bat speed, balance, and if you're always reflecting upon those issues, they are going to apply to almost any sport. That is a constant reinforcement." He believes the best hitters keep it very basic, very simple. "There's no secret."

The bulk of the development and instruction is done in the fall. Unlike most four-year college programs, junior colleges can have a robust fall practice schedule that might include 20 games. The coaching staff uses this period to identify the strengths and weaknesses in individual hitters. During this time they try to make adjustments, but not dramatic ones. The coaches also determine which players are more of an instructional/verbal learner versus a visual learner (video) and provide their guidance accordingly.

During the regular season, it's much more simplistic. "If I have a hitter walking up to the plate and he's thinking about his hands, his front side, not dipping, and what kind of pitch is this guy throwing, he's screwed from the get-go" says Arrington. "We have to allow his instincts to take over at that point, with all of the knowledge he had hopefully obtained in the fall ... just focus on pitch recognition. In the spring we attack the mental game more than anything else."

*The number one spot in the order has not been kind to the Palominos: four at-bats, four strikeouts. Daniel Alonzo gets the pinch-hit assignment and works a walk against Clyde. Chris Corrigan is brought into the game to try and close it out. This brings up James Green, and he has had the exact opposite result of his fellow lead-off hitters: four at-bats, four walks. To break the trend, he singles on the first pitch and Alonzo moves over to third. Everybody expects Green to steal his way into scoring position. He bluffs on the first two pitches, which Salmon takes for strikes. On the third pitch, Green runs and steals second.*

*Corrigan strikes out Salmon for the first out. Vitale then hits a grounder to Hines at short. He bobbles the ball momentarily, double-clutches, and his throw gets the out by one step. The Gators get the second out, but Alonzo scores and Green is poised to score the tying run.*

*Ethan Wagner is the player standing in the way of a series sweep for the Gators. He hits a ground ball to Hammack at first. Hammack fields it and lobs a throw to Corrigan, who runs over to cover first. The third out is recorded and the Gators end the weekend the same way they started it, with a 5–4 win.*

LAREDO COMMUNITY COLLEGE PALOMINOS VS.
SAN JACINTO COLLEGE GATORS
MARCH 17, 2007 AT HOUSTON, TEXAS
JOHN RAY HARRISON FIELD

### Laredo (13–15, 4–6)

| Player | AB | R | H | RBI |
|---|---|---|---|---|
| Miranda, Humberto dh | 1 | 1 | 0 | 0 |
| Green, James cf | 4 | 2 | 2 | 0 |
| Pifer, Cody lf | 2 | 0 | 1 | 1 |
| Vitale, Carson c | 3 | 0 | 0 | 0 |
| Wagner, Ethan 1b | 2 | 0 | 0 | 0 |
| Roman, Angel pr | 0 | 0 | 0 | 0 |
| Salmon, Jose rf | 3 | 0 | 1 | 0 |
| Callihan, Wes 3b | 2 | 0 | 0 | 0 |
| Aitken, Brad 2b | 3 | 0 | 0 | 0 |
| Schneider, Wes ss | 2 | 1 | 0 | 0 |
| Garcia, Anthony p | 2 | 1 | 0 | 0 |
| Brown, Matt p | 0 | 0 | 0 | 0 |
| Totals | 22 | 4 | 4 | 1 |

### San Jacinto (15–12, 4–6)

| Player | AB | R | H | RBI |
|---|---|---|---|---|
| Hines, Tanner ss | 2 | 1 | 0 | 0 |
| Miller, Kris lf | 4 | 0 | 2 | 1 |
| Belt, Brandon dh | 3 | 1 | 1 | 1 |
| Fry, Eric cf | 2 | 1 | 2 | 0 |
| Barfield, Jeremy rf | 4 | 0 | 1 | 0 |
| Godre, Nicholas c | 0 | 0 | 0 | 0 |
| Hammack, Taylor 1b | 3 | 1 | 1 | 1 |
| Sperring, Trey 3b | 2 | 0 | 1 | 1 |
| Kinart, Killan c | 2 | 0 | 0 | 0 |
| Luquette, Quentin rf | 0 | 0 | 0 | 0 |
| Kelso, Kevin 2b | 2 | 1 | 1 | 0 |
| Williamson, Hank p | 0 | 0 | 0 | 0 |
| Coburn, Matthew p | 0 | 0 | 0 | 0 |
| Totals | 24 | 5 | 9 | 5 |

### Score by Innings

| | | | | | | | | | | | R | H | E |
|---|---|---|---|---|---|---|---|---|---|---|---|---|---|
| Laredo | 2 | 0 | 0 | 0 | 2 | 0 | 0 | – | – | – | 4 | 4 | 1 |
| San Jacinto | 2 | 1 | 0 | 0 | 2 | 0 | X | – | – | – | 5 | 9 | 1 |

2B — Miller; Sperring. SF — Luquette.

| Laredo | IP | H | R | ER | BB | SO |
|---|---|---|---|---|---|---|
| Garcia, Anthony | 4⅓ | 7 | 5 | 5 | 5 | 1 |
| Brown, Matt | 1⅔ | 2 | 0 | 0 | 2 | 0 |

| San Jacinto | IP | H | R | ER | BB | SO |
|---|---|---|---|---|---|---|
| Williamson, Hank | 5 | 4 | 4 | 2 | 3 | 5 |
| Coburn, Matthew | 2 | 0 | 0 | 0 | 2 | 4 |

Win — Williamson. Loss — Garcia. Save — Coburn.

Start: 12:00. Time: 2:21. Attendance: 50

## LAREDO COMMUNITY COLLEGE PALOMINOS VS.
## SAN JACINTO COLLEGE GATORS
## MARCH 18, 2007 AT HOUSTON, TEXAS
## JOHN RAY HARRISON FIELD

### Laredo (13–17, 4–8)

| Player | AB | R | H | RBI |
|---|---|---|---|---|
| Miranda, Humberto dh | 1 | 1 | 0 | 0 |
| Granados, Enrique ph | 1 | 0 | 0 | 0 |
| Alonzo, Danny ph | 0 | 1 | 0 | 0 |
| Green, James cf | 1 | 1 | 1 | 0 |
| Salmon, Jose lf | 4 | 0 | 0 | 0 |
| Vitale, Carson c | 5 | 1 | 2 | 2 |
| Wagner, Ethan 1b | 4 | 0 | 0 | 0 |
| Aitken, Brad 2b | 3 | 0 | 1 | 1 |
| Callihan, Wes 3b | 4 | 1 | 1 | 0 |
| Schneider, Wes ss | 4 | 0 | 1 | 0 |
| Roman, Angel rf | 3 | 0 | 0 | 0 |
| Lishanko, Trevor p | 0 | 0 | 0 | 0 |
| Wilson, Jake p | 0 | 0 | 0 | 0 |
| Totals | 32 | 4 | 6 | 3 |

### San Jacinto (17–12, 6–6)

| Player | AB | R | H | RBI |
|---|---|---|---|---|
| Hines, Tanner ss | 2 | 0 | 1 | 1 |
| Miller, Kris lf | 4 | 0 | 0 | 0 |
| Belt, Brandon p, dh | 3 | 1 | 1 | 0 |
| Fry, Eric cf | 3 | 1 | 1 | 0 |
| Barfield, Jeremy rf | 4 | 1 | 1 | 0 |
| Luquette, Quentin rf | 4 | 1 | 1 | 0 |
| Hammack, Taylor 1b | 3 | 0 | 1 | 1 |
| Sperring, Trey 3b | 3 | 2 | 1 | 0 |
| Kinart, Killan c | 3 | 0 | 1 | 1 |
| Kelso, Kevin 2b | 2 | 0 | 1 | 1 |
| Clyde, Garrett p | 0 | 0 | 0 | 0 |
| Corrigan, Chris p | 0 | 0 | 0 | 0 |
| Totals | 27 | 5 | 8 | 4 |

### Score by Innings

| | | | | | | | | | | | R | H | E |
|---|---|---|---|---|---|---|---|---|---|---|---|---|---|
| Laredo | 2 | 0 | 0 | 0 | 0 | 1 | 0 | 0 | 1 | – | 4 | 6 | 1 |
| San Jacinto | 0 | 2 | 1 | 0 | 1 | 0 | 0 | 1 | X | – | 5 | 8 | 2 |

2B — Callihan; Barfield; Kinart; Fry.

| Laredo | IP | H | R | ER | BB | SO |
|---|---|---|---|---|---|---|
| Lishanko, Trevor | 2 | 2 | 3 | 1 | 6 | 0 |
| Wilson, Jake | 6 | 6 | 2 | 2 | 2 | 5 |

| San Jacinto | IP | H | R | ER | BB | SO |
|---|---|---|---|---|---|---|
| Belt, Brandon | 5⅓ | 5 | 3 | 1 | 6 | 5 |
| Clyde, Garrett | 2⅔ | 0 | 1 | 1 | 2 | 3 |
| Corrigan, Chris | 1 | 1 | 0 | 0 | 0 | 1 |

Win — Belt. Loss— Lishanko. Save — Corrigan.

Start: 11:00. Time: 2:55. Attendance: 50

# 7

# Eastern Connecticut State University Warriors

Eastern Connecticut State University Warriors *vs.*
University of Southern Maine Huskies
April 7, 2007
ATHLETIC-ACADEMIC BALANCE
One Grade at a Time

*It is Monday morning, two days after Eastern Connecticut State University (ECSU) played a doubleheader against Southern Maine. Jimmy Jagodzinski stands in the office doorway and hesitates momentarily before speaking to his coach. His hair and sideburns are longer than most on the ECSU baseball team and certainly longer than the short hair coach Bill Holowaty wears.*

*"Coach, is it okay if I miss the game this afternoon?" asks Jagodzinski. "I've got a test tomorrow and two papers to finish." The game he refers to is a Monday contest at 4:30 P.M. against Babson College.*

*His request seems reasonable on two levels. First, he pitched eight innings on Saturday against Southern Maine, which means his baseball services would not be needed this afternoon. Second, he is a student-athlete, after all.*

*"Are you going to get your workout in?" asks Coach Holowaty, leaning back in his office chair. His voice is matter-of-fact.*

*"Yes, I'm going there right now," responds Jagodzinski. "So, is it okay?"*

*"Yes," Holowaty says and nods his head. The conversation between player and coach is done.*

ECSU is either in Willimantic or Windham, Connecticut, depending who one asks. Windham was incorporated in 1692 and includes the city of Willimantic, a city within a town concept. Willimantic is about 30 miles southeast of Hartford. It is the type of town that is shown on a map in small, non-bolded font. Willimantic was originally a borough of Windham, then became its own city in 1893. Ninety years later Windham and Willimantic consolidated, but the college indicates Willimantic as its address. The baseball field, about a mile from the main campus, is in the adjoining town of Mansfield.

Willimantic is a quaint town with a population of about 17,000. Perhaps its only flaw is that retail redevelopment is still waiting to happen. Main Street generally follows the curves of the Willimantic River; the university is straight up a fairly steep hill from Main Street. If one stays on Main Street long enough it leads into a group of impressive buildings that were once the mill for the American Thread Company. These buildings are in the process of being converted to office and residential use.

Thread understandably accounts for one of the themes for the town; the other, not so intuitive, is frogs. The frog story dates back to 1754, in which the residents of the area were awakened in the middle of the night by a terrifying sound. Some concluded it was some horrific incident connected to the French and Indian War. The true answer became apparent the following morning when the townsfolk saw hundreds of dead frogs, who had been en route from a drought-reduced pond towards the Willimantic River, desperately in search of water.

Up the hill from Main Street, within blocks of the ECSU campus, is the "Hill Section" of the town with over 800 Victorian-style homes. Many were built in the late nineteenth century, some of which the owners have cared for impeccably. Others are just a paint job or a landscaping project away from being showcase-ready.

The university has an enrollment of about 5,000, and its buildings are nicely spaced on a 180-acre campus. It is a visually appealing college with a nice blend of old and new, primarily new. The ubiquitous college brick-and-tree theme is done well. The Smith Library, completed in 1998 on the site of the former baseball field, and the Foster Clock Tower are two relatively recent additions to the campus. But not every day in Willimantic is a day in late spring.

When the University of Miami began its 2007 home season on February 2 against Mercer, the south Florida city registered a high of 87 degrees that day. In eastern Connecticut, the high was 37 degrees with snowing falling in the area. On that February day, the Warriors were still 54 days away from playing their first home game. Actually, ECSU had yet to have a practice on the Eastern Baseball Stadium field.

The Warriors' home field was completed in 1997 and has the look of a nicely built minor league park. It is not what one normally expects when a Division III facility is imagined. Two large brick grandstands with aluminum bleachers (with blue back-rests) are symmetrically built alongside the press box and the behind-home-plate concessions stands. The listed seating capacity is 1,500. There are grass knolls at the end of the grandstands, beyond first and third base. The outfield fence, made up of green wooden slats, is covered with advertisements ranging from local business (such as Windham Hospital and Willimantic Waste Paper Company) to national products (Dunkin' Donuts, Gatorade and Barnes & Noble).

Ironically, although the University of Connecticut is regarded by most as the elite state-supported university in Connecticut, ECSU has a ballpark similar to many Division I programs while UCONN has a well-maintained but Division III looking facility. UCONN is only six miles up the road in the town of Storrs, which has a smaller population than Willimantic.

ECSU's ballpark is in contrast to the surrounding area. Although a small community called the Villages at Freedom Green are across the street from the sports fields, nearby are open fields and small forests. A few hundred yards beyond the center field fence is the Pleasant Valley Cemetery where the oldest burial appears to be that of Eliphalet Martin (1796–1873).

*The first game of the doubleheader against the University of Southern Maine begins at 12:01 P.M. As a few of the home fans trickle in, they comment how cold it is. If the locals think it is cold, it's cold. The sun intermittedly shines brightly, but the gentle breeze blows right through multi-layers of clothes. The infield and outfield grass is a shade of gray-green since it has not yet benefited from the warming of the spring sun.*

*Not far away on the Willimantic Road exit from U.S. 6, icicles have survived into the fourth month of the year and melt slowly during the day. At least it's not snowing. Just the day before, in Cleveland, Opening Night against Seattle was called in the fifth inning due to heavy snow. On television replays, one could see the Mariners' Jose Lopez mention to the home plate umpire that he couldn't see the ball. Today, in Mansfield, at least everyone can see the ball.*

*Shawn Gilblair gets the start for ECSU on the mound, and he will hit fourth in the batting order. As a pitcher he is 3–1 with a 2.86 earned run average. As a batter, he is hitting .360 with a team-leading three home runs and 19 runs batted in. The Warriors are wearing white uniforms, coordinated with blue socks, sleeves, and caps. The jersey shows "Eastern" written in blue script and the caps have an embossed block-style "E" in red.*

*Gilblair retires the first two Huskies before right fielder Ryan Borque comes up. In the 13 games Southern Maine has played, Borque is hitting .431 and has the same number of home runs and RBIs as does Gilblair. Borque hits the second pitch towards the gap in right-center field. There seemingly is just a light breeze blowing from left to right, but the ball continues to carry and goes over the fence. The inning ends with Max Arsenault grounding out, but the Huskies strike first.*

The University of Southern Maine squad, from Portland, drove about 200 miles and traveled within four states to reach Willimantic. Along with

ECSU, the Huskies have been consistently strong in the Little East Conference. In the past ten years ECSU has been the regular-season conference champion five times and Southern Maine four times. Such constitutes a baseball rivalry.

The league also includes Keene State (Keene, New Hampshire), UMass Boston, UMass Dartmouth, Plymouth State (Plymouth, New Hampshire), Rhode Island College (Providence) and Western Connecticut (Danbury). What is unusual about this conference is that all of the schools are state-supported. By comparison, 80 percent of the Division III schools nationwide are private colleges.

Most Division III colleges are only regionally known, as just a few have national name recognition. The exceptions include schools like Amherst, Tufts and Vassar, which are traditional colleges with histories going back to the mid–1800s. Johns Hopkins is known as much for its lacrosse program (the only Division I sport at the school) as its academic excellence. Mount Union has a national reputation as a Division III football power. The Coast Guard Academy, the "other" military academy, is the one that is not a Division I program.

The athletes in a Division III program generally participate because of their love of the sport. They work hard in relative obscurity. Most people on the East Coast have never heard of the La Sierra Golden Eagles (Riverside, California). Similarly, few folks on the West Coast are familiar with the Medaille College Mavericks (Buffalo, New York). However, since the number of Division III members is growing close to 500, there is some thought about creating a Division IV to accommodate the smallest of the Division III programs.

*Chris Burleson is the Southern Maine pitcher, and he starts lead-off hitter Ismael Bolorin with three straight balls. Home plate umpire Tim McCaffrey says "That's outside" or "That's upstairs" to explain the close pitches. Unlike what one normally sees in Division I and Division II games, a two-man crew oversees this contest.*

*After Bolorin pops up and Zack Thomas flies to right, Randy Re works a walk. Burleson is well aware of Re's speed, given the latter has 10 stolen bases in 11 attempts. He throws over to first four times before Gilblair hits a dying pop-up to center. Ryan Pike makes a diving, tumbling attempt to catch it, but base umpire Greg Noyes signals "safe" and the Warriors have runners on first and third. A warm-up jacket is immediately brought from the dugout to keep Gilblair's arm warm, or at least warmer. The inning ends when Melvin Castillo hits a curving line drive that holds up for Ryan Borque.*

*Gilblair works very quickly to the appreciation of his defensive teammates* and the fans. He throws 11 pitches, 10 of them for strikes, in the top of the second. Three up and three down. The bottom of the inning is equally as uneventful as the Warriors hit three ground balls to the shortstop, Nick Vardaro, for outs.

Gilblair duplicates his second-inning success with another 11-pitch effort in the top of the third. The bottom of the inning begins innocently enough as Bolorin pops up to the first baseman for the second consecutive time. Zack Thomas follows with a dying soft line drive to left and then Gilblair walks. Melvin Castillo, the shortstop and number five hitter, swings at the first pitch and hits what appears to be a routine fly to right field. A "Coors Field effect" seems to have taken over the ball as it continues to carry until it clears the fence. Perhaps Burleson is stunned as much as anyone as he proceeds to walk the next two batters. The Huskies' bullpen begins to stir and some pitchers start warming up. However, Burleson regroups and gets a ground out force play to third.

Going into the fourth, Gilblair has thrown 11 pitches in each of the first three innings. He throws 12 pitches in the fourth; one of those he would like to have back. With two outs, Max Arsenault hits a drive to deep left field. There is no wind-aid to this hit. It clears the left field fence easily, and it is now a 3–2 game. When Gilblair gets a ground out to end the inning, what is important for the Warriors is that he is getting ahead of the hitters, not walking anyone, and keeping the home runs to solo shots.

Gilblair is a hometown guy who attended Windham High School right across the street from ECSU. In his freshman year at ECSU, he went 8–1 with a 1.65 ERA. As a batter, he hit an even .300 with 31 runs batted in during the 50 games he played, primarily as a designated hitter. He was a first-team Division III All-American, a rarity for a freshman. He was the MVP for both the Little East Conference tournament and the NCAA regionals. It is only a matter of time before Gilblair will have a circular plaque on the perimeter wrought-iron fence commemorating the ECSU All-Americans.

He is sturdily built at 5'11" and 220 pounds and his expression shows both a confidence and intensity. He admits, however, that it takes a few games into the season before he really feels that confidence on the mound. "We spend a few weeks in the gymnasium and basically pitch off of wooden mounds," says Gilblair, describing winter baseball. "We don't ever get a feel for a real mound until our first game out there (in California). I guess the nerves are much higher than what it would be if we were playing in Texas or California. It's real tough playing these teams that may be eight to ten games ahead of us and we're just playing our first game."

Just across the foyer to the entrance of the gym, the Warriors' winter "practice field" is a set of double doors that lead into the sports administration offices. Residing in one interior office is Trece Hayslett, Assistant Athletic

Director for Student-Athlete Development. Just because ECSU is a Division
III program doesn't mean the school does not have NCAA compliance challenges. Hayslett, a former hurdler at the University of Memphis, has famil-
iarity with the rules with her prior experience as a student-athlete, coach and
administrator.

The NCAA Division I Manual, containing the constitution and bylaws,
consists of 424 pages. The Division III manual is a mere 288 pages long. One
significant difference between the two publications is Article 15, covering
financial aid. In the Division I manual, it takes 23 pages to explain what can
or cannot be done with respect to athletic scholarships. It takes only four
pages to cover the same topic in the Division III manual due to one basic reason — Division III programs cannot award athletic scholarships.

A Division III student-athlete may receive financial aid but only if it is
awarded on the same basis as any other student at the college (i.e., it cannot
be "based on athletic ability, participation or performance"). In other words,
an athlete better be really smart or not too wealthy for financial aid to be possible.

Historically, only two Division III baseball programs are listed in the
NCAA's database as having a "major infraction." Coincidently, Southern
Maine is one of the two and the infraction was settled in early 2007. In the
2003–04 school year, 37 athletes, including five baseball players, were found
to have received fraudulent work-study monies. It was not a jaw-dropping
offense as the total overpayments made to all 37 athletes amounted to less
than $11,000. However, it involved unethical behavior, including players who
did not clock out but were still paid pursuant to planned arrangements.

Hayslett is primarily concerned about Article 14, "Eligibility: Academic
and General Requirements." While it reads simple enough, sometimes it is
not easy for all of the athletes to meet three basic standards: (1) be a "full-
time" student (i.e., enrolled in 12 units per semester); (2) be in good academic standing; and (3) make satisfactory progress toward a degree. Perhaps
to a good, self-disciplined student, these standards are not burdensome. However, with the physical and mental fatigue that three or four baseball games
a week can produce, it can be a real challenge to some. Sometimes it takes
summer school or winter session to keep an athlete eligible.

The Division I athletes also have to abide by a 40/60/80 rule whereby 40
percent of a specific degree requirement must be met before entering the third
year of college, 60 percent before entering the fourth year of college and 80
percent before entering the fifth year of college. Division I programs must
also concern themselves with the NCAA's Academic Performance Program,
which measure a so-called academic progress rate and a graduation success
rate to determine whether a college has a its athletes on track to graduate. A

school must meet these measures to avoid a possible loss in scholarships or the ability to compete in post-season tournaments.

Hayslett is constantly preaching to athletes about the need for time management. She cautions against the dangers of procrastination and lauds the concepts of to-do lists, priority setting, and goal management. The message is particularly important for those athletes with part-time jobs or for freshmen who are used to a scholastic existence in high school in which administrative tasks were done for them.

*The fifth, sixth and top of the seventh go by quickly. Not only is Gilblair working smoothly, but Burleson has been in a good rhythm as well. Bolorin leads off an inning for the third time when he takes his at-bat in the seventh. With a 3–2 count, he takes his Ichiro-like swing and hits a routine off-field single to left. His all-out hustle turns the hit into a double. This marks the end of Burleson's day as a pitcher. He will remain in the game as the number two hitter, but now he is the designated hitter.*

*Pat Foley comes in to relieve and gets Zack Thomas on a solid line drive to center that holds up just long enough for Ryan Pike to make the catch. Foley has an unusual delivery in which he taps his lead foot during the start of his motion. The Huskies decide to intentionally walk Re; besides being a good base stealer, he is also a .485 hitter. Out goes Foley and in comes Andrew Stacey, a left-hander, to face the left-handed hitter Gilblair. He strikes out Gilblair to keep him off the bases for the first time. Out goes Stacey and in comes Tim Therrian.*

*Melvin Castillo, whose three-run home run was hit with two outs in the third inning, is up in a similar situation in the seventh. After falling behind 1–2, Therrian throws a pitch low and very outside, which provides Bolorin and Re with the opportunity to steal third and second, respectively. Castillo hits the next pitch to the right of Vardaro at short, who fields it but has no play. Bolorin scores and Re moves over to third. Tristan Hobbes then hits a routine fly to short left field and Eddie Skeffington decides to pull up and let the ball fall in rather than make a dive for a possible catch. The decision allows not only Re to score easily, but Castillo also scores after stealing second the pitch before.*

*With the way Gilblair is pitching, a 6–2 lead is looking solid for the Warriors. He keeps the momentum with ECSU with a seven-pitch, six-strike top of the eighth. In the bottom of the inning, after getting a ground ball out, Adam Ross comes in as the last reliever for the Huskies. He gets two ground ball outs to send the game into the ninth.*

*Gilblair comes out for the ninth having thrown just ninety pitches. He has walked no one and has only gone to three balls on two batters. He has given up but three hits. Although the Huskies manage an infield and off-field single in the inning, Gilblair strikes out Josh Mackey to end the game. Despite the opposition's pitching changes and eight combined runs scoring, Gilblair does his part to keep the game time to two hours and 25 minutes. The win is number 1,191 of Bill Holowaty's career. It adds to his distinction as having the most wins among the active Division III coaches. (Gordie Gillespie of St. Francis of Illinois is the all-time leader with 1,709 wins in his 54 years of coaching.)*

Holowaty didn't exactly anticipate becoming a baseball coach 38 seasons ago. He thought he would be a coach, all right, but in basketball. He grew up in Mohawk in upstate New York. He went to UCONN and played basketball and then he remained with the Huskies as an assistant coach after he graduated. Although he was convinced that he would become a head basketball coach at a major college, he hesitantly took a job at ECSU to be the assistant basketball and baseball coach.

Decades later, he still hasn't landed the head coaching basketball job, but he has won four national titles in baseball and has made it to the NCAA regionals seven other times. He was inducted into the American Baseball Coaches Hall of Fame in 2002.

Holowaty fits the image of a good Division III coach. He is a tenured professor of health and physical education and teaches golf and bowling. He thinks sports at all levels is often over-emphasized and sometimes out of balance with the college mission. He feels the player is most important as a person rather than as a "stupid baseball player." He uses the word "stupid" in an existential manner. His players are anything but the literal use of the word; they are well prepared, fundamentally sound and competitive.

He readily accepts what Mother Nature throws at Willimantic during the winter months and seems to relish the challenge without using it as an excuse. His practices in the gym are "highly organized and aggressive" because the baseball program is one of six teams that uses the facility before intramurals take over. Besides the gym, the team will work out on squash courts and hallways. When the weather is incrementally better, they make use of the tennis courts and the parking lot outside of Eastern Stadium.

Over time, Holowaty became more focused on the process as opposed to the end results. "When I first got here, I loved winning and I think my values were not appropriate," admits Holowaty. "Now I believe, like in business, if you develop your people, you make money; if you develop your ballplayers, you get wins. We develop kids here and I'm very proud of that."

In addition to Holowaty's impressive longevity with the program, third base coach Bob Wojick has been on the coaching staff for 31 seasons and was named as an American Baseball Coaches Association National Assistant Coach of the Year. Also, first base coach Len Reed is in his 16th season as an assistant. Both Wojick and Reed played for Holowaty at ECSU.

To the left on the Warriors' dugout entrance, a folding table has a tray full of peanut butter and jelly sandwiches and a case of assorted Gatorade drinks. Baseball is one of the few sports in which eating shortly before the contest, particularly between a doubleheader, is not unusual.

Most of those attending the first game stay for the second. The attending fans are primarily family and friends. Behind the third base dugout housing the ECSU team, about 35 spectators are seated in the aluminum blue bleachers. A slightly smaller number of fans are seated behind Southern Maine's dugout. Another 15 people, mainly ECSU students, are seated in the blue plastic box seats behind the home plate screen. Nobody is opting to sit on the two grass knolls beyond the first- and third-base dugouts. Perhaps it will be more inviting in May.

For the second game of most doubleheaders, there are generally a few lineup changes. One might expect a change in catchers, but Matt Cooney is written in as the starting catcher for game two. In fact, unlike the Huskies, the same nine Warriors are in the batting order for the second game, although there is some minor juggling of the exact placement.

Shawn Gilblair, fresh off his complete-game victory less than a half-hour earlier, is the designated hitter. Jimmy Jagodzinski, with the fashionable long hair and sideburns, has a 2–0 record and a 2.84 ERA. Opposing batters are hitting only .227 against him.

Southern Maine sends out Collin Henry, who played center field and got two hits in the first game. Coming into the series, his 3.60 ERA is numerically similar to his .350 batting average.

The first four innings pass by quickly as both teams send up the minimum 12 batters.

ECSU's Zack Thomas gets a first-inning off-field single, but he is forced out as part of an unassisted double play. In the top of the second, Collin Henry hits a ball that Jimmy Jagodzinski deflects to second baseman Zack Thomas, who cannot make a play in time. However, with the very next pitch, Henry is caught stealing on Cooney's strong throw. Those were the only two runners and their time on the bases was short-lived.

Matt Cooney is one of six seniors on the team. He is from Arlington, Massachusetts, just northwest of Boston and about 90 miles from Willimantic. He seems like a New Englander, in a Matt Damon kind of way.

Cooney is a co-captain of the team, a role he had on his high school football and baseball teams. He is in his third year as the starting catcher.

In reflecting back on his first three-and-a-half years of college studies, he observes that nobody makes one get up, nobody makes one go to class, but one better or problems will quickly develop. To make both parts of the student-athlete role work, people try different things. Some players get up early, or, at least earlier on the weekends to study. Cooney is an advocate of the incremental approach to schoolwork. "I've got to break it up. Not a lot of kids can sit there and cram in one night and I'm not like that. I break it up into little pieces with a partner, so whenever I have time in between classes or, if we don't have practice for an hour, we'll study a little bit or make note cards."

Cooney was part of the Little East Conference tournament in 2006 that is almost legendary, not just for the baseball, but for academics as well. The Warriors won four games in 27 hours and five games overall. They finished on a Sunday night in Bangor, Maine, and got back to Willimantic at 3:30 A.M. Monday. Some of the players had to take finals scheduled for 8:00 A.M. On Tuesday morning, the team got back on a bus to go to Auburn in upstate New York to begin the NCAA regionals. Fortunately, the professors were cooperative and allowed the players to take their exams afterwards.

*The top of the fifth seems like more of the same. Huskies first baseman Max Arsenault and designated hitter Collin Henry both ground out to the third baseman, Will Moran. Henry's out is very close and the call is questionable. Josh Mackey follows with a solid single to left and advances to second on a wild pitch. When Andrew Stacy follows with another single to left, one wonders what might have happened if Henry was ruled safe. That speculation is quickly interrupted when left fielder Eric O'Toole fires a throw to third baseman Will Moran, who relays it to Matt Cooney at home. Mackey is out. The inning is over.*

*With one out, Melvin Castillo comes up. His home run in the first game was a surprise when the ball cleared the fence. Not this time. With the advantage of a 2–0 count, he drives the pitch deep over the left field fence to give the Warriors the lead. The home run brings on the same air-raid siren sound effect that was played for Castillo in the first game. Today's home runs are unexpected. Coming into this game, Castillo had not hit a home run, and the team had hit just eight in its first seventeen games.*

*With the solid pitching performances by both teams so far, every run seems important. Jagodzinski's 1–0 lead seems precarious when Ryan Gaffney hits a one-out double off the base of the fence. Jagodzinski is intent on keeping Gaffney close to second and throws back to the bag a couple of times. His efforts are for naught when the lead-off hitter, Nick Vardaro, hits a solid single and Gaffney scores easily. Vardaro steals second on the first pitch to Chris Burleson, and then Burleson works a walk. With the number three and four hitters due up, the game suddenly is at a pivotal moment. However, Jagodzinski needs only six pitches to strike out both Ryan Borque and Max Arsenault. It has taken just a little over an hour to reach the bottom of the sixth with a 1–1 tie.*

After two consecutive foul pop-up outs to the catcher, Eric O'Toole singles to center. Pat Foley throws over to first to keep O'Toole close. The Warriors like to run, averaging two stolen bases a game. O'Toole has stolen successfully each of the seven times he has tried. Only Randy Re has run more: Re has stolen 10 out of 11 attempts. On the pitch immediately after the pickoff throw, O'Toole gets a great jump towards second. The Huskies have no chance to throw him out. The potential two-out rally ends as Zack Thomas strikes out.

Collin Henry leads off the seventh with a soft fly to right. Ismael Bolorin gets a late jump on the ball and it falls in front of him for a single. Jagodzinski then gets his sixth strikeout of the game as Josh Mackey goes down on three swings. Andrew Stacy comes up and Jagodzinski becomes concerned with Henry running. He throws over to first. On the first pitch to the plate, Henry takes off for second. If a double play is a "pitcher's best friend," then Jagodzinski finds out just how good a friend it can be. With Henry running, shortstop Castillo runs over to cover second in anticipation of a throw. Stacy hits a hard grounder up the middle. It deflects off Jagodzinski and right to Castillo, who is moving towards the base. The latter steps on the bag ahead of Henry and throws to Hobbes at first to finish the double play.

Re is the first hitter in the seventh and, thus far today, he has not hit the ball out of the infield. He grounds the 0–2 pitch to third and reaches first on an error. On a hit-and-run, Gilblair connects on the first pitch for a bloop hit to left-center and, with the ball in Re's sight as he runs, he makes the easy decision to go to third.

The Huskies bring in Pat Foley, who pitched to two batters in the first game. Melvin Castillo welcomes him with a shot down the third base line for a double. Re scores and Gilblair holds at third.

Although it is a welcomed sight to see the sun come back out, the pace of the game has slowed when the Huskies bring in their second pitcher of the inning, Tim Therrian. Therrian also pitched in the first game, facing four batters. Tristan Hobbes faces Therrian first and hits a bloop single to left, scoring Gilblair and moving Castillo to third. Although only two runs have come in, the inning has the feel of a camp fire that is about to spread into a forest fire.

Matt Cooney, the catcher, uses the element of surprise and lays down a bunt that provides Therrian with only one option — to get the out at first. Castillo comes into score the third run of the inning and Hobbes moves up to second. After the second out results from a grounder to second, Ismael Bolorin comes up. In the first game Bolorin hit lead-off; in the second game he is hitting ninth. He rips the second pitch down the left field line and the ball rolls all the way to the fence. Hobbes scores, Bolorin races to third, and the Warriors are only a home run from hitting for the cycle in the inning. O'Toole, the eighth batter of the inning, grounds into the third out.

On campus while wearing glasses, Tristan Hobbes might be stereotyped as a student without the "athlete" part in the title. In that way, it is not surprising to know that Hobbes was a National Honor Society student in high school. He is one of only three New Yorkers on the roster, an all-state player who led Notre Dame High School (Utica) to a state title.

It takes five or six games during the warm weather trip at the beginning of the season for Hobbes to feel comfortable at the plate. The Warriors' hitters usually don't see live pitching before the season starts. The batting practice in the gym is against pitches from only 20 feet away. One doesn't get the feeling of a true curveball since it is difficult to get the read of a good off-speed pitch from such a distance.

Getting ready for the season defensively is also a challenge. Hobbes takes ground balls in the gym, but good luck getting experience with bad hops on the smooth hardwood floors. Some areas the defense is very prepared for are the multi-player situations, such as bunt coverage and run-down plays.

When it comes to balancing sports with academics, Hobbes is progressing very well with a 3.7 grade point average. "Traveling is the tough part about it," says Hobbes. "If we're on the road, you say you are going to do work on the bus, but before games you are psyched about the game and you really can't concentrate. Then after the game, you are just tired and you really don't want to do work."

"A lot of times having the strict schedule of baseball helps with the schoolwork because you know you have to get it done." Procrastination is not an option. "With baseball, you have to get it done or you're not going to get it done."

*Provided with a four-run lead, Jagodzinski is looking for a shut-down inning in the top of the eighth. After Joe McGhee leads off with a pop-up for the first out, Ryan Gaffney singles to right. After taking the first pitch for a strike, Nick Vardano spins away from a pitch he senses is coming inside. He loses his balance, and as he falls down, the pitch hits his bat and the ball rolls fair. Jagodzinski races to the ball and throws to second, attempting to force Gaffney out. His throw to Castillo is too high, but Castillo throws to first in plenty of time to get an understandably confused Vardano. He apparently never worked much on his home-to-first speed from the supine position. It is one of the most bizarre outs one will ever witness.*

*After ECSU's breakthrough in the bottom of the seventh along with Vardano's ground out in the eighth, the Warriors have all of the momentum. ECSU goes down somewhat quietly in the bottom of the eighth while facing Adam Ross, who in a consistent pattern also relieved in the first game. With two outs Gilblair hits a single to left. Although the box score will show this hit just like the one he*

## University of Southern Maine Huskies vs. Eastern Connecticut State University Warriors April 7, 2007 at Mansfield, Connecticut Eastern Baseball Stadium

### *Southern Maine (9–6, 2–2)*

| Player | AB | R | H | RBI |
|---|---|---|---|---|
| Vardaro, Nick ss | 4 | 0 | 1 | 1 |
| Burleson, Chris cf | 3 | 0 | 0 | 0 |
| Bourque, Ryan rf | 4 | 0 | 0 | 0 |
| Arsenault, Max 1b | 4 | 0 | 0 | 0 |
| Henry, Collin p/dh | 4 | 0 | 2 | 0 |
| Mackey, Josh 3b | 3 | 0 | 1 | 0 |
| Stacy, Andrew lf | 3 | 0 | 1 | 0 |
| McGhee, Joe c | 3 | 0 | 0 | 0 |
| Gaffney, Ryan 2b | 3 | 1 | 2 | 0 |
| Foley, Pat p | 0 | 0 | 0 | 0 |
| Therrian, Tim p | 0 | 0 | 0 | 0 |
| Ross, Adam p | 0 | 0 | 0 | 0 |
| **Totals** | **31** | **1** | **7** | **1** |

### *Eastern Connecticut (13–6, 5–0)*

| Player | AB | R | H | RBI |
|---|---|---|---|---|
| O'Toole, Eric lf | 4 | 0 | 1 | 0 |
| Thomas, Zack 2b | 4 | 0 | 1 | 0 |
| Re, Randy cf | 4 | 1 | 0 | 0 |
| Gilblair, Shawn dh | 4 | 1 | 2 | 0 |
| Cousineau, Joe pr/dh | 0 | 0 | 0 | 0 |
| Castillo, Melvin ss | 3 | 2 | 2 | 2 |
| Hobbes, Tristan 1b | 3 | 1 | 1 | 1 |
| Cooney, Matt c | 2 | 0 | 0 | 1 |
| Moran, Will 3b | 2 | 0 | 0 | 0 |
| Bongiovanni, Trey ph | 1 | 0 | 0 | 0 |
| Dalton, Jon 3b | 0 | 0 | 0 | 0 |
| Bolorin, Ismael rf | 3 | 0 | 1 | 1 |
| Jagodzinski, Jimmy p | 0 | 0 | 0 | 0 |
| LaVorgna, Jason p | 0 | 0 | 0 | 0 |
| **Totals** | **30** | **5** | **8** | **5** |

### Score by Innings

| | | | | | | | | | | | R | H | E |
|---|---|---|---|---|---|---|---|---|---|---|---|---|---|
| Southern Maine | 0 | 0 | 0 | 0 | 0 | 1 | 0 | 0 | 0 | - | 1 | 7 | 1 |
| Eastern Connecticut | 0 | 0 | 0 | 0 | 1 | 0 | 4 | 0 | X | - | 5 | 8 | 0 |

2B — Gaffney (4); Castillo (5). 3B — Bolorin (6). HR — Castillo (2).

| *Southern Maine* | IP | H | R | ER | BB | SO |
|---|---|---|---|---|---|---|
| Henry, Collin | 6 | 4 | 3 | 2 | 0 | 3 |
| Foley, Pat | 0 | 1 | 1 | 1 | 0 | 0 |
| Therrian, Tim | 1 | 2 | 1 | 1 | 0 | 0 |
| Ross, Adam | 1 | 1 | 0 | 0 | 0 | 0 |

| *Eastern Connecticut* | IP | H | R | ER | BB | SO |
|---|---|---|---|---|---|---|
| Jagodzinski, Jimmy | 8 | 7 | 1 | 1 | 1 | 6 |
| LaVorgna, Jason | 1 | 0 | 0 | 0 | 0 | 2 |

Win — Jagodzinski (2–0). Loss— Henry (1–3). Save — None.

Start: 2:51. Time: 1:56. Attendance: 100

# 8
# Louisiana State University Tigers

Louisiana State University Tigers *vs.*
University of Florida Gators
May 11–13, 2007
FAN SUPPORT
Inside the Box

*It is about 20 minutes before game time on Saturday. For those fans who parked in the Tiger Stadium lot across Nicholson Drive, they are reminded of the significance of their presence. On the back side of billboards facing the interior of Alex Box Stadium is a sign that reads "Home of College Baseball's Greatest Fans" and "The Nation's Leader in College Baseball Attendance."*

LSU is consistently at or near the top of college baseball attendance. Why fans do or do not attend college baseball games is based on a combination of factors. A winning team. A history of success. A nice facility. An enjoyable game-day experience. Loyal fans. Limited alternative entertainment choices. Good weather. Media exposure.

LSU is a flat, sprawling campus of 2,000 acres in the western section of Baton Rouge. It is about 80 miles northwest of New Orleans. The part of the campus boundary that ends at River Road is only hundred yards-plus from the Mississippi River. The east side of the campus is adjacent to University Lake and the upscale homes that were built around it.

Baton Rouge, Louisiana's capital with a population of about 230,000, has its roots going back a few centuries. The area was previously under French, then Spanish control. It has a stately capitol building and tower, the Shaw Center for the Arts, and a riverfront casino, but much of what it has is LSU.

The campus has traditional architecture, such as the Memorial Tower (1923) and the buildings on the perimeter of the quadrangle. It has contemporary structures like the Cox Communications Academic Center. It has the facilities in the grand scale, such as Tiger Stadium and Livestock Exhibit Building, and those smaller structures like the tiger habitat that is home to Mike VI, a Bengal tiger. There are over 250 buildings, and the 30,000 enrollment easily blends into the large campus.

There are not any real baseball competitors attempting to draw fans away from Alex Box Stadium. Across town, Southern University, another Division I program, usually draws a few hundred to its games. The New Orleans Zephyrs, a New York Mets AAA affiliate, are over an hour's drive away. The Houston Astros are the closest major league team, requiring at least a four-hour drive.

When the fans enter the front gate of Alex Box Stadium, Ted Stickles is determined to make sure it is a good experience.

Stickles is over 2,000 miles away from his hometown of San Mateo, located in the San Francisco Bay Area. He was an accomplished swimmer at Hillsdale High School before attending the University of Indiana in the early 1960s. He set several world records in individual medley events. Once his swimming career was over, he went on to coach, first at the University of Illinois and then at LSU.

When Stickles retired from coaching, he remained at LSU and took on the position of director of event/game management. He officially retired from the position in 2003, but continues to work on a contract basis just for baseball games. He enjoys the task.

With his walkie-talkie frequently in use, he coordinates big things, little things and everything in between. He works with ticket takers, marshals, parking attendants, police officers, concession workers (from non-profit organizations), television crews, umpires, and visiting teams. Sometimes the duties go beyond the routine. When lightning strikes in the vicinity, Stickles checks with ImpactWeather (a nationwide, full-service weather monitoring company) to determine the precise location. If it is within a six-mile radius, he notifies the umpires and the game is automatically suspended for 30 minutes.

To Stickles, the answer as to why LSU has been so successful in drawing fans to the baseball games begins with Skip Bertman. Now the school's athletics director, Bertman was head coach from 1984 through 2001. He led the Tigers to five national championships, the first in 1991. Stickles comments that Bertman was a coach, a promoter, and an organizer. "You got to give him so much credit for what he has done here," says Stickles. "There was nothing but the grandstands at the time, then we had to add a set of bleachers." Originally a 1938 Works Progress Administration project, the grandstand could seat 2,700. Under Bertman's direction, one set of bleachers led to another and another and another and another.

*"LSU Fighting Tiger baseball is on the air. Welcome to LSU Fighting Tiger baseball. This afternoon, game two of the three-game weekend series between the LSU Fighting Tigers and the Florida Gators. Hey everybody, Jim Hawthorne, along with Charles Hanagriff, with you here on a bright, hot afternoon at Alex Box Stadium.*

*"The Florida Gators jumped on LSU pretty good last night and won the opening game of this final home series of the year, the final games of the year, and downed LSU 19–3 last night."*

Hawthorne's radio voice is smooth and pleasant, with a hint of a Southern drawl. His looks are a combination of actor Kurt Russell and basketball coach Mike Montgomery. His announcing is well known in Louisiana as he broadcasts LSU football, basketball and baseball games. The 2007 season marks his 24th year announcing the play-by-play of the LSU baseball games. He called each of the five national championship baseball victories.

His voice is heard not only on the flagship station WDGL-FM in Baton Rouge, but on nearly 20 affiliates as well. The broadcasts reach parts of Mississippi and Arkansas.

While Hawthorne provides the radio broadcast for each game, there is television coverage for many contests. At least 17 LSU games are telecast during the regular season.

*"We are in the Bayou for a warm afternoon of Southeastern Conference baseball. A team that has dominated the college baseball scene for a number of years, trying to get back up the ladder, but they are fighting for their SEC tournament lives. We are at LSU, where the Tigers will play host to the Florida Gators from Alex Box Stadium.*

*Hello again everybody, I'm Dave Neal, partner Larry Conley, so glad you could join us. A very important couple of weekend games left of SEC baseball on the way. There are only two weekends left before we all convene at Hoover, Alabama, at Regents Park for the SEC baseball tournament...."*

Neal recorded the opening of the pre-game segment for the Fox Sports Net telecast, which aired a few minutes before game time. After a commercial break, the broadcast team returned live just before the Tigers took the field. Neal, a former sports anchor in Tallahassee, does SEC football and basketball in addition to the baseball broadcasts. He also hosts the show "SEC-TV Weekly" for its nine months of broadcasts. Conley has been primarily a basketball commentator during his nearly 30-year broadcasting career.

While Fox Sports Net has the responsibility for certain games, Cox Sports Television and the Jumbo Sports Network televise most of the selected LSU games.

Cox has the broadcast team of Lyn Rollins and Ben McDonald. Rollins is a veteran announcer who also covers LSU football. McDonald, a native of nearby Denham Springs, is probably LSU's most famous baseball alumnus.

In the 1989 season, his junior and final year with LSU, he was *Baseball America*'s national player of the year and the USA Baseball's Golden Spikes award winner as the top amateur baseball player in the country. McDonald was a first-team All-American in both 1988 and 1989, and he still holds the school's single-season strikeout record of 202. He was the first player taken in the 1989 major league draft, going to the Orioles. McDonald pitched for nine years in the major leagues before shoulder injuries finally ended his career with the 1997 season.

*When Cole Figueroa grounds out to Michael Hollander at shortstop, it is a moral victory for the Tiger fans. The previous night Figueroa singled on the second pitch of the game and proceeded to produce three of the 21 total hits the Gators generated.*

Friday night was a fireworks promotion night. Unfortunately, most of the home crowd was not in the mood for fireworks, especially the variety launched by Florida hitters. Matt LaPorta hit two home runs; Chris Petrie had a grand slam; Jon Townsend clubbed a two-run homer. By the time the game ended at 10:37 P.M., the spectators had dwindled by the thousands.

Shortly after the final out, Carl Dubois, the *Advocate*'s (Baton Rouge's main newspaper) sports writer interviewed Coach Paul Maineiri as loud fireworks exploded beyond the outfield fences. Dubois is one of three beat writers who regularly covers the games. He held his recorder practically against Maineiri's neck, as if he were taking the latter's pulse, to hopefully pick up his voice amid the background noise. Perhaps it was the sound quality, but there were no quotes from Mainieri or anyone else in Dubois' article, which ran in the paper Saturday morning. Perhaps there is nothing enlightening to say or write about after a 16-run loss.

*Jon Townsend strikes out on the only pitch he swings at. The strikeout puts Anita Haywood, known by some as the "K lady," into motion. She sits in the second row of Section D in the grandstand. She looks fortyish, with a braided ponytail under her LSU visor. She reaches into a square LSU travel bag and pulls out a placard with the letter "K." This is not a hastily photocopied symbol of the strikeout, but a metal placard, with a purple background and a gold letter. She holds it aloft, a technique that is a cross between a minister displaying a missal and a boxing ring card model holding up the round number. She jogs 50 feet to a section of the backstop near the beginning of the baseline. The placard remains overhead for the entire jog.*

*Haywood affixes the "K" to the top rail of the backstop and returns to her seat with one finger in the air. It signifies the number of cumulative Tiger strike-outs for the game. On Friday night, she eventually got to hold up eight fingers in an otherwise-disastrous night for LSU pitching.*

*After the first two outs, Matt LaPorta bats in his usual third spot.*

LaPorta is one of the nation's most feared hitters. He comes into the game with 19 home runs and a .443 average for the season. His average is within the top ten in NCAA Division I baseball. LaPorta is having this offensive success despite having a strained quadricep. In 2006, he had an oblique injury that limited him to starting 43 games. In 2005, he hit 26 home runs with 79 RBIs and had a .328 average. He was a big part of the Florida team that made it all the way to the 2005 finals before losing to Texas.

*Charlie Furbush, the starter for LSU, makes it clear how he intends to pitch to LaPorta; everything is well inside. Furbush begins his motion from the far left side of the rubber and uses a very slow delivery. After falling behind 3–1, Furbush intentionally walks LaPorta. Sean Ochinko does not bother to hold him on at first given he cannot run faster than a jog. Although Brian Leclerc's single and Austin Pride's fly out are sharply hit, they do not result in a first-inning score. It is another moral victory.*

*Bryan Augenstein makes the start for the Gators. On the first pitch of the game, Jared Mitchell grounds out to second. Nicholas Pontiff, the designated hitter, hits a foul ball down the right field line. Leclerc goes all out for it. He dives for the ball and crashes into a gate. He cannot make the catch, but he earns the applause of the crowd for his effort. On the next pitch, Pontiff hits a bloop single, just like a drop shot in tennis, that falls in front of Pride. That, however, is the extent of the Tiger offense in the bottom of the first.*

*Before the start of the next inning, the public address announcer, Bill Franques, informs the crowd of LSU's extra-inning, 1–0, SEC softball championship win over Florida. The announcement gets more than a perfunctory cheer from the fans.*

*Furbush gets a one-two-three second. In LSU's turn, two consecutive one-out singles go for naught when the runners attempt a double steal on J.T. Wise's full count. Wise strikes out and the Gator catcher, Hampton Tignor, makes a good throw to third ahead of Ryan Schimpf's slide.*

*Clayton Pisani leads off the third with a single. Although Furbush's delivery is relatively slow from the stretch, he nonetheless neutralizes potential running by being a left-hander that looks right at the runners. After two line-drive*

*outs, the Tigers intentionally walk LaPorta. The strategy works again as Leclerc*
*grounds out to end the threat.*

   *Coach Mainieri has a brief television interview for the Fox Sports Network*
*outside of the dugout. He then jogs to his usual spot as the third base coach. For*
*LSU it is three up, three down in the bottom of the third; the same result occurs*
*for both teams in the fourth and fifth innings.*


   While many college baseball teams do not have any radio coverage, LSU
supplements the game broadcasts with "The Paul Mainieri Show." It airs
every Monday for an hour. In addition to the radio show, Mainieri is featured
in a weekly television show, "Inside LSU Baseball."

   Mainieri has a challenging job, but slightly less challenging than that of
predecessor Smoke Laval. It is less challenging because Laval was first to succeed Skip Bertman. In Laval's last season, in 2006, the Tigers lost seven of
their last nine games and failed to get selected for the NCAA tournament for
the first time since 1988. Laval moved on. Mainieri inherited an expectation
level that, in addition to the national championships, was built on 13 SEC
titles, 13 College World Series appearances since 1986, and nine 50-win seasons. The Tigers are 28-21-1 overall and 11-12-1 in the SEC when Florida
arrives in town.

   Not only have the teams been successful, but many of the players have
been as well. Besides Ben McDonald, the Tigers have had other former players with successful major league careers: Albert Belle (played at LSU in the
1985-1987 seasons); Paul Byrd (1989-1991); Mark Guthrie (1984-1987); and
Todd Walker (1992-1994). More than 50 LSU players have reached the major
leagues.

   Although Mainieri was recently associated with Notre Dame, his roots
are southern. He went to Columbus High School in Miami and played for a
season at LSU and the remainder at the University of New Orleans. He ultimately graduated from Florida International. He then got a master's degree
and began coaching at St. Thomas (Miami Gardens, Florida, a Division II program). He has been coaching college ball for almost 25 years. His Notre Dame
teams frequently reached the NCAA regionals, and his winning percentage
there was an impressive .714.


   *The sixth inning begins ominously for LSU. The Gators' number two bat-*
*ter, Jon Townsend, turns to bunt and Furbush's pitch is far inside, hitting*
*Townsend on the leg. Up comes LaPorta, who has been intentionally walked*
*twice. Furbush starts him off with an inside fastball for a strike. He comes back*
*with an off-speed pitch and LaPorta hits a grounder that Furbush fields and*
*throw to first for the out.*

*Leclerc then hits a chopper right down the first base line, narrowly alluding Sean Ochinko's glove. His double scores Townsend for the first run of the game. Pride grounds out to J.T. Wise, and it looks like Furbush has a good chance to limit the damage. He intentionally walks Cody Neer. It was not a routine intentional walk as the second pitch almost floats in for a strike and the third one requires Robert Lara to leap to catch it. This time the intentional walk does not work so well.*

*With Jonathan Pigott up, Furbush throws a wild pitch, advancing the runners to third and second. With a 2–0 count, Pigott lays down a surprise bunt to the right side. Both Furbush and Ochinko converge for the ball, but they have no play and Leclerc scores. Tignor adds to LSU's two-out misery with a bloop hit to center that scores Neer.*

*After LSU goes down one-two-three in the bottom of the sixth, Florida has the top of the order up. Figueroa lines the first pitch perfectly between Schimpf in left and Mitchell in center, and it rolls to the fence for a double. Townsend follows with a shot to the left field fence. Nolan Cain now is warming up with greater urgency. LaPorta is intentionally walked for the third time this game. Furbush still looks uncomfortable, purposely throwing balls.*

*Leclerc takes a first-pitch ball and then crushes the next pitch in the general direction of the Athletic Administration Building. Ironically, his home run is hit over the billboard known as "The Intimidator," which sits just beyond the right field fence. It displays the large profile of a tiger with "National Champions" in bold lettering above the five years LSU won the College World Series. Most schools are not bashful about boasting of national championships; using a billboard to do so is different. Just like that the score is 7–0. The way Augenstein is pitching, this lead seems formidable. The home run sucked most of the enthusiasm out of the crowd.*

"The Intimidator" is but one unique feature of Alex Box Stadium. It is the grandstand structure that is such a throw-back to baseball in the early twentieth century. In the middle of the grandstand are yellow plastic seats, some with slightly rusted metal armrests. Seven steel pillars support the large overhang. About 3,200 fans can sit under the roof, which shields the faithful from the hot Louisiana sun. At the top of each pillar are large oscillating fans angled downwards towards the seats. A bird nest or two has been built on some of the metal cross supports.

In center field, above the 20-foot-high green wall, is a huge American flag accompanied by five national championship flags. Two flags are purple (1991 and 1997), two are white (1993 and 2000), and one is yellow (1996).

Three sets of aluminum bleachers are symmetrically placed along the left and right field foul lines. Another three sets of bleachers are in left field. At the back of the bleachers are flags of each team in the Southeastern Conference (SEC). Behind these is a parking lot in which tailgating is a regular occurrence.

The SEC is made up of two divisions for baseball, the Eastern and Western. The Eastern Division consists of Florida, Georgia, Kentucky, South Carolina, Tennessee and Vanderbilt. The Western Division features Alabama, Arkansas, Auburn, LSU, Ole Miss and Mississippi State. In 2007, the SEC is considered the strongest baseball conference in the country.

*The Tigers don't have an answer in the bottom of the seventh, but they try to get something going in the eighth. Buzzy Haydel leads off the inning by striking out. Steve Broschofsky pinch-hits for Wise and hits a shot towards third. Townsend can't make the play cleanly and draws the error. Jason Lewis pinch-hits for Robert Lara and singles to left. It is back to the top of the order and Mitchell hits the first pitch hard for a single up the middle. Chris McGee, who pinch-ran for Broschofsky, comes in to score. Now, it is starting to get just a little interesting.*

*Pontiff grounds out to third for the second out, but Lewis comes in to score. Blake Dean then rips a ball along the left field line for a double, and Pontiff scores. That is the final batter Bryan Augenstein will face, and David Hurst, a left-hander, enters the game. Michael Hollander greets him with a single right up the middle, scoring Dean. When Hollander and Ochinko hit back-to-back singles, the crowd is really back into the game. It's 7–4, and when Jordan Mayer, a right-handed pinch-hitter, comes up to face the left-handed Hurst, he is both the ninth batter of the inning and the potential tying run. But his fly out to right ends the inning.*

*At a minimum, LSU is looking to shut down Florida in the ninth to still have a chance. Shane Ardoin is given the assignment as the third Tiger pitcher of the afternoon. It does not start out well when he walks Chris Petrie on four pitches. It gets worse when Neer and Pigott hit back-to-back singles to load the bases. Paul Bertuccini gets the unenviable task of coming into the game with the bases loaded and no outs. He doesn't exactly get out of it when he walks Tignor on five pitches. Bertuccini does get the double-play grounder, a home-to-first variety, but it is a batter too late.*

*Falling short in the bottom of the eighth and giving up an added run in the ninth seems to take something out of the Tigers. In the bottom of the ninth, they fail to score, getting just one base runner on a walk. They have been outscored 28–7 in the first two games. It is not just discouraging; it is embarrassing.*

LSU had a paid attendance of 7,674 for Saturday's game. When LSU had its 2007 home opener on Friday night, February 9, the paid crowd was 7,492. The Tigers beat Saint Mary's College, 4–3.

Saint Mary's had its season opener two weeks earlier and drew a crowd of 322. Admittedly, it was a 1:00 P.M. start on a Friday afternoon; nobody was expecting a large walk-up business. The Gaels, who play their home games on an idyllic campus in Moraga, 20 miles east of San Francisco, drew 722 and 478, respectively, for the weekend series against the University of Nevada. The attendance was hardly a sign of indifference for the Gaels or the Wolf Pack. For most college games, the norm is a few hundred spectators.

LSU is not a normal team. The SEC is not a normal league. LSU has led the nation in attendance for the past ten years. In 2004, the Tigers set an average attendance record of 7,898 per game. In 2003, they set a total attendance record of 291,676. While LSU's strong season-ticket base has guaranteed the big-ticket sales, the actual number that walk through the gate can be substantially smaller for any given game. Also, the increased losses in the past seasons have taken a minor toll on attendance. Average attendance slipped a little between 2005 and 2006, but rebounded slightly in 2007.

Arkansas is very close to LSU's attendance figures and Mississippi State is not far behind. As a conference, the SEC draws over 1.6 million aggregate fans. Even those colleges at the bottom of the SEC list are averaging over 1,500 fans. Chuck Dunlap, the SEC's associate director of media relations and a Mississippi State graduate says, "I think SEC fans are just a different kind of fan than fans from any other conference. SEC fans have more pride and more passion, I believe, than any other group of fans."

After LSU's Skip Bertman and Ron Polk of Mississippi State showed the rest of the country how to build successful programs, both on the field and in the stands, the rest of the SEC teams eventually began to follow. In recent years, most of the SEC teams have either built new stadiums or made significant renovations to existing ones.

According to Dunlap, ironically, what LSU started more than 20 years ago may have indirectly made the national championship goal more challenging for the Tigers for the indefinite future. "What LSU had a major part of doing was, all the other administrations in the SEC saw that baseball could be a revenue producer, baseball could be an exciting sport, baseball could be something that would pack the stands and create a great deal of excitement throughout the end of June. You've seen the other administrations start putting a ton of money into their facilities, into their coaching salaries, into recruiting, and you've seen baseball in the SEC go from two to three programs to a complete, rounded out, very even, ultra-competitive top twelve schools. There's not much room in between one and twelve in the SEC. We don't have those two or three dominant programs anymore, but we've got twelve really, really good ones."

*"Ladies and gentlemen, boys and girls, good afternoon and welcome to Alex Box Stadium for today's Southeastern Conference game between the Florida Gators and the LSU Fighting Tigers. Today's game is sponsored by McDonald's...."*

It is the public address announcer, Bill Franques. His voice is deep and steady. His diction is so refined that one would expect to hear it continuously at airports. "The train to terminal C will arrive in two minutes."

Franques knows a thing or two about LSU baseball. He grew up in Lafayette, Louisiana, and attended LSU sporting events as a kid. He worked in the sports information office as an intern, and the timing of his graduation from LSU was perfect as there became a full-time opening. His first assignment was with the baseball program, where he saw first-hand the impact of Skip Bertman on LSU baseball as a coach, a recruiter and a marketer. Bertman discussed with Franques the important role the media had in publicizing the team and ultimately drawing fans into the park.

"He came up with marketing ideas as far as the ticket plans that were sold," Franques says about Bertman. "He was comprehensive. He was his own marketer and brought in different promotional ideas. His attention to details spread to the concession areas. He said the 'coffee has to be hot, the bathrooms have to be clean.' He did as much as he could to enhance customer relations so that people would want to come back. Of course, the recruiting, the quality of play, and the winning had a huge amount to do with it as well."

During the game Franques is seated on the top row in the unusual unenclosed press box in Alex Box Stadium. Alongside him, a person enters information into a laptop for the GameWatcher software, which allows Internet users to track the action almost live. In the row below him are the radio broadcast team of Hawthorne and Hanagriff, and to their right is the person who maintains the statistics for the LSU website. Within an hour after the game is over, fans can log in and get a summary description of the highlights as well as the box score. Seated in front of Franques is the official scorer, either long-time columnist Joe Macaluso of the *Baton Rouge Advocate* or his son, Chris. In the middle of the press box sits the scoreboard operator and a second person keeping up-to-date statistical information that is shown to spectators throughout the game.

Most of the remainder of the press box usually has a collection of print media personnel: the student newspaper reporter, a Gannett Newspaper reporter (which owns five newspapers in Louisiana), the *Times-Picayune* (New Orleans) reporter, the beat writer for the visiting team, and Carl Dubois of the *Advocate*. Alongside of them, for the many televised games, is the television broadcast team, either from Cox or Fox.

As an associate sports information director, Franques' duties go well beyond PA announcing. Besides coordinating media requests for practices and games, he joins Jim Hawthorne and Charles Hanagriff on the radio for road games. He compiles the 207-page baseball media guide that has received regional and national awards from the College Sports Information Directors of America. In general, because of the school's sports website, he issues more press releases than in years past.

*About six minutes before the first pitch, "Eye of the Tiger" pumps from the speakers, "acoustical cannons," mounted to the roof of the grandstand. A moment later, the national anthem is sung. Then, right according to script, at 1:05 P.M., the LSU fight song is played followed by Bill Franques telling the crowd, "Here come the LSU Fighting Tigers!" and the team takes the field.*

*Ryan Byrd starts the game and faces the lead-off hitter, Cole Figueroa, inducing him to a bouncer to first. Buzzy Haydel fields the ball on the short-hop and, just as he is about to flip the ball to Byrd, he slips. Haydel still manages to toss the ball and Byrd catches it bare-handed and behind his back as he touches the bag. Perhaps it is a good omen for LSU to have a fortuitous result on the first play. Byrd is a lanky 6' and he comes right over the top in his delivery. Townsend flies out to center for the second out. With LaPorta up, the Tigers continue their pitching approach: pound him inside.*

*Once Byrd falls behind LaPorta 2–0, he throws two intentional balls. It is followed with a ground ball to second for an easy fielder's choice.*

*Chris McGhee receives the start at second and gets the crowd into the game immediately with a base hit up the middle. Florida starter Billy Bullock is concerned about McGhee running and throws over to first four times with Nicholas Pontiff at the plate. Pontiff hits an opposite-field single to right. McGhee goes to third on the hit and Pontiff takes second on the throw from right field.*

*A "Here we go Tigers, here we go" chant echoes through the crowd. Chris Guillot is the man responsible for starting the cheers. His voice is deep, but on occasion it teeters on becoming raspy. He stands as much as he sits and, when he sits, it usually is an alternating pattern between sections B and C on the grandstands. Moments later he starts a chant of "L-S-U!"*

Guillot, a season-ticket holder and a member of the Coaches Committee, has been attending LSU baseball games since he graduated from the university with a degree in engineering in 1986. But for an occasional conflict, he attends most of LSU's home and away games. He has been to the College World Series about 18 times.

"The difference in college baseball fans and anywhere else, the difference in LSU fans and anywhere else, is that we are family," says Guillot. "Welcome to our family." When it comes to cheering, he comments, "The difference in a LSU fan is 'I'm not waiting for it to happen, I going to try to make it happen.' That's the secret of what a LSU fan is. I've seen it. Every one of them believes the more we yell it, the better we perform." Guillot is not an "in-your-face, put the other team down" type of fan; he has a healthy respect for college baseball and all of its participants.

The 2008 season is the last for what will become known as the "old" Alex Box Stadium. The new one is being built a quarter-mile away. It got to the point that the necessary repairs were continual and, by definition, it is an old facility. In the view of many, it was outdated. The new stadium will have a general layout similar to the old, but it will have an increased capacity of about 1,000 (to 8,786) with 19 suites and an expanded number of full seats (versus bench seating) in the grandstand. The restrooms and concessions will be greatly expanded, as will the pressbox. There will be a club lounge and hall of fame room.

Guillot fully expects to be leading cheers in the new Alex Box Stadium. He is philosophical about the new stadium. "Nobody in life likes change," says Guillot. "The players and coaches will make (the new stadium) an experience. I'll yell and get the fans into it. It will be home again."

*Blake Dean hits a grounder to first for an out, but it is enough to score McGhee. It is the first time this series the Tigers have had a lead. Michael Hollander pops up for the second out, but it is anything but routine. Cole Figueroa can't locate the ball in the bright sky from his shortstop position and left fielder Austin Pride hustles in to make the catch. Jared Mitchell is up next and looks at a series of pitches, all away, and draws a walk. Sean Ochinko follows with a solid single between third and short that easily scores Pontiff for the second run.*

*Ryan Schimpf gets hit by a pitch to load the bases. This brings up the eighth hitter of the inning, Buzzy Haydel. Haydel hits what looks to be a bloop single to right, but it lands on the edge of the infield dirt. Second baseman Avery Barnes fields it on one hop, but he double clutches and his throw is too late. Mitchell scores and the bases are still loaded. The inning ends with J.T. Wise striking out.*

*The home crowd is feeling good. There are expectations that the Tigers are not going to get swept. But they could. Austin Pride reinforces that possibility with a lead-off homer for Florida in the second. The ball hits the left field bleacher railing and comes back onto the field, but third base umpire A. J. Lostaglio signals a home run. Neer singles and Pigott, after fouling off a bunt, hits a fly that Mitchell dives but just misses. The ball is relayed to shortstop Hollander, who throws towards home, but the throw gets past Ochinko, towards the Florida dugout. With nobody covering home, Pigott scores. The first-inning optimism is replaced with second-inning concerns.*

*Tignor walks, still with nobody out, which gets the bullpen warming up. Byrd regroups and retires the next three batters. During the half-inning break, some young soldiers with LSU connections are acknowledged as part of a veteran's salute. They are either going to or coming back from the Middle East. Both teams and the fans give a standing ovation.*

The all-time single-game attendance records have been played at neutral sites. When Petco Park in San Diego first opened, San Diego State drew 40,106 in a game against Houston in 2004. Later that year, a Georgia-Georgia Tech game drew 28,836 at Turner Field in Atlanta, which was, in part, a fundraiser. That 2004 activity surpassed the 2002 record of 27,673 in a game between LSU and Tulane at the New Orleans Superdome.

At the College World Series, the largest crowd occurred on a semi-final day when 30,335 saw two games: North Carolina-Cal State Fullerton and Oregon State-Rice.

The largest on-campus crowds regularly go to Mississippi State, in which Dudy Noble Field can hold almost 15,000 due to the capacity of its outfield terrace and drive-up "left field lounge." Back in 1989, the Bulldogs drew 14,991 in a doubleheader against Florida.

*LaPorta leads off the top of the third in the most unusual manner: he takes a called first strike. He then grounds to third but barely runs half-way to first on the putout due to his hamstring injury. The Gators do not mount a threat in the inning, nor do the Tigers.*

*As the Gators are back up to bat in the fourth, the five LSU championship flags in center field blow from left the right to clearly show their wording. With one out, Pigott hits a line drive to left-center that, despite Ryan Schimpf's bobble, is a double all the way. Tignor follows with a bloop single, but Pigott advances only to third. Avery Barnes, who showed he could lay down a bunt in the second inning, does so again; this time the squeeze brings home a run. The LSU bullpen is back in action, but Byrd stops a rally and keeps the Tigers within a run.*

*Bullock begins the inning with, for him, a dreaded walk. Not only does the walk put the tying run on base, but it puts the bullpen into action. When Haydel tries to sacrifice Schimpf over, his bunt is pushed too hard and Bullock gets the force at second. Wise follows with a single, which results in a pitching change as Josh Edmondson comes in. Edmondson throws sidearm, almost submarine. McGhee, who has reached base safely in his two previous at-bats, hits the ball between Neer and Barnes for a single. Haydel is running hard as right fielder Leclerc comes up throwing. The on-deck batter, Pontiff, emphatically signals Haydel to slide as the throw heads towards home. But the throw is errant, to the foul side of the first base line, and suddenly the air traffic controller, Pontiff, has to run for cover as the ball reaches the general plate area. On the error, Wise comes in to score and McGee advances to second. When Pontiff then singles to drive in McGee, the crowd erupts. The LSU dugout erupts. Pontiff claps his hands powerfully once; he's pumped.*

*The Tigers settle for the three and take a 6–4 lead into the fifth. Given the manner in which the series had gone so far, a two-run lead is hardly safe, especially with LaPorta up first. Byrd falls behind 3–0, and Ochinko looks to the LSU dugout as he normally does between pitches. Somewhat unexpectedly, he does not get the sign to intentionally walk LaPorta. The next pitch is ripped to deep center but it is just a long out. Byrd gets out of the inning, keeping the lead intact.*

*After LSU strands Haydel on second and fails to score in the bottom of the inning, the fans dispassionately watch a three-legged race with teams consisting of a mom and child. It is Mother's Day, after all. Byrd is done for the afternoon and T.J. Forrest comes in to relieve.*

After the end of the fifth inning of every home game, the infield dirt is dragged smooth. The men doing the work are not part of the paid grounds crew or reserves on the team. They are part of the Coaches Committee.

This booster group started out with about 20 members and met in the locker room. Now the Coaches Committee has a membership of almost 300 that provides financial and volunteer assistance to the program in addition to being season-ticket holders. The group was formed under Skip Bertman, and it provides a connection to the program for alumni and community supporters that is stronger than the spectator-only experience. The Coaches Committee has purchased baseball equipment and assisted with stadium improvements over the years.

*Forrest, besides being right-handed, is taller and lankier than Byrd. He also has more of a three-quarters arm delivery.*

*Forrest does give up a one-out pinch-hit double to Chris Petrie, but the Gators follow that with two ground ball outs and do not score.*

*For the third time, McGhee is the lead-off batter, but this time he strikes out on three pitches. Pontiff and Dean reach safely on a hit-by-pitch and a single, respectively; the latter is a hard, high chopper past Neer at first. Hollander then tries to bunt home a run, but it is a safety squeeze and Pontiff wisely remains at third with the putout made to first. Jared Mitchell approaches the plate for the thirteenth time this series, and, for the thirteenth time, the Jay-Z lyrics that introduce him come from the grandstand speakers.*

*Mitchell hits a hard chopper right up the middle, and when the middle infielders' momentum carry both players into the outfield, Mitchell alertly advances to second with nobody covering. His hit scores two. The Tigers finally appear to be in control.*

*The seventh inning was an impressive pitching effort for Forrest. He faced and retired consecutively the two through four hitters in the batting order on eight pitches. Most impressive is a three-pitch strikeout of LaPorta in which Forrest delivered an off-speed pitch for the called last strike.*

*When the Tigers bat in the seventh with the bottom of the order, it is time to manufacture some offense. Steve Broschofsky pinch-hits for Schimpf and hits a ball off his fists to Townsend at third. Townsend fields the ball cleanly on the run, but he cannot get the ball out of his glove to make a throw. Haydel squares around to bunt and takes a first-pitch ball. Broschofsky has wandered off first too far and the catcher, Neer, who had changed positions in the sixth, has his pick-off throw go right into the colliding runner and first baseman (Pride). The throw bounces away and Broschofsky advances to second. Haydel gets a pitch to bunt and his sacrifice moves the runner to third. Wise singles to score Broschofsky, but Chris Petrie hustles to the ball and easily throws out Wise trying to stretch the hit into a double. With a 9–3 score, the fans feel they can relax and enjoy the final two innings. They do.*

When the inning ends, a couple of LSU Bat Girls spring into action and pick up the bat and bring extra balls or water to the umpire. There are 10 LSU Bat Girls working each home game. Thirty students are selected each year to be part of the group from the many that sign up. It is considered to be a privilege to be a member of this group. Some colleges would be happy if 30 students simply attended a home game, let alone volunteered to help out an entire season. The Bat Girls work under the direction of the Marketing and Promotions Department and sell programs and retrieve foul balls in addition to standard "batboy" duties.

The Marketing and Promotions Department is headed by Guy Gaster. He works to improve upon an already impressive season-ticket holder base. The "gold seats," yellow full-seats, were first made available in the 1990s. There are over 400 holders of these seats directly behind home plate, and the owners have generally held onto these seats since they were first made available. There are almost 2,200 season-ticket holders in the purple bench-style seats in the grandstand. There are about 3,900 season-ticket holders in the bleachers. That provides a season-ticket holder base of about 6,500.

The right field bleachers are designated for LSU students. They are a group that tends to arrive late and leave early, and they come out most frequently for higher-ranked opponents. The remaining bleachers are typically filled by families. Many of the baseball promotional activities are aimed towards children to allow them to be part of the college baseball experience. While LSU's approach to fan promotions is similar to those found at many minor league parks, Gaster also tries to be careful that "we don't try to over-entertain them."

*Forrest and LSU close out the eighth and ninth innings, allowing a couple of walks and an infield hit in total. Despite the win, it is bittersweet for many of the fans. The win continues the Tigers' mathematically possibility of partic-ipating in the SEC tournament. Even the sound of that is hollow. The LSU faith-ful are used to watching their team play in the NCAA Regional Tournament and the College World Series. Having just a slim chance to only play the confer-ence tournament is far below expectations. Happy Mother's Day.*

---

UNIVERSITY OF FLORIDA GATORS VS.
LOUISIANA STATE UNIVERSITY TIGERS
MAY 12, 2007 AT BATON ROUGE, LOUISIANA
ALEX BOX STADIUM

---

Florida (27–25, 14–12 SEC) | | | | LSU (28-23-1, 11-14-1 SEC) | | | |

| Player | AB | R | H | RBI | Player | AB | R | H | RBI |
|---|---|---|---|---|---|---|---|---|---|
| Figueroa, Cole ss | 6 | 1 | 1 | 0 | Mitchell, Jared cf | 5 | 1 | 1 | 1 |
| Townsend, Jon 3b | 4 | 2 | 2 | 1 | Pontiff, Nicholas dh | 4 | 0 | 1 | 1 |
| LaPorta, Matt 1b | 2 | 1 | 0 | 0 | Dean, Blake rf/lf | 4 | 1 | 1 | 1 |
| Leclerc, Brian rf | 5 | 2 | 3 | 4 | Hollander, Michael ss | 4 | 0 | 2 | 1 |
| den Dekker, Matt cf | 0 | 0 | 0 | 0 | Ochinko, Sean 1b/c | 4 | 0 | 2 | 0 |
| Pride, Austin lf | 3 | 0 | 0 | 0 | Schimpf, Ryan lf | 2 | 0 | 1 | 0 |
| Petrie, Chris ph/lf | 1 | 1 | 0 | 0 | Mayer, Jordan ph/1b | 1 | 0 | 0 | 0 |
| Neer, Cody dh | 4 | 1 | 1 | 0 | Haydel, Buzzy 2b/3b | 4 | 0 | 1 | 0 |
| Pigott, Jonathan cf/rf | 5 | 0 | 3 | 1 | Wise, J.T. 3b | 2 | 0 | 0 | 0 |
| Tignor, Hampton c | 4 | 0 | 2 | 2 | Broschofsky, Steve ph | 1 | 0 | 0 | 0 |
| Pisani, Clayton 2b | 5 | 0 | 1 | 0 | McGhee, Chris pr/2b | 0 | 1 | 0 | 0 |
| Augenstein, Bryan p | 0 | 0 | 0 | 0 | Lara, Robert c | 2 | 0 | 0 | 0 |
| Hurst, David p | 0 | 0 | 0 | 0 | Lewis, Jason ph/rf | 2 | 1 | 1 | 0 |
| | | | | | Furbush, Charlie p | 0 | 0 | 0 | 0 |
| | | | | | Cain, Nolan p | 0 | 0 | 0 | 0 |
| | | | | | Ardoin, Shane p | 0 | 0 | 0 | 0 |
| | | | | | Bertuccini, Paul p | 0 | 0 | 0 | 0 |
| Totals | 39 | 8 | 13 | 8 | Totals | 35 | 4 | 10 | 4 |

| Score by Innings | | | | | | | | | | | R | H | E |
|---|---|---|---|---|---|---|---|---|---|---|---|---|---|
| Florida | 0 | 0 | 0 | 0 | 0 | 3 | 4 | 0 | 1 | - | 8 | 13 | 1 |
| LSU | 0 | 0 | 0 | 0 | 0 | 0 | 0 | 4 | 0 | - | 4 | 10 | 0 |

2B — Figueroa (9); Townsend (12); Leclerc (12); Dean (12). HR — LeClerc (3).

| Florida | IP | H | R | ER | BB | SO |
|---|---|---|---|---|---|---|
| Augenstein, Bryan | 7⅔ | 8 | 4 | 0 | 0 | 7 |
| Hurst, David | 1⅓ | 2 | 0 | 0 | 1 | 0 |

| LSU | IP | H | R | ER | BB | SO |
|---|---|---|---|---|---|---|
| Furbush, Charlie | 6 | 8 | 7 | 7 | 4 | 3 |
| Cain, Nolan | 2 | 3 | 0 | 0 | 1 | 3 |
| Ardoin, Shane | 0 | 2 | 1 | 1 | 1 | 0 |
| Bertuccini, Paul | 1 | 0 | 0 | 0 | 1 | 0 |

Win — Augenstein (6–5). Loss— Furbush (3–8). Save — None.

Start: 3:09. Time: 3:03. Attendance: 7,674

---

UNIVERSITY OF FLORIDA GATORS VS.
LOUISIANA STATE UNIVERSITY TIGERS
MAY 13, 2007 AT BATON ROUGE, LOUISIANA
ALEX BOX STADIUM

---

Florida (27–26, 14–13 SEC)       LSU (29–23, 12-14-1 SEC)

| Player | AB | R | H | RBI | Player | AB | R | H | RBI |
|---|---|---|---|---|---|---|---|---|---|
| Figueroa, Cole ss | 4 | 0 | 0 | 0 | McGhee, Chris 2b | 5 | 2 | 2 | 1 |
| Townsend, Jon 3b | 5 | 0 | 1 | 0 | Pontiff, Nicholas dh | 4 | 2 | 2 | 1 |
| LaPorta, Matt dh | 4 | 0 | 0 | 0 | Dean, Blake rf | 4 | 1 | 1 | 1 |
| Leclerc, Brian rf | 5 | 0 | 0 | 0 | Waguespack, Steven ph/rf | 1 | 0 | 1 | 0 |
| Pride, Austin lf/1b | 4 | 1 | 3 | 1 | Hollander, Michael ss | 2 | 0 | 0 | 0 |
| Neer, Cody 1b/c | 4 | 1 | 1 | 0 | Mitchell, Jared cf | 3 | 1 | 1 | 2 |
| Pigott, Jonathan cf | 3 | 2 | 2 | 1 | Lewis, Jason ph/cf | 1 | 0 | 0 | 0 |
| den Dekker, M. ph/cf | 0 | 0 | 0 | 0 | Ochinko, Sean c | 4 | 0 | 1 | 1 |
| Tignor, Hampton c | 1 | 0 | 1 | 0 | Schimpf, Ryan lf | 0 | 0 | 0 | 0 |
| Petrie, Chris ph/lf | 1 | 0 | 1 | 0 | Broschofsky, Steve ph/lf | 2 | 1 | 1 | 0 |
| Barnes, Avery 2b | 2 | 0 | 0 | 1 | Haydel, Buzzy 1b | 3 | 1 | 2 | 1 |
| Bullock, Billy p | 0 | 0 | 0 | 0 | Wise, J.T. 3b | 4 | 1 | 2 | 1 |
| Edmondson, Josh p | 0 | 0 | 0 | 0 | Byrd, Ryan p | 0 | 0 | 0 | 0 |
| Porter, Steven p | 0 | 0 | 0 | 0 | Forrest, T.J. p | 0 | 0 | 0 | 0 |
| Keating, Patrick p | 0 | 0 | 0 | 0 | | | | | |
| Hurst, David p | 0 | 0 | 0 | 0 | | | | | |
| Totals | 33 | 4 | 9 | 3 | Totals | 33 | 9 | 13 | 8 |

### Score by Innings

| | | | | | | | | | | | R | H | E |
|---|---|---|---|---|---|---|---|---|---|---|---|---|---|
| Florida | 0 | 3 | 0 | 1 | 0 | 0 | 0 | 0 | 0 | - | 4 | 9 | 3 |
| LSU | 3 | 0 | 0 | 3 | 0 | 2 | 1 | 0 | X | - | 9 | 13 | 1 |

2B — Pigott (6); Petrie (7); Mitchell (8); Haydel (4). 3B — Pigott (1). HR — Pride (11).

| Florida | IP | H | R | ER | BB | SO |
|---|---|---|---|---|---|---|
| Bullock, Billy | 3⅓ | 5 | 5 | 5 | 3 | 3 |
| Edmondson, Josh | 0 | 2 | 1 | 1 | 0 | 0 |
| Porter, Steven | 1⅓ | 1 | 0 | 0 | 1 | 0 |
| Keating, Patrick | 2⅓ | 4 | 3 | 3 | 0 | 2 |
| Hurst, David | 1 | 1 | 0 | 0 | 0 | 0 |

| LSU | IP | H | R | ER | BB | SO |
|---|---|---|---|---|---|---|
| Byrd, Ryan | 5 | 7 | 4 | 4 | 3 | 0 |
| Forrest, T.J. | 4 | 2 | 0 | 0 | 2 | 4 |

Win — Byrd (6–1). Loss— Bullock (2–6). Save — Forrest (1).

Start: 1:05. Time: 3:02. Attendance: 7,092

# 9
# University of Miami Hurricanes

University of Miami Hurricanes *vs.*
Florida State Seminoles
April 27–29, 2007
MAJOR LEAGUE DRAFT
Signability

*When the lineup card is completed for tonight's game against Florida State, University of Miami head coach Jim Morris will have to play without Mark Rogers, Gio Gonzalez and Dexter Fowler. He also is missing Chris Perez, Jon Jay, Ricky Orta, Tommy Giles, Danny Valencia and Eddy Rodriquez. It was expected.*

Rogers, Gonzalez and Fowler are all would-be Hurricane juniors if they had chosen to go to college; however, all signed a professional contract three years ago and opted not to attend the University of Miami.

Perez, Jay, Orta, Giles, Valencia and Rodriquez are all would-be Hurricane seniors; however, all signed a professional contract last year and opted not to return for their senior season at Miami.

Mark Rogers was selected in the first round, the fifth pick overall of the 2004 draft, by the Milwaukee Brewers. Highly regarded during his years at Mount Ararat High School on Orr's Island, Maine, Rogers was named the Gatorade National High School Player of the Year. On June 18, about two months before the remote chance of starting his freshman season at Miami, he signed a contract with a signing bonus reported at $2.2 million.

Gio Gonzalez was also a first-round pick of the 2004 draft, albeit in the supplemental phase of the first round. The Chicago White Sox made him the 38th pick overall. Instead of making a short trip to UM in Coral Gables, he played his first season for the Kannapolis Intimidators, more than 750 miles away in North Carolina. He had a signing bonus reported at $850,000.

Dexter Fowler was a 14th-round pick of the Colorado Rockies. The prevailing logic was "if you can't sign him, don't choose him." He is a financial-page example of how a player's stock plummets if teams are convinced he is highly likely bound for college. Bound, that is, unless the money is significant. His reported $975,000 signing bonus was better than amounts agreed to by most second-round picks. It was enough to lure him away from college.

The major league draft (a.k.a. the Rule 4 draft or the amateur draft) is held in the first part of June, usually a couple of weeks before the College World Series is completed. There are 50 rounds of selections, plus a supplemental round, which occurs between the first and second rounds. While most teams select every round, a few stop making picks around, or soon after, the 35th round.

The supplemental round attempts to compensate major league teams that have lost "Type A" (statistically, the top 20 percent players at their position) or "Type B" (statistically, the top 40 percent players at their position, but less than the top 20 percent) free agents who have signed with another team.

The earliest an amateur player can be selected is after graduation from high school but before he attends either a four-year or junior college. Junior college players can be drafted after their freshman and/or sophomore seasons. Four-year college players can be selected at the earliest following the completion of their junior (or senior) year or upon reaching age 21. The unique rule for junior college players is a compelling reason for some to choose that route.

It is estimated that only 5 percent of drafted players will ever reach the major leagues. Thus, the signing bonus or other guaranteed money is very important to the player because pursuant to the Collective Bargaining Agreement for a rookie professional player, the minor league minimum salary is $30,000 per season in 2007 (increasing to $31,250 in 2008 and $32,500 in 2009).

If any ballplayer deserves the title "Mr. Rule 4," it has to be Matt Harrington. Harrington went to Palmdale High School, north of Los Angeles in the eastern foothills of the San Gabriel Mountains. He reportedly could throw in the mid–90s, was *Baseball America*'s High School Player of the Year, and was considered among the top prospects in the 2000 draft. As the draft approached, the word was out that he expected a $4.5 million signing bonus. The Colorado Rockies selected him as the seventh pick in the first round. No agreement with the Rockies was ever signed. There was disagreement as to what was supposedly said and promised. Harrington and his agent reportedly turned down a signing bonus of at least $3.7 million.

Agents typically receive 4 percent to 10 percent of the value of the contract;

five percent is frequently stated as the norm. Some agents opt for an hourly fee in lieu of taking a percentage. The practice is similar to the law profession, and some agents are attorneys.

Eligible for the 2001 draft, Harrington's stock fell and the San Diego Padres selected him in the second round. Harrington passed on a $1.2 million signing bonus. No agreement was signed. In the 2002 draft, the Tampa Bay Devil Rays selected him in the 14th round. No agreement was signed. In the 2003 draft, the Cincinnati Reds selected him in the 24th round. No agreement was signed. In the 2004 draft, the New York Yankees selected him in the 36th round. No agreement was signed. When he went unselected in the 2005 draft, he became a free agent and ultimately signed a minor league contract (without a signing bonus) with the Chicago Cubs in 2006. He was released in March of 2007.

*Miami came into Friday night's contest with a four-game winning steak. The Hurricanes beat Stetson two days earlier and swept Virginia Tech the prior weekend. The Virginia Tech series in Blacksburg was memorable. Winning three from the Hokies was not that much of a surprise. Going into the series, Virginia Tech was in last place in the Atlantic Coast Conference's Coastal Division with a 4–15 league record and 17–20 overall.*

*However, these Hokies were not the same team that had played five days earlier. Just four days prior to their match-up with Miami, Seung-Hui Cho shot and killed 31 students prior to his succumbing as well.*

*The first game brought out a record crowd of 3,132, which was likely looking to demonstrate school spirit while searching for an emotional respite from their grief. They were probably only momentarily disappointed when left fielder Nick Freitas snatched a ball going over the fence to prevent the Hokies' shortstop, Warren Schaeffer, from tying the game in the bottom of the ninth.*

It is ironic that the University of Miami baseball stadium is named for a former highly promising high school recruit who never played an inning for the Hurricanes. Miami baseball is played at Mark Light Field in Alex Rodriguez Park. While both benefactors to the facility, the latter donated $3 million-plus to make improvements to the facility. The improvements have been phased in since 2005, and full completion is expected after the 2008 season.

Even without the Rodriguez Park upgrades, it is a nice college venue. The grandstand is traditional with green seats close to the field and bench seating above the aisles.

The marked contrast is the comparison of the view in right field versus left field. Just beyond the right field fence is a five-level parking garage. To left-center are 17 palm trees. The area adjoining the right field foul line is generally inaccessible to spectators.

Along the left field foul line fans can get very close to the visitor's bullpen. There is some relief from the sun with a set of smaller bleachers, set back from the left field line fence and under a large banyan tree with its intriguing downward root growth. The scoreboard in left field is a perfect blend of looks and functionality for a college stadium. It has the message board that continually provides stats, but its best feature is the "U," the dual-hands clock and the "Hurricanes" lettering along the top. Below the scoreboard is a banner acknowledging the four national championships, and to the right are five palm trees.

*An early "statement" is often an overstatement in a baseball game. Players who have quick success or teams that jump out to a big lead often find themselves struggling over the duration of a game. When Tony Thomas, Jr. hits the first pitch of the game for an opposite-field single, neither pitcher Scott Maine nor the Hurricanes were concerned. Sure enough, Thomas is stranded at second when the half-inning comes to an end.*

Maine was highly touted out of Dwyer High School in Palm Beach Gardens. The Seattle Mariners selected him in the 15th round, but he opted to go to Miami. Little did he know what his college years had in store for him.

He not only had Tommy John surgery just prior to his sophomore season, but he also suffered a severe head injury the summer before his junior season. He spent two of his 22 days at North Broward Medical Center (Deerfield Beach, Florida) in a drug-induced coma after a serious auto accident. While he recuperated, he lost 45 pounds, but he amazingly was ready to pitch by the second series of the year when he started and got the win against UCLA.

*Blake Tekotte leads off against Bryan Henry and hits an off-field single. Roger Tomas, the second of five consecutive left-handed hitters, also hits an opposite-field single with the third baseman on the infield grass expecting a bunt. Yonder Alonso hits a shot to deep right field, but it is caught. Tekotte tags up and advances to third. Dennis Raben then hits a hard grounder, the full story of which never appears in a box score. The first baseman, Brandon Reichert, bobbles it, decides he no longer has a chance for the double play, and gets the unassisted out at first. Tekotte scores. There is no official error, but the slight miscue may have precluded a scoreless inning.*

*Two strikeouts sandwiching a pop-up to right nullified any Florida State offense in the second. The bottom of the inning started similarly for the Hurricanes with a tepid ground out and a pop-up to right. Then Richard O'Brien hits the first pitch for a home run, barely clearing the left field fence. After O'Brien has touched first base, veteran public address announcer Jay Rokeach calls out, "And you can kiss it goodbye! It's a Richard O'Brien home run! It's a Hurricane home run!" His voice is filled with enthusiasm, somewhat surprising for a person who has announced games for more than 35 years. It's also the first time he has had to make that particular announcement all season. It is O'Brien's first home run this year.*

O'Brien certainly comes from outside of Miami's typical recruiting footprint of Florida, particularly southern Florida. He went to Catholic High School in Little Rock, Arkansas, and Connors State Junior College in Warner, Oklahoma. The Chicago White Sox drafted him out of high school in the 47th round. With that late draft selection and little incentive to turn pro, he opted for Connors State, a program with a good national reputation and one O'Brien felt did a good job of developing catchers. The draft actually pushed O'Brien to junior college with the hopes of improving his position in future drafts.

After O'Brien's freshman year, the Chicago White Sox once again drafted him in the 47th round. Again there was not much incentive for him to sign, particularly since his goal was to go to junior college, attend a four-year school for one season, and then turn pro. When the White Sox selected him, he was under the process known as "draft and follow," which ceased with the 2007 draft. Teams used to be able to select a player in June, evaluate him in junior college through his season in the spring of the following year, and then have until the week before the next draft date to sign him. Now, teams only have about two months, until August 15, to sign players. Players who are not signed are eligible to be selected in next draft.

His play at Connors produced more interest than he received in high school, and before his sophomore season, he committed to Texas A&M. When long-time Aggie head coach Mark Johnson was fired from A&M (he has since relocated to Sam Houston State), O'Brien determined his role would not be the same under the new coaching staff. He was released from his commitment provided he did not attend another Big 12 school.

He had considerable interest from schools like Kentucky, Alabama, Loyola Marymount, and, of course, Miami. He chose Miami. "My opportunities seem to be very good here. They had Eddy Rodriquez, a great catcher, but when you play at a big school or a tough conference in D-I, you need two catchers. They only had one and they needed another guy to back up so I knew that coming in." His analysis was sound as he got to play in 42 games and started seven during his junior year.

*Scott Maine has another shut-down inning after the offense has scored. He is nicked by a leadoff single by Ruairi O'Connor. After Reichert looks intently into the Seminole dugout for a sign, he winds up swinging away and hits a deep drive to left for an out. Thomas pops out and Hallberg follows with a deep drive to left for the third out.*

*With one out, Roger Tomas hits a high chopper up the middle. Thomas fields the ball but has no play. Yonder Alonso then hits a shot just slightly left of straight-away center. There is no doubt it will clear the fence, and suddenly Rokeach is back with his home run acknowledgment, "And you can kiss it good-bye! It's a Yonder Alonso home run! It's a Hurricane home run!" Just like that, Miami has a 4–0 lead. It is Alonso's 13th home run of the season.*

*It's another shut-down inning opportunity for Maine, but he has the heart of the order challenging him. Posey leads off with a hard grounder to Gus Menendez at third, who is playing in. After diving for the ball that hits off his glove, he stays with it and gets the runner by a step. A few pitches later, Jack Rye hits another grounder to third. This time it is more routine, and the second out is recorded. Travis Anderson then hits a ball to deep center that Tekotte seemingly has locked in for the third out. At the last moment, Tekotte slips yet still makes a vain attempt to catch the ball from his knees. Anderson reaches third with a triple.*

*Stidham follows with a fly to left-center for which Tekotte makes a diving attempt, only this one is far more graceful than the previous dive. He catches the ball, but only for an instant. It trickles out of his glove before he can control it, and Stidham has a double. Mark Gildea then hits a shot past Menendez' back-hand attempt, and as quickly as the Hurricanes jumped out to a lead, the Seminoles have cut it in half. O'Connor continues to make it interesting, hitting a deep drive that Tekotte is able catch for the third out.*

*Miami doesn't have an answer in the bottom of the inning when Henry strikes out three around a two-out walk. Maine has similar success in a quiet top of the fifth, needing only 10 pitches to get three fly-ball outs.*

*In the bottom of the fifth, Tekotte again does what he is designed to do by leading off an inning for the third time. After he flies out to left, Tomas follows with a single. With Alonso up, Tomas runs on the fourth pitch. Alonso hits a very high foul pop-up that catcher Buster Posey has plenty of time to think about whether the ball will land and stay in his glove. It doesn't. The error gives Alonso new life. On the next pitch, he hits a shot that glances off the top of the "Hurricanes" wording on the right portion of the scoreboard. "And you can kiss it goodbye! It's a Yonder Alonso home run! It's a Hurricane home run!" It's a 6–2 game when the half-inning is done.*

Alonso looks like a hitter. He is 6'2" and 215 pounds with a powerful left-handed swing. He speaks confidently. He grew up three blocks away from

UM in Coral Gables. He verbally committed to Miami the summer after his sophomore year of high school, a full year before most players have an opportunity to make a decision. Yet despite his dream to play baseball for the Hurricanes, he still maintained the dream of playing major league baseball. The draft has an effect on the decision process. Leading up to the draft, conversations with major league teams' representatives were constant. There was contact from one of eight teams almost daily. They knew his cell phone number and his high school class schedule. "It does affect you a little bit, just because you don't know what to do," says Alonso. "Then, right after the draft comes around and you see where you go, it becomes a little bit easier."

Not that the process has an abrupt end. The Minnesota Twins selected Alonso in the 16th round, but he was of the impression he might go within the top six rounds. However, the draft is a bit of a self-fulfilling prophecy. If major league teams think a player is likely to go to college unless he is a very high draft pick, they will try to avoid potentially wasting a high pick, but still select the player in a lower round. His parents urged him to go to college. The day before he was about to start school at Miami, the Twins were still negotiating with him.

Since the 2000 draft, "slot money" is a term that has entered baseball's lexicon. The Commissioner's Office provides recommendations as to what a draft choice in each of the first five rounds should receive, which is designed to keep a spending discipline around signing players. It is not a requirement, and teams can and frequently do exceed the slot money, as was the case for Dexter Fowler.

*Baseball America* reported that the slot money for the number one pick for 2007 is approximately $3.6 million and the last pick (30th) of the first round is about $945,000. The estimated slot money for the 100th (third round, depending on the number of supplemental round picks) selection is $347,000. The fifth round ranges from about $150,000 to $125,000.

*Posey leads off the sixth with the crowd energized. Maine gets ahead in the count 1–2 and the fans begin staccato clapping. Two pitches later, Posey swings and misses, the bat flying out of his hands. It ignites a roar. Rye routinely grounds to third for the second out. Anderson, who hit the unusual triple a couple of innings prior, takes a swing at the first pitch, and seconds later, the ball lands over the palm trees in left field. Stidham follows with a grounder up the middle that just alludes Maine, Tomas and then Jackson. Maine stops any notion of a two-out rally by getting Mark Gildea to hit into a force play.*

*Sobolewski starts the bottom of the sixth with his own version of the up-the-middle grounder, his ticking off Henry's glove and continuing into center field. The hit gets the Florida State bullpen active. Menendez executes the sacrifice, but neither O'Brien nor Jackson can produce the RBI hit.*

*In the seventh, O'Connor leads off with an off-field double down the right field line. Reichert follows with a grounder to short, and O'Connor makes an ill-advised decision to break for third. Jackson fields the ground ball then throws to Menendez at third for the putout. Thomas then hits a perfect double-play ball to Jackson, who tosses to Tomas for the force, but the latter's relay throw sails over the head of first baseman Alonso. The wall parallel to the visitor's first base dugout provides a handball-like bounce back to Alonso, who races over to tag Thomas. Thomas made a turn to the left, into the field of play, and he is the third out. This inning is not Florida State's best example of base running.*

*Miami has an uneventful bottom of the seventh, failing to get a runner on for the first time in this game.*

*Maine starts off the eighth with a four-pitch walk. The last pitch goes all the way to the backstop. As Maine gets a visit from the coaching staff, an elevated Metrorail train passes by the first base side of the stadium. Maine regroups to get two consecutive fly outs, but the decision is made to pull him for Danny Gil. Gil falls behind O'Connor 2–0 and then hits him. Things don't improve much as Gil falls behind Stidham 3–0, which gets the Hurricane bullpen back into action. Stidham then takes two borderline strikes before swinging and missing to end the inning.*

Gil is an aberration in major college baseball as a fourth-year senior. Most college players don't make it that far with the same school. When Miami published its media guide for the 2004 season, Gil's freshman year, he was one of eight freshmen listed on the roster. Only Scott Maine (technically, a red-shirt junior) and Roger Tomas remained as Hurricanes four years later. In fact, these three plus Jemile Weeks are on the cover of the 2007 program.

There are at least four reasons why same-school baseball seniors are unusual. First, a few players just don't find college, in general, to be a fit and they leave school. A second reason is that some students stop playing due to an injury or a decision that the reward versus effort simply isn't there. Third, some players conclude they will have a better baseball experience at another school and transfer. There will likely be a curtailment of transferring given the rule that has an effective date of August 1, 2008, requiring Division I baseball players who transfer to another Division I school to sit out a year. This matches the requirement in football, basketball and ice hockey.

Lastly, many players leave after their junior year because they are selected in the major league draft and sign a professional contract. Jon Jay, Ricky Orta, Chris Perez and Eddy Rodriguez were part of Danny Gil's freshman class and these four signed contracts after their junior year. Perez, Jay and Orta were selected in the supplemental first round, the second round and the fourth round, respectively, while Rodriguez was a 20th-round pick.

A major league team's decision to draft a particular player starts with scouting evaluations. Each major league team has a scouting operation that uses about 20 scouts; some teams have more, some less. In addition, major league baseball controls the Major League Scouting Bureau, which provides the input of about 35 scouts for the benefit of all teams.

The hierarchy and titles may differ among the teams, but usually there are area scouts doing much of the grassroots evaluation and reporting their findings to a regional supervisor. These lower level recommendations are reviewed by a regional and/or national cross-checker. The information then filters up to the amateur scouting director for the team.

Position players are evaluated on the so-called five tools: speed, arm strength, fielding, hitting ability and hitting power. Pitchers are evaluated on velocity, control, movement, and mechanics. In both cases, the player is also evaluated as to his physical build and mental approach. Besides observing a player, the area scouts like to visit the family to get a more complete picture of the prospect. While many scouts can correctly observe the objective characteristics of a player's skills, the more difficult challenge is to get a correct read on the intangibles, health or signability of a player. As important as it is to choose the right players, it is equally as important to pass on ones that aren't.

*Miami goes out one-two-three in the eighth, and since the Alonso home run in the fifth, Henry has pitched solidly.*

*The Hurricanes are either confident or hopeful that Gil will find the strike zone and his rhythm. He doesn't. The leadoff batter, Gildea, walks on four pitches. This results in a parade of substitutions, the most interesting of which is the right fielder, Dennis Raben, coming in to pitch. He switches his outfield glove for a smaller pitcher's glove. Florida State counters the appearance of the left-handed pitcher with a right-handed pinch-hitter, D'Vontrey Richardson. After falling behind 0–2, Richardson works to an even count and then fouls off three straight pitches before hitting a pop-up along the right field line. The ball lands fair, and Richardson nearly runs up the back of Gildea, who had to wait to determine if the ball would be caught. Richardson ends up on second and Gildea on third.*

*On the first pitch to the next batter, Reichert, a called strike gets by O'Brien for a passed ball. Gildea comes in to score and Richardson moves up to third. Reichert battles, but he finally strikes out on a high pitch, the ninth he has seen. Raben has thrown 18 pitches to his first two batters, but he is now two outs away from ending the game with a Hurricane victory. Raben starts off the leadoff hitter, Thomas, with a perfect breaking ball for a strike. The next pitch stuns the crowd. Thomas has a perfectly timed swing and the result is a deep drive to left to tie the game.*

*Since the first inning, this game had been steadily drifting into Miami's win column, only to have a hurricane-like ninth inning knock the team on its backs. As some Miami fans finish checking their scorecard to determine which Hurricanes will come up in the bottom of the ninth to hopefully untie the game, Hallberg hits the ball to deep right field, giving the visitors back-to-back home runs. After the ball clears the fence, the second baseman Tomas, in a moment of deep frustration, takes off his glove and slams it to the ground. The embolden FSU fans bring out the tomahawk chop and chant for the first time this evening. David Gutierrez comes in to relieve, but Raben does not have the opportunity to deal with the stunning development in the dugout or locker room, for he is sent back to right field.*

*Gutierrez walks his first challenge, Posey, on four pitches. He is overthrowing. With the four and five hitters in the order coming up, the Hurricanes have to regroup just to keep it a one-run game. Rye pulls a single, but Gutierrez retires Oravetz and Stidham to finally get out of the inning.*

*The offensive damage is significant: nine batters come to bat and four of them score. The score is 7–6 going into the bottom of the ninth.*

*Danny Rosen comes in to relieve Henry and surrenders an off-field hit to Menendez leading off for Miami. Rye cuts the ball off quickly and limits a potential double to a single. Keeping the leadoff hitter from getting into second is important in a one-run game. O'Brien, the next batter, sacrifices Menendez to second and Miami still has two outs to work with. Chris Petralli pinch-hits for Jackson, and his first-pitch swing results in a pop-up to the shortstop. Down to the last out, only the most optimistic fan could expect something good to happen. It doesn't. Tekotte flies out to right field and the game is over. This one really stings the Canes.*

Mark Light Field is located in the southwest part of campus, where Ponce De Leon Boulevard appropriately becomes Ron Fraser Way. Fraser, a coach at Miami for 30 years, guided the national championship teams in 1982 and 1985.

Miami University, the "U" as it is know to locals, is actually in Coral Gables, less than 10 miles southwest of downtown Miami. It is a private university whose annual cost for tuition and books is about $35,000. Near downtown are the bridges that lead traffic to trendy Miami Beach. While the Coral Gables neighborhood surrounding the campus is made up of middle-class homes, further to the west, towards the water of Biscayne Bay, the homes get more exclusive. Eventually, one winds up in the ultra-exclusive area called Tahiti Beach, where the homes routinely are in excess of $10 million.

The campus is sizeable but walkable, and the Hurry'Cane shuttle is available for those who choose not to walk. While it is a pleasant enough campus, there is something missing for the first-time visitor. Of course, there is no football stadium, as the Hurricanes played at the Orange Bowl through the 2007 season and at Dolphin Stadium beginning in 2008. Something else is missing. The college does not have a landmark building the likes of a Hoover Tower (Stanford), Notre Dame's golden domed Main Building or the University of Texas Tower. Lake Osceola in the middle of campus is nice, but for an 80-plus-year-old school, it does not have an 80-year-old landmark.

The reason is due to money and timing as much as anything. When the school moved beyond a concept into reality, it faced a major downturn of south Florida real estate, a destructive hurricane, the Great Depression and a world war. Thus, the design of a grand Spanish Renaissance-style building never reached fruition. Instead, the college began in the leased Anastasia Building, a partially constructed hotel, and then took hold at its present campus site in the late 1940s when the war ended.

*Despite all of the clichés that have been created to describe a new beginning, a fresh start, nobody was surprised the funk that resulted from Friday night's game translated into a loss on Saturday. After a 37-minute delay for a lightning alert, Miami spotted Florida State four runs in the first and ultimately lost, 13–8.*

*Sunday is a character-testing game. While it is a difficult task to beat the Hurricanes three straight at Miami, it is not too improbable once the visitors have won the first two.*

In recent decades Miami has not worried too much about series sweeps. UM has qualified for the NCAA tournament 34 consecutive times coming into the 2007 season. Besides the two national championships under Ron Fraser, head coach Jim Morris led the Hurricanes to the College World Series title in 1999 and 2001. Miami has produced more than 30 major league players, including Pat Burrell, Alex Cora, Greg Vaughn and even Mike Piazza (one season, nine at-bats and a .111 average before transferring to Miami-Dade Community College). It is one of the elite programs in the country.

*Sunday is hot and muggy even by Florida's springtime standards. The Hurricanes did their pre-game drills in orange basketball shorts and green short-sleeve shirts. By game time, they are wearing the traditional white pants and sleeveless white shirts with a green short-sleeve shirt underneath. Over the left breast is the orange and green "U" with the number beneath it. The Miami Maniac, in full mascot gear, cannot be comfortable. However, the ominous lightning and rain clouds that delayed the start of Saturday's game by 37 minutes are not seen above Mark Light Stadium. Today's game has a get-away travel curfew; no new inning can start after 3:30 P.M.*

*Eric Erickson gets the start for Miami. When he gets Thomas to fly out to start the game, it is a minor moral victory. Thomas has reached first safely in his two previous at-bats to lead off the game. More than a moral victory, he takes just seven pitches to retire the side.*

*In the bottom of the inning, Tomas works a one-out walk and advances to second on Alonso's single to right. Danny Rosen, the starting pitcher for the Seminoles, has an unusual delivery: he rocks slightly backwards and drops his arm angle, sometimes completely sidearm. Raben follows with a soft drive to left that Tomas reads very well and scores easily with his good base running on the hit. Sensing early-game troubles, head coach Mike Martin makes a visit to the mound. Whatever he said may have worked as Rosen strikes out Weeks and Sobolewski, both fooled on swinging third strikes.*

*After Rye singles to lead off the second, Erickson is concerned about him running and throws over to first a couple of times. Travis Anderson battles for nine pitches before popping up to second for the first out. On the second pitch to Stidham, Rye takes off and gets a good jump. Erickson's pitch is very high and inside and grazes Stidham to put runners on first and second. However, another high pitch works to his favor as he strikes out O'Connor on a high fastball, and then Gildea grounds out.*

*Before the bottom of the inning, a couple guys connected with WVUM (90.5 FM, "the voice of the University of Miami") throw bags of sunflower seeds from the top of the stands as part of a "Seeds of the Second" promotion. It's a quiet inning for the Hurricanes, as the only base runner, O'Brien, is thrown out easily trying to steal second.*

*The press box set-up is unusual in this pre-renovated stadium. The public address announcer, official scorer and newspaper media are in the upstairs of a separate structure along the left field line. During the game, Jay Rokeach occasionally opens a window to his side, like a passenger in a car, while providing his PA announcements. At the top of the grandstands, behind home plate, are a series of portable orange canopies that provide some shield from the elements for the radio and television crews. The pair from WVUM are seated among this group.*

*The Seminoles' third inning is similar to the preceding half-inning. Thomas' one-out single is short-hopped by Sobolewski, but he is quickly erased from the base paths as Erickson picks him off. Although the left-hander is somewhat slow to the plate, his pick-off move is effective. He ends the inning with a nine-pitch strikeout of Hallberg.*

*Before the bottom of the inning, the entire FSU team takes a quick jog down the left field line. After retiring the first two batters, Rosen walks Alonso and gives up a Raben infield single, but the two-out rally dies when Weeks pops out to second.*

*In the fourth, Erickson has his best inning of the game so far by handling the Seminoles' heart of the batting order with successive fly outs to right, center and left field, respectively.*

*Rosen continues his trend of a walk an inning, but it does not result in any Miami scoring. Of the seven Miami base runners, only one has scored, and it is still a 1–0 game.*

*Stidham leads off the fifth with a single, just the fourth Seminole to reach base. Using nine pitches, Erickson disposes of the seventh, eighth and ninth batters.*

*Tekotte leads off an inning for the third time. After a ground out and fly out in his previous at-bats, he hits an off-field single that splits the third baseman and shortstop. After Rosen throws three times to first, Tomas lays down a bunt along the first base line and eludes Reichert's tag. Two runners on, no outs, and Alonso coming up to bat; not the result Rosen had hoped for in a tight game. However, he gets Alonso to do more than what he could have hoped for by inducing a ground ball right back to the mound. With a double play in sight, Rosen fires his throw right between the shortstop and second baseman and into center field. Tekotte comes in to score and Tomas makes it safely into third. Mike Martin decides on a pitching change and brings in Travis Burge.*

*Burge gets ahead in the count but surrenders a single to Raben that scores Tomas. The game may well be at a tipping point. Can Florida State limit the scoring damage or will Miami get the big inning? Weeks lays down a great bunt in front of the mound. Burge fields it and should have Weeks out by two steps, but his throw is to Reichert's glove-side just as Weeks arrives at the bag. Weeks stumbles, falls and doesn't get up as the throw gets past the first baseman. The bad news for the Hurricanes is that Weeks does not get up to advance to second; the good news is that Weeks is not injured. Alonso scores the third run of the inning.*

*Burge is replaced after facing two batters in favor of right-hander Jimmy Marshall. Sobolewski works the count to 3–2. On the next pitch Weeks is running, and with Sobolewski's single to center, Weeks easily advances to third. Six batters have come up and all six have reached base safely. The big inning is still alive.*

*Menendez follows with a sacrifice fly to right field for the first out of the inning. On the fly out, Sobolewski is unaware where the ball is hit while Thomas and Hallberg pretend a double play is in process. Once Sobolewski realizes he is being deked, he scrambles back to first, beating the right fielder's throw by a few strides. O'Brien ends the inning with a double play, but Miami now has a 6–0 lead.*

Sobolewski is a freshman and was a high school teammate of Eric Erickson. Although his consistent high school play at Sarasota High drew the attention of some colleges, he really got noticed thanks to three days in Atlanta in June. Perfect Game USA, a company that produces several showcases for individual players and hosts summer team tournaments, held its national showcase at Turner Field in Atlanta. Sobolewski did well and attracted the attention of a number of professional scouts and Division I coaches. When July 1 came, the day Division I programs can call a player who has finished his junior year, he received 35 calls.

Sobolewski felt Miami would prepare him best for professional baseball. He certainly had options since his baseball talents and 4.0 grade point average would gain him entrance to just about any college. Georgia Tech, Stanford and Florida were all on his list, but the tradition of Miami was too much to pass.

A player's senior year is when the professional scouts really start taking notice. "They are at a bunch of games," recalls Sobolewski. "They start calling, they try to come to your house and get some information on you. Signability, some guys would like to go in the tenth round for $50,000; other guys would say, 'If it's not in the first round, I'm going to college.'" Sobolewski, who made it clear it would take something special to derail his dreams of going to college, was selected by the Houston Astros in the 20th round. Thanks, but no thanks. The New York Yankees had contacted him on draft day with respect to the fourth round, but Sobolewski reiterated his college plans.

*Erickson would like nothing more than to have a shut-down inning in the sixth. His first pitch to Thomas is hit off the left field wall and he advances only to third, conservatively, when Hallberg singles to center. The back-to-back hits get David Gutierrez throwing in the bullpen. Posey follows with a hit that scores Thomas, and a full-fledged threat is on. Erickson regroups and gets three consecutive pop-ups, including a foul behind home plate, to end the half-inning.*

*Jackson leads off with a hit to the gap in right-center in which Gildea falls down trying to field the ball. It looks like the Hurricanes have a great opportunity to get back the run they surrendered in the top of the inning. With the infield playing in, Tekotte hits a grounder right to the second baseman, who holds Jackson before throwing out Tekotte. Tomas grounds to Reichert at first, who gets both the putout at first and follows with a throw home for a double play.*

*Erickson is done for the day, having pitched a solid six innings. Gutierrez comes in to face the bottom of the order. He is very lean and seems lighter than the 160 pounds listed in the program. His first pitch is hit for a ground out to second. His fourth pitch is hit to left field and the batter reaches second on a hustle double. But that is as far as he can advance when the inning ends on a ground ball that Tomas ranges far to his left to throw out Hallberg.*

*Alonso leads off the bottom of the inning and is hit by the first pitch thrown by the new reliever, Michael Hyde. Alonso has reached first base four different ways in this game: a hit, walk, error and hit-by-pitch. With a somewhat unusual strategy, the number four hitter Raben sacrifice bunts Alonso to second. Weeks follows with a single to right, but Alonso holds at third. Sobolewski then hits a routine fly to center that Gildea catches, but for no apparent reason falls and drops the ball. He alertly springs up and throws the ball to second, but it is too late to get the force out of Weeks. Sobolewski is credited with a sacrifice fly when Miami's seventh run touches home plate. Menendez' line drive to shortstop ends the inning.*

Weeks went to Lake Brantly High School in Altamonte Springs, just outside of Orlando, about 250 miles north of Coral Gables. He knows more than a little bit about the major league draft as his brother, Rickie, was the second overall pick for the Milwaukee Brewers in 2003. Amazingly, Rickie went undrafted out of high school, yet went on to become just about everyone's college player of the year in 2003. His signing bonus was reported at $3.6 million.

Younger brother Jemile has been an outstanding player as well. In his freshman year he was the starting second baseman, and his .352 average was second best on the team. He was selected to the *Baseball America* Freshman All-American team. Coming into the Florida State series, he is hitting .275 but has missed 11 games due to an injury he sustained while trying to leg out a bunt.

As is the case with most talented high school players, Weeks committed in November of his high school senior season to play for Miami. The only other schools high on his list were Texas and Georgia Tech. About one-third of the way into his senior season, about ten professional teams would contact him to discuss signability. The Milwaukee Brewers selected Weeks in the eighth round. While his parents and brother supplied input on the college versus professional baseball dilemma, the decision was Weeks to make. Jemile Weeks explains his brother's advice, saying, "What he told me was that I got two great decisions. I can either come to Miami or, [since] I got drafted pretty well, play pro ball. Whichever one you pick, if you are led that way, is probably the right way to go."

*Danny Gil, begins to warm up in the bullpen, doing his best to forget the sub-par outing Friday night. However, Gutierrez is still in as the reliever and starts out with a "wince result," a lead-off walk. He ends the inning in an opposite manner, striking out Danesh, freezing him on an off-speed pitch. In between, a Tommy Oravetz pinch-hit single ultimately results in runners stranded on first and second.*

*Miami has a relatively quiet bottom of the eighth in which the action is* limited to a Tekotte single and stolen base. The safe call on the stolen base brings Martin out to argue, but, of course, nothing results from that.

Carrying a 7–1 lead into the ninth seems very safe, safer than the 6–3 lead Miami had in Friday night's game. Appropriately, Danny Gil is sent in to relieve, a bit of "getting back on the horse." Gil was brought in to close out Friday's game, only to give up a lead-off four-pitch walk in the ninth. Although Raben surrendered the back-to-back home runs, Gil was culpable in the unraveling.

He starts out with two straight balls on D'Vontrey Richardson, who had a pinch-hit double in Friday's disastrous ninth inning. But this is a different day, a different inning, and a different game. Richardson strikes out swinging, as does Reichert. Although Thomas is hit by a pitch and advances to second on a wild pitch, Gil regroups to get Hallberg to fly out to center. No need for the curfew rule to be invoked. Game over.

---

### #1 FLORIDA STATE SEMINOLES VS. UNIVERSITY OF MIAMI HURRICANES
### APRIL 27, 2007 AT CORAL GABLES, FLORIDA
### MARK LIGHT FIELD

---

**Florida State (38–6, 16–3 ACC)**

| Player | AB | R | H | RBI |
|---|---|---|---|---|
| Thomas Jr., Tony 2b | 5 | 1 | 2 | 2 |
| Hallberg, Mark ss | 3 | 1 | 1 | 1 |
| Posey, Buster c | 4 | 0 | 0 | 0 |
| Rye, Jack rf | 5 | 0 | 1 | 0 |
| Anderson, Travis dh | 3 | 2 | 2 | 1 |
| Oravetz, Tommy dh | 1 | 0 | 0 | 0 |
| Stidham, Jason, 3b | 5 | 1 | 2 | 1 |
| Gildea, Mark cf | 3 | 1 | 1 | 1 |
| O'Connor, Ruairi lf | 3 | 0 | 2 | 0 |
| Danesh, Ohmed lf | 0 | 0 | 0 | 0 |
| Richardson, D'Vontrey ph | 1 | 1 | 1 | 0 |
| Reichert, Brandon 1b | 4 | 0 | 0 | 0 |
| Henry, Bryan p | 0 | 0 | 0 | 0 |
| Rosen, Danny p | 0 | 0 | 0 | 0 |
| **Totals** | **37** | **7** | **12** | **6** |

**University of Miami (26–10, 11 ACC)**

| Player | AB | R | H | RBI |
|---|---|---|---|---|
| Tekotte, Blake cf | 5 | 1 | 1 | 0 |
| Tomas, Roger 2b | 4 | 2 | 3 | 0 |
| Alonso, Yonder 1b | 4 | 2 | 2 | 4 |
| Raben, Dennis rf/p | 3 | 0 | 0 | 1 |
| Weeks, Jemile dh | 4 | 0 | 0 | 0 |
| Diego, Kevin lf | 0 | 0 | 0 | 0 |
| Gutierrez, David p | 0 | 0 | 0 | 0 |
| Sobolewski, Mark lf | 4 | 0 | 1 | 0 |
| Freitas, Nick lf/rf | 0 | 0 | 0 | 0 |
| Menendez, Gus 3b | 3 | 0 | 1 | 0 |
| O'Brien, Richard c | 2 | 1 | 1 | 1 |
| Jackson, Ryan ss | 3 | 0 | 0 | 0 |
| Petralli, Chris ss/ph | 1 | 0 | 0 | 0 |
| Maine, Scott p | 0 | 0 | 0 | 0 |
| Gil, Danny p | 0 | 0 | 0 | 0 |
| **Totals** | **33** | **6** | **9** | **6** |

**Score by Innings**

| | | | | | | | | | | | R | H | E |
|---|---|---|---|---|---|---|---|---|---|---|---|---|---|
| Florida State | 0 | 0 | 0 | 2 | 0 | 1 | 0 | 0 | 4 | - | 7 | 12 | 1 |
| University of Miami | 1 | 1 | 2 | 0 | 2 | 0 | 0 | 0 | 0 | - | 6 | 9 | 0 |

2B — Stidham (10); O'Connor (9). 3B — Anderson (1); HR — Thomas (8); Hallberg (3); Anderson (1); Alonso 2(14); O'Brien (1).

| Florida State | IP | H | R | ER | BB | SO |
|---|---|---|---|---|---|---|
| Henry, Bryan | 8 | 8 | 6 | 4 | 1 | 7 |
| Rosen, Danny | 1 | 1 | 0 | 0 | 0 | 0 |

| University of Miami | IP | H | R | ER | BB | SO |
|---|---|---|---|---|---|---|
| Maine, Scott | $7\frac{2}{3}$ | 8 | 3 | 3 | 1 | 4 |
| Gil, Danny | $\frac{1}{3}$ | 0 | 1 | 1 | 1 | 1 |
| Raben, Dennis | $\frac{1}{3}$ | 3 | 3 | 3 | 0 | 1 |
| Gutierrez, David | $\frac{2}{3}$ | 1 | 0 | 0 | 1 | 0 |

Win — Henry (11–0). Loss — Raben (1–2). Save — Rosen (8).

Start: 7:00. Time: 2:43. Attendance: 2,763

---

## #1 FLORIDA STATE SEMINOLES VS.
## UNIVERSITY OF MIAMI HURRICANES
## APRIL 29, 2007 AT CORAL GABLES, FLORIDA
## MARK LIGHT FIELD

---

### Florida State (38–6, 16–3 ACC)      Miami (26–10, 11 ACC)

| Player | AB | R | H | RBI | Player | AB | R | H | RBI |
|---|---|---|---|---|---|---|---|---|---|
| Thomas Jr., Tony 2b | 3 | 1 | 2 | 0 | Tekotte, Blake cf | 5 | 1 | 2 | 0 |
| Hallberg, Mark ss | 5 | 0 | 1 | 0 | Tomas, Roger 2b | 4 | 2 | 1 | 0 |
| Posey, Buster c | 3 | 0 | 1 | 1 | Alonso, Yonder 1b | 2 | 2 | 1 | 0 |
| Rye, Jack rf | 4 | 0 | 1 | 0 | Raben, Dennis rf | 3 | 1 | 3 | 2 |
| Anderson, Travis dh | 3 | 0 | 0 | 0 | Weeks, Jemile dh | 4 | 1 | 2 | 0 |
| Oravetz, Tommy ph | 1 | 0 | 1 | 0 | Sobolewski, Mark lf | 3 | 0 | 1 | 2 |
| Stidham, Jason, 3b | 3 | 0 | 1 | 0 | Menendez, Gus 3b | 2 | 0 | 0 | 1 |
| O'Connor, Ruairi lf | 2 | 0 | 0 | 0 | O'Brien, Richard c | 3 | 0 | 0 | 0 |
| Danesh, Ohmed ph/lf | 2 | 0 | 0 | 0 | Jackson, Ryan ss | 4 | 0 | 1 | 0 |
| Gildea, Mark cf | 3 | 0 | 1 | 0 | Erickson, Eric p | 0 | 0 | 0 | 0 |
| Richardson, | | | | | | | | | |
| D'Vontrey cf | 1 | 0 | 0 | 0 | Gutierrez, David p | 0 | 0 | 0 | 0 |
| Reichert, Brandon 1b | 4 | 0 | 0 | 0 | Gil, Danny p | 0 | 0 | 0 | 0 |
| Rosen, Danny p | 0 | 0 | 0 | 0 | | | | | |
| Burge, Travis p | 0 | 0 | 0 | 0 | | | | | |
| Marshal, Jimmy p | 0 | 0 | 0 | 0 | | | | | |
| Hyde, Michael p | 0 | 0 | 0 | 0 | | | | | |
| Tucker, Luke p | 0 | 0 | 0 | 0 | | | | | |
| Totals | 34 | 1 | 8 | 1 | Totals | 30 | 7 | 11 | 5 |

### Score by Innings

| | | | | | | | | | | | R | H | E |
|---|---|---|---|---|---|---|---|---|---|---|---|---|---|
| Florida State | 0 | 0 | 0 | 0 | 0 | 1 | 0 | 0 | 0 | - | 1 | 8 | 3 |
| Miami | 1 | 0 | 0 | 0 | 5 | 1 | 0 | 0 | X | - | 7 | 11 | 0 |

2B — Thomas (25); Gildea (6). 3B — Jackson (2); SF — Sobolewski (1).

| Florida State | IP | H | R | ER | BB | SO |
|---|---|---|---|---|---|---|
| Rosen, Danny | 4 | 5 | 4 | 3 | 4 | 3 |
| Burge, Travis | 0 | 2 | 2 | 2 | 0 | 0 |
| Marshal, Jimmy | 2 | 2 | 0 | 0 | 0 | 0 |

| Florida State | IP | H | R | ER | BB | SO |
|---|---|---|---|---|---|---|
| Hyde, Michael | 1 | 1 | 1 | 1 | 0 | 0 |
| Tucker, Luke | 1 | 1 | 0 | 0 | 0 | 2 |

| Miami | IP | H | R | ER | BB | SO |
|---|---|---|---|---|---|---|
| Erickson, Eric | 6 | 6 | 1 | 1 | 0 | 3 |
| Gutierrez, David | 2 | 2 | 0 | 0 | 2 | 1 |
| Gil, Danny | 1 | 0 | 0 | 0 | 0 | 2 |

Win — Erickson (6–3). Loss — Rosen (1–1). Save — None.

Start: 12:06. Time: 2:51. Attendance: 3,000

# Epilogue

Late May and early June is an exciting time for college baseball. It starts with several conferences that have playoffs. The major league draft is held. The regionals, super regionals and national championships take place. College baseball reaches the front page of the sport sections in the same newspapers that practically ignore the sport for much of the regular season.

To rephrase a proverb, "A season of 78 games begins with a single pitch." Because the college baseball season is so long for the ultimate champion, one has to respect the teams that deal with all of the highs and lows. For example, the highly improbable 2008 Division I champion, Fresno State, lost 12 of its first 20 games. The Bulldogs were not ranked among the top 30 teams in the National Collegiate Baseball Writers Association poll going into NCAA regionals; they weren't even in the category of "others receiving votes." Between the regionals and the College World Series championship game, Fresno State fought through six games in which a loss would have eliminated their chance for the trophy.

Although Oregon State's NCAA championship in 2007 was not nearly as unexpected as Fresno State's in 2008, it did surprise many people. The Beavers finished 10–14 in the PAC-10 and were ranked 25th, but the returning champions won 11 out of 12 games in the NCAA tournament, including the last 10.

It's exciting to watch both the teams and the individual players late in the season. Within a period of a few weeks, an eligible player could get drafted, help his team have success in the Junior College or College World Series, and then play professional baseball. That scenario is dramatically different from the four months college football players must wait for the NFL draft after the end of their season.

For those players who do sign a professional baseball contract, they often head for the higher-rated short-season New York–Penn or Northwest leagues or one of the rookie leagues (Appalachian, Pioneer, Arizona or Gulf Coast), which begin in mid–June.

If things go well, a player will advance to a Class A League the following year. If things don't go so well, a player's professional baseball career may consist of just that one season. Given that each year many of the 40 to 50 major league teams' draft picks will sign contacts, the business laws of attrition come into play.

While this book's chapters focused on a 2007 conference series for each of the nine teams, a lot took place after those series concluded. What follows is a brief college-by-college summary of what happened once those series were completed.

## University of Southern California

The euphoria that USC had when Lucas Duda hit the walk-off home run on March 25, 2007, was short-lived. The win put the Trojans' overall record at 17–12, and they were 1–2 in the PAC-10. As expected, their number 19 ranking going into the Arizona State series slipped to number 25 the following day in the *Baseball America* poll. That was before USC lost seven of its next nine games and completely dropped out of the polls.

After that losing streak, they had 18 games left . Trojans lost ten of those, including a sweep by Stanford at home in the final series of the year. That series pushed USC to a losing record of 27–29 overall, and 8–16 in the Pac-10. That series loss also put them in the highly unusual position of finishing ninth and in last place in the Pac-10 standings (Oregon's program will be reborn in the 2009 season, hence only nine Pac-10 teams). It was only the third time since playing games at Dedeaux Field (which began in 1974) that USC had a losing home record.

However, there is no disgrace in having a difficult Pac-10 season. Oregon State finished tied for sixth and ultimately won the 2007 national championship. The league has parity.

It wasn't a situation in which the Trojans had an very young lineup. While they started three freshmen in the last game of the series against Arizona State, there were also five juniors and a senior in the batting order. The four main starters for the year were three sophomores (Cook, Milone, and Vasquez) and a freshman (Boxberger). The sophomore pitchers had experience coming into the season, but they were not as experienced as juniors generally are. When the season was done, the team's ERA of 4.90 was about 50 basis points higher than that of their opponents.

With a challenging schedule, even the slightest edge over their opponents could result in a losing record for the season.

Nobody from USC made the All-Pac-10 team, but Grant Green, along with UCLA's Gabe Cohen, were the Pac-10 Co-Freshmen of the Year. Arizona State's Brett Wallace was the Pac-10 Player of the Year as well as a consensus first-team All-American as determined by *Baseball America*, the National College Baseball Writers Association and *Collegiate Baseball*.

When the 2007 major league draft began on June 7, USC was finished for the season. Outfielder Lucas Duda was selected in the seventh round and signed with the New York Mets. He played for the Brooklyn Cyclones of the New York–Penn League and progressed to begin the 2008 season with the St. Lucie Mets in the Class A Advanced Florida State League.

Second baseman Matt Cusick was selected in the tenth round and signed with the Houston Astros. He had a solid first season in professional baseball with the Tri-City ValleyCats (Troy, New York) of the New York–Penn League hitting .306, and was selected to the league's All-Star team. He advanced to begin the 2008 season with the Lexington Legends (Kentucky) in the South Atlantic League before being promoted to the Tampa Yankees in the Class A Florida State League.

The Los Angeles Dodgers selected Paul Koss, the Trojans' senior closer, in the 11th round. He played in 2007 for the Ogden Raptors (Utah) in the rookie Pioneer League and began the 2008 season with the Inland Empire 66ers (San Bernardino) in the advanced Class A California League.

Shawn Olsen (pitcher, 28th round by the San Diego Padres), Hector Estrella (infielder, 40th round by the Los Angeles Angels) and Johnny Bowden (catcher, 41st round by the Colorado Rockies) were Trojans selected in the later rounds. Bowden, who followed a winding path to USC from Springfield, Oregon, made his way closer to home when his professional career began with the Tri-City Dust Devils of the Class A (short-season) Northwest League. George Brett is the principal owner of the team located in Pasco, Washington. In 2008, Bowden advanced to begin the season with the Modesto Nuts in the California League and then rejoined the Dust Devils.

Dave Lawn, the pitching coach and recruiting coordinator, left in June 2007 to take the head coaching position at Servite High School in Anaheim. He had an opportunity to stay closer to home while serving as a head coach for the first time during a school season, although he has been the head coach for a Cape Cod League summer team.

Servite is an all-male Catholic school that competes in the highly regarded Trinity League which includes national power Mater Dei High School (Santa Ana). The Servite Friars even publish an 18-page "media guide" for their baseball program. Servite typically produces a couple of Division I players each year and its 1999 class had three players who made it to the major leagues: Ryan Garko (Cleveland Indians), Brian Wolfe (Toronto Blue Jays) and Ben Francisco (Cleveland Indians). The team finished 14-11-1 overall and 7–8 in its league in Dave Lawn's first season.

The 2008 season was marginally better for the USC Trojans. They needed a bases-load double-play in the ninth inning against Washington State in the last game of the season to secure an overall record of 28–28 and an 11–13 mark in the Pac-10. Once again, their schedule was one of the most challenging in the country, and they did win series against Arizona, Cal and UCLA, all ranked teams.

Shortstop Grant Green had another great year, earning All Pac-10 honors and being named a *Baseball America* third team All-American. He hit .390 for the season, had 46 RBIs and a team-leading nine home runs, which far exceeded his 2007 numbers of .316, 24 and 2, respectively. Green was a key to an improved Trojan offense. Derek Perren, Roberto Lopez and Anthony Vasquez also had good seasons at the plate, far exceeding their contributions from the prior year. If Robert Stock's final at-bat of the season was a hit instead of a ground out to the shortstop, he would have finished the year at .305 rather than the .299 that is in the official records. Stock also made 11 pitching appearances and had three saves that, surprisingly, tied him for the team lead. Paul Koss had 16 saves the previous year.

Unlike the offense, the pitching and defense did not improve from 2007 to 2008. The team ERA increased from 4.90 to 5.64, their opponents collectively scored 43 more runs, and the Trojans committed 16 more errors for the season. It was not unexpected for the team's pitching stats to be off from 2007. Starting in 2008, the beginning of the season was pushed back a few weeks, but the end of the season remained the same. This meant the same number of games in a shorter period of time. The new scheduling rules put pressure on all pitching staffs, but USC did not match their opponents' overall performances.

Sophomore pitcher Kevin Couture stepped into the starting rotation, joining returning starters Brad Boxberger, Ryan Cook and Tommy Milone. The group had periodic success, but they were not consistently dominant. Milone, a 2008 10th round selection, signed with the Washington Nationals and began his professional career with the Vermont Lake Monsters (Winooski) in the New York–Penn League and progressed to the Hagerstown Suns (Maryland) in the Class A South Atlantic League.

Besides Milone, Nick Buss, who was a regular in center field, was a relatively high draft pick, selected in the eighth round by the Los Angeles Dodgers. He started with the Ogden Raptors in the Pioneer League.

Hank Conger and D'Arby Myers were originally committed to USC and scheduled to be classmates of Grant Green, Robert Stock and Brad Boxberger, but they signed professional contracts after the 2006 draft. Conger followed a good 2007 minor league season with solid offensive numbers in 2008 with the Rancho Cucamonga Quakes in the California League. Myers spent 2008 splitting time between the Lakewood BlueClaws (New Jersey) in the Class A

South Atlantic League and the Williamsport Crosscutters (Pennsylvania) in the New York–Penn League. One will never know if their choice to forgo USC was a good one.

That leaves a core of good players who were recruited in 2004–2005, sophomores in the 2008 season, and in 2005–2006 to represent USC for the 2009 season with the hope they are back on the path to the NCAA tournament and eventually the College World Series.

## University of Texas

Texas took the first two games against Oklahoma on a very warm weekend in Austin in the spring of 2007. However, on April Fool's Day, the Sooners won their first game at Disch-Falk Field since 1997; they had lost 15 straight. Despite the loss, the Longhorns moved up to seventh in the national rankings.

Texas played well the rest of the 2007 regular season. They lost only one series the entire year when they dropped two against Missouri in early May. They finished conference play with an impressive sweep of Texas A&M and followed that with an opening round Big 12 tournament win over Kansas State, 19–10. Those 19 runs set a tournament record.

Texas had a momentary setback when the team lost to Texas A&M in the second game of the Big 12 tournament. Just a week before, James Russell scattered eight hits and four runs, earning a 6–4 win against the Aggies. In the rematch, he forced home a run with a hit batsman and then gave up a grand slam in a game the Longhorns eventually lost, 7–4.

Despite falling short in the Big 12 tournament, it was no surprise that Texas was selected as a host school for the NCAA regionals. However, there were two changes from the norm. Preston Clark, the starting catcher, was injured while jogging just prior to the start of the regionals. Also, due to the construction still in process at Disch-Falk Field, the host site was at nearby Round Rock, the home of the Express, Houston's AAA affiliate. Texas normally plays a few games there each season.

The Longhorns beat Brown, 8–2, in the opening game before matching up against UC Irvine, a team they had never played. Irvine's head coach, Dave Serrano, was a former player at Cal State Fullerton under then-head coach Augie Garrido. The Anteaters took the first game, 3–1. Texas bounced back to defeat Wake Forest, 7–4, in a 12-inning game to set up a rematch with Irvine.

The drama was spread over two days as the game was suspended due to rain, with Irvine leading, 6–5, in the seventh inning. The following day Irvine scored three in the eighth and the score was 9–6 when the Longhorns left the bases loaded in the top of the ninth. Chais Fuller grounded into a force play to end the game. Eleven days later, the undrafted Fuller signed a free-agent contract with the Atlanta Braves. He played in the Gulf Coast League that summer before moving to Danville (Virginia) in the Appalachian League to begin the 2008 season.

Perhaps the most anticipated development after the 2007 season ended was the future of Kyle Russell. He finished leading the nation with 27 home runs, was a first-team All-American, and was one of four finalists for the Dick Howser trophy, which ultimately went to David Price of Vanderbilt. He was selected by the St. Louis Cardinals in the fourth round but he did not sign with them.

While Kyle Russell did not sign a professional contract in 2007, several other Longhorns did. Bradley Suttle, selected as a third-team All-American, was picked in the fourth round by the New York Yankees. He played a few games during the 2007 summer with the Gulf Cost League Yankees (Tampa, Florida) and moved on to their Class A South Atlantic League team, the Charleston RiverDogs (South Carolina), for the 2008 season.

Pitchers Randy Boone and Adrian Alaniz were selected in the seventh and eighth rounds, respectively. Boone, who finished his senior season, went to the Toronto organization. He signed late in the summer and did not play professionally in 2007, but he began his pro career in 2008 with the Lansing Lugnuts (Michigan) in the Class A Midwest League and then moved to the Dunedin Blue Jays in the Florida State League. Alaniz signed with the Washington Nationals and had a very good first season (8–2, 2.39) with the Vermont Lake Monsters (Winooski) in the New York–Penn League. He followed that with an excellent start to 2008 (9–0, 2.62) with the Potomac Nationals (Woodbridge, Virginia) in the Class A Carolina League and earned a promotion to the Harrisburg Senators (Pennsylvania) in the Class AA Eastern League.

Also selected in the "teens" rounds were pitcher James Russell (14th round by the Chicago Cubs), pitcher Joseph Krebs (14th round by the Cincinnati Reds), first baseman Chance Wheeless (17th round by the Arizona Diamondbacks) and outfielder Nick Peoples (19th round by the St. Louis Cardinals).

Russell had limited playing time in 2007 while in the Arizona League before being promoted to the Peoria Chiefs (Illinois) in the Class A Midwest League late in the season. He split time in the 2008 season with Daytona in the Class A Advanced Florida State League and the Tennessee Smokies (Kodak) of the Class AA Southern League. Krebs spent 2007 with the Billings Mustangs (Montana) in the Pioneer League before moving on in 2008 to the

Dayton Dragons (Ohio) in the Class A Midwest League and then the Sarasota Reds in the Class A Advanced Florida State League. Chance Wheeless divided his 2007 season between the Missoula Osprey (Montana) in the Pioneer League and the Yakima Bears (Washington) in the Northwest League. He spent the 2008 season with the South Bend Silver Hawks (Indiana) in the Class A Midwest League.

Nick Peoples had spent his 2005 and 2006 summers in beautiful Santa Barbara playing for the Foresters in the California Collegiate League. His last game as a Longhorn determined his fate for the summer of 2007. In the first inning of the NCAA regional game against Wake Forest, he dove for a drive off the bat of Dustin Hood. He made the catch, but in doing so broke his collarbone. Baseball would have to wait. He began playing professionally in 2008 for the Quad Cities River Bandits in the Class A Midwest League. He was no longer spending his summers near the Pacific Ocean, but he was still near water. Modern Woodman Park in Davenport, Iowa, is on the banks of the Mississippi River. In April and June 2008, flooding damaged much of eastern Iowa and sandbag levees surrounded the park to keep floodwaters away.

The returning Longhorns were scattered throughout the U.S. Jordan Danks was selected to play on the USA National baseball team. Five players went up to the prestigious Cape Cod League, including pitcher Hunter Harris, who played for the Hyannis Mets. Travis Tucker was a member of the Coppell Copperheads, joining several other players in the Texas Collegiate League.

Going into the 2008 season, expectations were pretty much the usual for Texas. The Longhorns were selected as the Big 12 regular season favorites for the seventh straight year and were a top 20 team in the national polls.

The renovations to Disch-Falk Field were completed. There were also significant renovations to the team given the usual impact of the draft and graduation. The Opening Day infielders were completely different, although Travis Tucker just moved from second to third. The starting first baseman was sophomore Brandon Belt, who transferred from San Jacinto College. He wound up with a good year by hitting .319 with 65 RBIs and 6 home runs.

Kyle Russell, Jordan Danks and Russell Moldenhauer were familiar players in the outfield and Preston Clark was behind home plate. A starting rotation of Kenn Kasparek, Austin Wood, Chance Ruffin and Riley Boening was a complete change from 2007. Kasparek missed the entire 2007 season due to an elbow injury, but he had College World Series experience dating back to the 2005 season. Ruffin became an unexpected success, as the freshman went 8–3 with a 1.96 ERA.

The season progressed reasonably well through April 8 when Garrido won his 500th game with the Longhorns. Then came April 11, the Friday night series opener against Missouri. Texas lost, 31–12. They also went on to lose seven of their next ten games and fell from a 12th national ranking to unranked. They did get back to winning games and ended the regular season with a three game sweep of Texas A&M. Then, although the Longhorns lost in extra innings, 3–2, to Missouri in the opening Big 12 tournament game, they won the next three to capture the Big 12 title. One of those wins was an 11–10 decision over rival Oklahoma as a result of a three-run bottom of the ninth rally.

Despite the team peaking at the right time, Texas did not get to host a NCAA regional tournament. Instead, the Longhorns traveled southeast to be part of the Houston regional hosted by Rice. After an unexpected opening round loss to St. John's, 2–1, the Longhorns bounced back to win the next two to force a regional championship game against Rice. Texas lost, 7–4, and was eliminated.

But as always is the case, when one baseball season ends, another begins. Kyle Russell, whose offensive numbers were still very good (.296, 19 home runs, 56 RBIs), but down from his stellar 2007 season, was selected by the Los Angeles Dodgers in the third round. He began with the Ogden Raptors (Utah) in the Pioneer League. Outfielder Jordan Danks went in the seventh round to the Chicago White Sox and he did not sign until mid–August, in time for the final two weeks of the Kannapolis Intimidators' (North Carolina) season. Pitchers Kyle Walker and Kenn Kasparek went in the 11th round (Colorado Rockies) and 12th round (Seattle Mariners), respectively. Walker began playing for the Casper Ghosts (Wyoming) in the Pioneer League. Kasparek first played for the Pulaski Mariners (Virginia) in the Appalachian League before moving on to the Everett AquaSox (Washington) in the Northwest League.

The 2008 National Collegiate Baseball Writers Association (NCBWA) Freshman All-American team selections included Chance Ruffin (first team) and catcher Cameron Rupp (second team). Ruffin also was selected by *Baseball America* as an All-American (third team). The future always looks bright in Austin.

Besides those who were drafted, other Longhorns went off to summer teams. Chance Ruffin participated in the USA Baseball national team trials. Brandon Belt became a member of the Harwich Mariners accompanying five other teammates who went to the Cape Cod League. Hunter Harris joined the East Texas Pump Jacks in the Texas Collegiate League. Some went to the Alaska League; some joined teams in the M.I.N.K. (Missouri, Iowa, Nebraska, Kansas) League; some headed to the Northwoods League; some went west to Santa Barbara in the California Collegiate League. They all were on a quest to improve their baseball skills to help the Longhorns in 2009 and beyond.

## California State Fullerton

When Long Beach State defeated Cal State Fullerton in the 2007 regular season finale, none of the Titans dwelled on it for long. The very next day the NCAA announced that Fullerton would be part of the regional tournament hosted by the University of San Diego. It was the 16th straight time that Fullerton would participate in the tournament.

Wes Roemer started the tournament with a complete-game 7–1 victory over the University of Minnesota. The Titans followed that game with 6–4 and 13–2 wins over Fresno State (a year before the Bulldogs would shock just about everyone and win the 2008 College World Series). Evan McArthur had a strong regional series, batting .429 with four RBIs and a home run. Bryan Harris came in and pitched effectively for four-plus innings in the third game to get the win. The sweep of the regional games earned the Titans the opportunity to host a Super Regional pairing with UCLA. During the regular season, Fullerton beat UCLA two out of three times in non-conference games.

In game one, Wes Roemer pitched another complete game and the Titans won, 12–2. Evan McArthur went 3–3 with three RBIs and Chris Jones had two hits and two RBIs. They followed that victory the next day with a 2–1 win to secure another trip to the College World Series. Bryan Harris got the save, getting through a tense ninth inning. With one out and a runner on third, McArthur fielded a ground ball, spun 360 degrees and threw out the runner at home. UCLA eventually left the potential tying run stranded on second.

The trip in 2007 marked the 15th time the Titans made it to the College World Series.

In the first game, Wes Roemer scattered three runs and seven hits, but Cal State Fullerton lost to Oregon State, 3–2.

Game two matched the Titans against another Big West team, UC Irvine. During the regular season Irvine took two out of three from Fullerton to win its first conference series against the Titans since 1980. The Anteaters were coached by Dave Serrano, a former player and assistant coach at Fullerton. Bryan Harris was charged with just one run in his career-high five innings of relief, but that one run was the difference in a memorable 5–4 loss to UC Irvine. The game time of 5 hours and 40 minutes was a College World Series record. For Evan McArthur, it was doubly disappointing because an ankle injury, later diagnosed as a fracture, forced him to watch his final college game from the bench.

Two days before Roemer's Super Regional win over UCLA, he was selected in the major league draft's supplemental first round by the Arizona Diamondbacks. He was followed by nine other Titans who were drafted:

outfielder Clark Hardman (Chicago Cubs in the 9th round); third baseman Evan McArthur (San Francisco Giants in the 11th round); catcher John Curtis (Chicago White in the 14th round); outfielder Nick Mahin (Chicago White Sox in the 16th round); Jared Clark, an outfielder who sat out the entire 2007 season due to an injury (Cleveland Indians in the 21st round); Bryan Harris (Seattle Mariners in the 22nd round); first baseman Matt Wallach (Los Angeles Dodgers in the 22nd round); pitcher Justin Klipp (Chicago White Sox in the 22nd round); and shortstop Joe Scott (Milwaukee Brewers in the 39th round).

Clark and Scott opted to return to Cal State Fullerton for the 2008 season. McArthur's ankle injury and Klipp's leg injury kept them out of professional games in the summer of 2007. For McArthur, as disappointing as another injury was, he had the experience in dealing with such circumstances. He would have to deal with another injury in 2008.

Roemer began his professional career with the Yakima Bears (Washington) in the Northwest League in 2007 and advanced in 2008 with the Visalia Oaks in the Class A California League. Clark Hardman started off with the Peoria Chiefs (Illinois) in the Midwest League and also played in the Arizona Rookie League in which he hit .351. He was reportedly rehabbing an injury during the 2008 season.

John Curtis played in 2007 for the Great Falls Voyagers (Montana) in the Pioneer League and moved up in 2008 with the Kannapolis Intimidators (North Carolina) in the Class A South Atlantic League. Nick Mahin played his 2007 season with the Bristol Sox (Virginia) in the Appalachian League and then, in 2008, after starting the season in Great Falls, joined Curtis at Kannapolis. Matt Wallach played for the Ogden Raptors (Utah) in the Pioneer League both in 2007 and 2008.

Bryan Harris, the unique third baseman-pitcher combination, continued to build on his solid late-season performances for the Titans. With the Everett AquaSox (Washington) in the Northwest League, he made 18 relief appearances in 2007, earned eight saves and had a 1.16 ERA. He continued his success with the Wisconsin Timber Rattlers (Appleton) in the Class A Midwest League to begin the 2008 season. He was then first promoted to the High Desert Mavericks (Adelanto, California) in the advanced Class A California League and then to the West Tenn Diamond Jaxx (Jackson, Tennessee) in the Class AA Southern League for a very short stint before returning to High Desert. His progress has been good for a 23rd-round pick.

The real Fullerton baseball news of the summer of 2007 did not concern the minor league developments of it former players, but rather head coach George Horton. He decided to take the head coaching job at the University of Oregon. Besides a good salary plus guaranteed monies derived from television and Nike contracts, Horton saw a unique opportunity. Oregon dropped its baseball program after the 1981 season, so not only would a new program have to be built to begin competing in the 2009 season, but facilities would have to be built as well. He has an opportunity to use his successful coaching and recruiting skills to compete in the Pac-10 and to develop a baseball rivalry against back-to-back national champion in 2006 and 2007 Oregon State.

Horton's departure led to bringing back Dave Serrano, who not only had a history at Fullerton, but his UC Irvine team beat the Titans just three months earlier in the College World Series. The UC Irvine position went to Mike Gillespie, who had coached USC from 1987 through the 2006 season.

Despite the change in of the coaching staff and the usual turnover of players, the 2008 season was an improvement over 2007. At the end of the 2008 regular season, the Titans were 37–19 (16–8 in the Big West) compared to 33–23 (10–11 in the Big West) the year before. Only Josh Fellhauer, the Joneses (Corey and Chris), Joe Scott and Joel Weeks (injured for much of 2007) were regular players in 2007 who were expected to play in 2008. Unfortunately for Chris Jones, the outfield was set with two talented newcomers, transfer Erik Komatsu (.355, 54 RBIs at the season's end) and true freshman Gary Brown (.292, five home runs).

Although the Titans lost their 2008 finale to Long Beach State, just like they did in 2007, they ended the year ranked 11th and were selected to host a NCAA regional tournament. The Titans beat UCLA twice in a row to advance to the Super Regional level where they hosted Stanford in the best-of-three format. This proved to be a difficult match-up. Stanford swept Fullerton in a three-game series in early March in Palo Alto. The home field did not change the result three months later when Stanford won back-to-back, 4–3 and 8–5. There was no trip to Omaha for the Titans.

Komatsu earned third-team All-American honors and Fellhauer, first baseman Jared Clark and freshman infielder Christian Colon made the USA Baseball national team.

Six players were drafted just a day before Fullerton's Super Regional match-up with Stanford. Komatsu went the highest (8th round, Milwaukee Brewers) and started playing soon thereafter with the Helena Brewers (Montana) in the Pioneer League. Closer Adam Jorgenson was taken in the 26th round (Colorado Rockies) and he took on a reliever role with the Casper Ghosts (Wyoming) in the Pioneer League. Starting pitchers Jeff Kaplan (11th round) and Cory Arbiso (22nd round) were selected by the New York Mets and New York Yankees, respectively. Kaplan became part of the Brooklyn Cyclones roster in the New York–Penn League. Arbiso started close by with the Staten Island Yankees.

Infielder Joe Scott and outfielder Jared Clark were late round selections going to the Milwaukee Brewers (41st round) and Los Angeles Angels of Anaheim (45th round), respectively. Scott kept his options open by playing for the Anchorage Glacier Pilots in the collegiate Alaska Baseball League, while Clark was a late addition to the national team and played in Europe against other national teams. Neither signed by the August 15 deadline.

## Lewis-Clark State College

The sweep of Albertson College, which months later would change its name back to College of Idaho, in April 2007 was much like any other conference game — a tune-up for the NAIA World Series. Lewis-Clark State College (LCSC) doing well in the NAIA playoffs is as predictable as the taste of bottled water.

The only surprise in the remainder of the 2007 regular season was a 1–0 loss to the University of British Columbia. Chris Kissock gave up a lead-off home run in the top of the seventh which produced his first loss of the season. That would be the first and only loss of the season for Kissock, who would finish with an 11–1 record. Perhaps even more impressive was Matt Fitts, who went 10–1 with a 2.08 ERA and an opposing hitters batting average of .198.

The Warriors went 3–0 in the regionals, yet needed 11 innings against Albertson to win the third game in Caldwell, Idaho. Mirroring the NCAA tournament format, LCSC then moved on to the NAIA Super Regionals hosted by Azusa Pacific University in southern California.

LCSC beat the Cougars two out of three games, but the surprising outcome was the Warriors were outscored an aggregate 38–34 and Fitts lost his only game all year. They figured to see Azusa again in the World Series because the Cougars would get an at-large bid.

In the ten-team, double-elimination tournament, LCSC's first game (the fifth of the day at Harris Field at LCSC) was against the Lee University Flames of Cleveland, Tennessee. Kissock struggled, allowing the Flames to out-hit the Warriors, but Lee's pitchers gave up 13 walks. Jesse Roehl was the hitting star, driving in six on a three-run double and three-run home run. In game two, Matt Fitts had a stellar performance as he pitched a complete-game shut-out (two hits, 12 strikeouts) for a 7–0 win against Spring Arbor University (Michigan). Beau Mills hit his 35th home run of the season with a solo shot in the fifth.

The following day, Brad Schwarzenbach and Brian Parker combined to shut down Bellevue University of Nebraska, 8–1. First baseman Ikaika Lester, who had been injured for much of the regular season, provided much of the offense by going 3–4 with a home run and five RBIs. In game four of the World Series, LCSC was matched against Houston Baptist University. Once again, Lester was the difference as his solo home run in the top of the eighth gave the Warriors an 8–7 win. The victory set up a championship game against Spring Arbor, and the Cougars would have to beat LCSC twice to capture the title. The expected match-up with Azusa Pacific never happened as *those* Cougars were eliminated when they lost to Lindenwood (Missouri) and Houston Baptist.

In front of a partisan crowd in excess of 5,000, LCSC had an easy time winning its 15th NAIA World Series with a 9–2 victory. Beau Mills had three home runs and an incredible eight RBIs; a fitting effort one week before the major league draft. He finished the season with a .458 average, 38 home runs and 123 RBIs— remarkable college stats. Mike Miller scattered seven hits over eight innings to pick up the win and ended the season with a 6–0 record.

Draft prognosticators foresaw Mills going in the first round. They were right. The Cleveland Indians selected him as the 13th pick in the first round. Within a couple of weeks, he was playing for the Mahoning Valley Scrappers (Ohio) in the New York–Penn League. That stint lasted but eight games before he moved on to the Lake County Captains (Eastlake, Ohio) of the South Atlantic League. He finished his summer in the same place he began the 2008 season, with the Kinston Indians (North Carolina) in the Class A Advanced Carolina League, where he was compiling solid offensive numbers.

Mills was not a one-hit wonder when it came to draft selections of LCSC players. Not only were seven other players selected, but they were chosen in relatively low rounds. Cleveland also selected Mark Thompson (8th round) and the infielder went to Mahoning Valley and was briefly a teammate of Beau Mills until the latter was promoted. Thompson moved up to the Lake County Captains for the 2008 season. In the ninth round, Philadelphia selected Chris Kissock; he spent the 2007 season with the Williamsport Crosscutters (Pennsylvania) in the New–York Penn League. In 2008, he played with the Lakewood BlueClaws (New Jersey) in the South Atlantic League.

In the 12th round, the Los Angeles Dodgers selected catcher Jessie Mier and the New York Mets selected pitcher Will Morgan. Mier spent 2007, and started 2008 with the Ogden Raptors (Utah) in the Pioneer League, and then moved up to the Great Lakes Loons (Midland, Michigan) in the Midwest League; Morgan went to Brooklyn in the New York–Penn League in 2007 and then advanced the following season to the St. Lucie Mets in the Class A Florida State League. He suffered an elbow injury that limited his playing time in 2008. Matt Fitts, who returned to play at LCSC in 2008, was selected by the Houston Astros in the 15th round. Pitcher Brian Parker was selected in the

19th round by the Baltimore Orioles. The Warriors' closer was 5–0 with nine saves and a 1.86 ERA. He split time in 2007 with Bluefield (West Virginia) in the Appalachian League and the Aberdeen IronBirds (a Cal Ripken-owned team in Maryland) in the New York–Penn League before advancing in 2008 to the Delmarva Shorebirds (Maryland) in the South Atlantic League.

Donnie Ecker was the final LCSC player selected when the Texas Rangers picked him in the 22nd round. He began in the Arizona League before moving on in 2008 to the Spokane Indians (Washington) in the Northwest League. Lastly, Zach Evangelho went undrafted, but he did sign as a free-agent with the Kansas City Royals. He played the summer of 2007 with the Idaho Falls Chukars in the Pioneer League and for 2008 advanced to the Burlington Bees (Iowa) in the Class A Midwest League.

With respect to LCSC players, it was a draft that even an elite NCAA Division I program would be very proud of.

Despite Lewis-Clark's consistent history of success, there had to be at least a little doubt about the 2008 season. Doubts related only to the NAIA World Series Championship, that is. There was no doubt the 2008 team would be successful in the NAIA; it had been for decades. However, when a team loses that many talented players, including a first-round draft pick, one had to wonder what would happen. Doubts were not too prevalent as LCSC received all 22 first-place votes in the NAIA pre-season poll.

Surprisingly, the Warriors lost their second game of the season to Whitworth University, a NCAA Division III program. About a week later, they lost, 3–2, in extra innings to College of Idaho. But then the Warriors ran off 23 straight wins including an 8–6 victory over the University of Washington and an 8–7 defeat of Gonzaga University. In rematches in May, Washington won, 6–2, and Gonzaga was defeated for a second time, 8–3. It is a credit to the two Washington schools that they continue to play LCSC; Division I opponents are increasingly more difficult for the Warriors to schedule.

LCSC went into the NAIA World Series with a 53–6 record. Except for the loss to Washington, all of the Warriors' defeats had been one-run games. Going into the postseason, LCSC was ranked second to the Lubbock Christian Chaparrals and their 50–2 record. However, Lubbock Christian did not make it to the World Series as they lost their regional series to Oklahoma City University.

In the regionals, LCSC outscored their opponents 37–7; in the Super Regionals, they swept Azusa Pacific in a pair of 4–3 games.

The first game of the World Series was a 19–0 blow-out of Embry-Riddle Aeronautical University (Daytona Beach, Florida). Despite the game being shortened to seven innings due to the 10-run rule, Ikaika Lester had four hits and five RBIs. The only hiccup in the next four games on the way to the championship game was a 5–2 loss to Lee University, which eventually won its first four games and thus had to be beaten twice for the title. In the first match-up, Matt Fitts found himself trailing the Flames, 6–2, at the end of six, but he shut them down in the final three innings and the Warriors rallied for three in the top of the ninth to win, 7–6. Catcher Brain Ward was the offensive star, hitting two home runs plus doubling home the go-ahead run in the ninth.

In the championship game, LCSC won, 8–3, in front of 5,500 fans. The win was a group effort, both hitting and pitching. It was their third straight national title and the 16th overall, all under coach Ed Cheff.

When the major league draft came a week later, infielder Kyle Greene, a hometown product, was selected in the 11th round by the Arizona Diamondbacks. He had a tremendous year for the Warriors hitting .428 with 19 home runs and 94 RBIs. Like Beau Mills the year before, Greene was selected as the NAIA Player of the Year. He signed and played with the Missoula Osprey (Montana) in the Pioneer League. Matt Fitts, who backed up his outstanding 2007 season with another good year (13–0, .297 ERA, .189 opposing batting average), was selected by the Oakland A's in the 16th round. His professional career began with the Vancouver Canadians (British Columbia) in the Northwest League.

Blaine Hardy (8–1, 2.48 ERA) went to the Kansas City Royals in the 22nd round; he began with the Idaho Falls Chukars in the Pioneer League. Brent Wyatt, who made a transition from the outfield to the infield, was selected in the 26th round by the Detroit Tigers; he played with the Oneonta Tigers (New York) in the New York–Penn League.

If 2007 and 2008 are samples of his work, Coach Cheff must be doing a lot of things right.

## California State University Chico

When Chico State got swept in its three-game series with Cal State Los Angeles in early March 2007, a signal was sent that the California Collegiate Athletic Association (CCAA) would provide challenges for the Wildcats. Besides CSULA, Sonoma State and UC San Diego were shaping up to be conference and Division II national powers. Chico didn't go into a tailspin, however; the Wildcats won 23 of their next 27 games going into the conference finale against the Sonoma State Seawolves.

By this point in the season, Sonoma had pushed its way to a number two national ranking and Chico was a very respectable number eight. The Seawolves took the first game, 5–1, handing Nick Bryant his first loss of the season. The Wildcats took the second game, 16–14, scoring six runs in the eighth and seven more in the ninth for the ultimate comeback win. The Wildcats hit four home runs, two of them by Aaron Demuth. The next day Billy Spottiswood hurled a complete-game five-hitter to lead Chico to a 3–0 win. In the second game of the doubleheader, Sonoma won, 4–1, but Chico at least knew that it was very competitive with the Seawolves.

In the conference tournament, Chico was matched up again with Cal State L.A. in the first game. Nick Bryant got the start against the Golden Eagles just as he did two months earlier. The first time he had a no decision in a 4–3 loss. This time he had a no-decision in a 3–2 win. In the top of the tenth, the Wildcats played small ball, using both a sacrifice and a Lorin Nakagawa squeeze bunt to push across the winning run. Chico was not as fortunate the following day when the Wildcats lost to both Sonoma State (7–1) and ninth-ranked UC San Diego (8–6), but they nonetheless fully expected an at-large bid to the NCAA Division II tournament.

The West Regionals had the top four CCAA teams, plus Mesa State of Grand Junction, Colorado, and Nebraska-Kearney as the other participants. Chico first faced — who else? — Cal State L.A. Once again Nick Bryant had a no-decision, but the Wildcats won the game 9–7 in 10 innings. Carl Fairburn, after failing to execute a sacrifice bunt, singled home the go-ahead run. Then an insurance run scored when Nakagawa's failed squeeze attempt resulted in a Greg Finazzo steal of home.

The next day Mesa State shut out the Wildcats, 6–0, forcing Chico to "win or go home." The following day Chico did beat Nebraska-Kearney, 3–0, on a superb complete-game, two-hit, nine- strikeout performance by Garrett Rieck. That evening, however, the Wildcats squandered a 6–0 lead and eventually lost, 9–8, to Mesa State. It was a frustrating end to a season for which the final three weeks provided some real tense games.

Cal State L.A. beat Mesa State twice in the Regionals' final games to advance to the National Championship tournament in Montgomery, Alabama. The Golden Eagles won a couple of games in the tournament, but they were eliminated as a result of their losses to the University of Tampa and Columbus State (Georgia). Tampa was the eventual winner for the second consecutive year.

When the National Collegiate Baseball Writers Association All-West Region team was named, four Wildcats were selected: Nick Bryant made the first team and Robby Scott, Edgar Sedano, and Daniel Code made the second team. However, when the season was finally done, the major league scouts projected only three Wildcats as professional players— pitchers Billy Spottiswood, Garrett Rieck and Chris Bodishbaugh.

The Arizona Diamondbacks selected Spottiswood in the 25th round and he was soon off to the Yakima Bears (Washington) in the Northwest League.

In 2008, he closed games with the South Bend Silver Hawks (Indiana) in the Class A Midwest League. The Cleveland Indians selected Rieck in the 29th round. In the summer of 2007, he was on the Mahoning Valley Scrappers (Niles, Ohio) in the New York–Penn League; he returned there for the 2008 season before moving up to the Lake County Captains (Eastlake, Ohio) in the South Atlantic League. Chris Bodishbaugh signed as a free agent with the Florida Marlins in 2007. In 2008, he started with the Jamestown Jammers (New York) in the New York–Penn League and shortly thereafter was pitching for the Greensborough Grasshoppers (North Carolina) in the Class A South Atlantic League before moving back with Jamestown.

After the 2007 season, Chico experienced significant attrition. If a team's strength are the positions up the middle, then Chico had numerous questions. In fact, of the 14 players who participated in the final 2007 game, the loss to Mesa State, only first baseman Matt Bitker, an occasional starter, center fielder Shane Farmer, Travis DeCoito, who pinch ran against Mesa, and starting pitcher Kyle Woodruff would return. Also, that final game lineup did not include starters Bryant, Spottiswood, Rieck, and Bodishbaugh or the closer, Martinez. All had moved on.

Pitching coach Alex Carbajal left Chico State and reports indicated that he took a position with the Upper Deck company. Lorin Nakagawa, whose college playing time ended with the 2007 season, came back as a graduate assistant for the 2008 season.

There was one big reason why no one at Chico was panicking at the thought of losing so many key players: transfers. Mainly from the strong California junior college programs, transfers brought instant experience and skills to a depleted Chico team. Joining returnees Farmer and Bitker to build an offense were transfers Josh Meagher (.379, 55 RBIs), Bret Ringer (.308, 47 RBIs), Cody Dee (.317, 8 home runs), and Jimmy Dodos (.361, 38 RBIs). With Kyle Woodruff switching from a starter to a reliever, transfers Mike Robbins and Andrew Pluta pitched well as starters. The other starter, Pete Mickartz, was the anomaly — a non-transfer player. He had a good season (13–4, 3.48 ERA) and was selected to the All-West Region team.

The Wildcats put together a good season going 42–17 and 24–11 in conference. They beat the teams they were expected to beat and faced challenges from the better teams in the conference. Cal State L.A., Cal State Stanislaus, and UC San Diego all took conference series from Chico, but none of them were sweeps. Chico split a four-game series with Sonoma State; the latter eventually climbed to a number three national ranking in the final poll.

Chico was the host team for the CCAA tournament and the Wildcats won their first two games against UC San Diego and Sonoma State, respectively. On the final Saturday, when Chico had to be beaten twice, Sonoma did just that. The first was a 4–3 loss as a result of the Seawolves pushing across two runs in the bottom of the ninth. The final was a less-climatic 7–4 loss.

Not only did Chico State host the CCAA conference tournament, they hosted the NCAA Division II West Regional. Just like 2007, four CCAA schools were selected (Chico, Sonoma, UC San Diego and Cal State Stanislaus) to join lower seeds Western Oregon University and Nebraska-Kearney. Chico won its first game, 4–2, against Stanislaus as both Mickartz and the Warriors' second-team All-American Marquis Fleming both pitched complete games. The Wildcats won their second game, 13–7, over UC San Diego with Shane Farmer not only hitting a home run but making a spectacular catch on a deep drive to center. The momentum was short-lived when Sonoma State beat Chico, 13–2. The Wildcats came back later in the evening to beat UC San Diego again, 3–2.

Saturday's win set up the championship on Sunday against Sonoma State, and the Seawolves would have to be beaten twice for Chico to advance to the NCAA Division II World Series. They weren't. Chico lost the game, 11–4, as Mickartz started on just two days rest. Sonoma State went on to reach the semifinals at the national championships (after a 19-inning, 6–5 win which started at 6:45 and ended at 3 AM the following morning). However, the Seawolves lost a pair of 2–1 games to the eventual runner-up, Ouachita Baptist University (Arkansas).

When the season concluded, the San Francisco Giants selected pitcher Kyle Woodruff in the 27th round. He began play a few weeks later in the rookie Arizona League.

The departures were assumed to be minimal, and Chico State anticipated bringing back many key players for what the Wildcats hoped would be a long run in 2009.

## San Jacinto Community College

Just as San Jacinto Community College has a target on its back for every opponent wanting to beat the historical powerhouse, the Junior College World Series has a target that San Jac aims for. By the time the Gators swept the series against Laredo in mid–March 2007, they appeared to be on track to get back to a good postseason.

San Jac ended the conference by going 19–3 and swept through its Region XIV tournament with convincing wins over Navarro (12–2), Angelina (15–5), Blinn (12–2) and Texarkana (11–5) to set up a trip back to Grand Junction, Colorado. They were ranked 11th nationally in the final NJCAA poll.

In their first game at the JUCO World Series, the Gators scored five runs on six hits in the bottom of the first and cruised to an 11–3 win in seven innings (there is a 10-run rule after five innings and an eight-run rule after seven innings). With the attendance in excess of 10,000 for the Sunday night game, Hank Williamson held Cowley County Community College (Arkansas City, Kansas) to just two multi-hit innings while striking out nine.

Two days later, they took on Western Nevada Community College (Carson City) and homered their way to a 12–5 win. Kris Miller, Brandon Belt, Try Sperring, and Kyle Henson all hit home runs. On top of that, the team collected eight doubles with Henson accounting for three of them. Lucas Luetge went eight innings and 144 pitches for the win.

In game three, the Gators met Chipola College (Marianna, Florida); and it was a see-saw game in the late innings. Trailing 4–0 going into the top of the seventh and having just surrendered three runs, the Gators sent up Quentin Luquette as a pinch hitter with two outs and two on. He hit a three-run homer, his first of the year. Chipola then added two runs in the bottom of the inning, but San Jac scored two in the top of the eighth. Chipola scored once more, in the bottom of the eighth, courtesy of a wild pitch. The Gators scored once in the top of the ninth, but stranded the potential tying run on third and lost, 7–6. In a double-elimination format, they still had life.

The following evening San Jac was matched up against New Mexico JC (Hobbs), and the Gators jumped out to a 7–1 lead through four innings. It was 7–2 after six innings with Matt Coburn pitching well, scattering four hits. The Thunderbirds chipped away for two runs in the seventh, leading up to a disaster for the Gators in the eighth. San Jac gave up six runs that inning, even with Williamson coming in as a reliever. The first three runs were by way of a home run and the last one scored via a wild pitch. The Gators answered with two runs in the bottom of the inning, but in the ninth, San Jac's potential tying run was stranded at second base. Game over. Season over. Chipola went on to win the World Series.

For several key players, the end of the season meant the end of their San Jac career. Eric Fry was in the last group of "draft-and-follow" players. Beginning with players selected in the 2007 draft, a team had until August 15 to sign a player unless he was a college senior. Previously, a team that drafted a player who went to junior college had exclusive rights to sign such a player up until one week before the following year's draft. Eric weighed his options—Oklahoma State or the Texas Rangers. He opted for the latter and began playing in the Arizona League before playing with the Spokane Indians (Washington) in the Class A Northwest League, where he returned to play in 2008.

Hank Williamson was selected by the Baltimore Orioles in the 14th round. He pitched during the summer of 2007 with Bluefield in the Appalachian

League before moving on in 2008 with the Aberdeen IronBirds (Maryland) in the New York–Penn League. Fellow pitchers Chris Corrigan (18th round selection of the Toronto Blue Jays) and Garrett Clyde (43rd round selection of the Chicago Cubs) were drafted, but Corrigan returned to San Jac and Clyde transferred to the University of Texas.

Brandon Belt also transferred to Texas where, as a sophomore, he became the starting first baseman for the Longhorns. He hit .319, was the team leader in RBIs with 65 and was an All-Big 12 honorable mention selection. Taylor Hammack also left after his freshman year and transferred to the University of Houston, where he was used as a pitcher primarily in relief. Trey Sperring went to the University of Oklahoma for his junior year and received frequent playing time at third base. Catcher Kyle Henson finished his second year at San Jac and moved on to Ole Miss, while pitcher Luke Luetge went to Rice University.

Coach Tom Arrington had little to be concerned about when the 2008 season began. If he was concerned, the juco baseball community wasn't; San Jac was picked eight in the national pre-season poll. He had his number one (Tanner Hines), two (Kris Miller) and five (Jeremy Barfield) hitters in the batting order returning. While he lost some key pitchers, Chris Corrigan was returning, as well as other sophomores who had limited action in 2007.

The Gators got off to a good start in 2008, winning their first 12 games. The only stumbles during the regular season were dropping doubleheaders to Temple College in February and Alvin Community College in March. Otherwise, the team went into the postseason with a 42–12 record. The Gators were consistently ranked between fourth and seventh in the national polls.

In the Region XIV tournament hosted by Northeast Texas Community College, the Gators defeated Panola College, 11–4, as Miller, Barfield, Devin Shines and Danny Hernandez all hit home runs. Jamie Bagley got the win in a long relief effort. Next up was Angelina College and Chris Corrigan was one out away from pitching a complete game; when he exited, he had allowed but five hits in 8⅔ innings. Although 12 Gators struck out, they had enough offense to win, 7–2.

The following day San Jac faced Alvin with whom the Gators split six regular-season games. The game was tied 5–5 through nine innings and after San Jac punched across a run in the tenth, they were one out away from a win. However, a two-out rally scored two and the Gators had lost game one. They had to then beat Wharton County Junior College who had lost five out of six games to San Jac during the regular season. On this day, they fell behind early and came up just short, losing 5–4. With the loss went their hopes to return to Grand Junction where they had spent many a mid–May.

Alvin was the regional winner and went 2–2 in the JUCO World Series, losing to the eventual champion, Grayson County College (Denison, Texas), a team San Jac had swept in an early season doubleheader. Grayson became the 2008 mythical national champion; one will never know how they would fare against, for example, the California champion, Sierra College (Rocklin).

After the season, Jeremy Barfield was drafted by the Oakland A's in the seventh round and began work right away for the Vancouver Canadians in the Class A Northwest League. Jamie Bagley, a sophomore pitcher, was selected in the 35th round by the Tampa Bay Rays and he began his professional career with the Princeton Devil Rays (West Virginia) in the rookie Appalachian League before going to the Hudson Valley Renegades (Fishkill, New York) in the New York–Penn League. Kris Miller was selected as a first team All-American and the Defensive Player of the Year and he announced that he would attend Lewis-Clark State College in the fall. Shortstop Tanner Hines committed to Stephen F. Austin State University (Nacogdoches, Texas) and Chris Corrigan committed to Ole Miss.

There is every reason to think that San Jac will keep adding to the years painted on the left field (World Series appearances) and right field (World Series championships) fences.

## Eastern Connecticut State University

When ECSU won a doubleheader against the University of Southern Maine on a frigid day in early April 2007, two things were certain: the weather would get warmer, and the Warriors would have a role the postseason.

After they began the season out west and a month behind other teams, the Warriors lost only four times leading up to the postseason, none of which were Little East Conference games. They finished the regular season 30–9 overall and 14–0 in conference. They won the 2007 Little East tournament, needing a Shawn Gilblair RBI in the bottom of the ninth against Keene State College (New Hampshire). The 11th-ranked Warriors received an automatic bid to the NCAA Division III Regionals.

In the first game of the regionals, they faced St. Joseph's College (Standish, Maine), and although Gilblair gave up 11 hits (10 singles), ECSU won convincingly, 10–2. In the second game, Jimmy Jagodzinski scattered seven hits and shortstop Melvin Castillo had four RBIs as ECSU beat Western New England (Springfield, Massachusetts), 6–3. In game three, Joe Esposito and Jason LaVorgna combined for a two-hitter to lead the Warriors to a 6–1 win over Keene State. Going into the game, they had previously won three out of four games against the Owls. Keene also did ECSU a favor by eliminating Wheaton College, the latter a team that had beaten the Warriors twice in a pair of one-run games during the season.

In the final of the Regionals, Keene got one more shot against ECSU. Tristan Hobbes produced five RBIs and he was one of four Warriors who hit home runs (his, a first-inning grand slam) in an 18–3 rout. By winning the New England Regional, ECSU earned its 12th trip to the Division III national tournament in Grand Chute, Wisconsin.

In the first game, Shawn Gilblair struggled and lasted but 2⅓ innings while giving up six runs (only three earned) on six hits in a 15–4 rout at the hands of Carthage College (Kenosha, Wisconsin). This immediately put ECSU in the loser's bracket with no margin for error. However, error was exactly what happened as Emory University (Atlanta, Georgia) scored four unearned runs and won 5–4. The Warriors uncharacteristically committed four errors (after committing five the game before) and had an eighth-inning balk which led to the eventual winning run. Jason LaVorgna suffered his first loss of the season.

In a little over 24 hours after starting tournament play, ECSU was done. Emory wound up losing the 2007 Division III championship to Kean University (New Jersey) in extra innings.

It was not the manner in which one would expect the Warriors to exit the national tournament. However, it was still a good season. In the final American Baseball Coaches Association (ABCA) poll, ECSU finished ranked first in the New England Region and eighth nationally. Shawn Gilblair and outfielder Randy Re were selected as ABCA first-team All-Americans and freshman Melvin Castillo was a third-team selection.

A couple weeks after ECSU was eliminated from the national tournament, the New York Mets selected closer Jason LaVorgna in the 35th round of the 2007 draft. He spent the summer of 2007 with the Kingsport Mets (Tennessee) of the Appalachian League where he also started in 2008 before advancing to the Savannah Sand Gnats in the Class A South Atlantic League. Shortly after the draft was completed, catcher Matt Cooney attended an open tryout with the Boston Red Sox organization and within a couple of weeks was playing with their rookie team in the Gulf Coast League. He finished the summer playing a few games with the Greenville Drive (South Carolina) in the South Atlantic Class A League. In 2008, he split time between Greenville and the Lowell Spinners (Massachusetts) in the New York–Penn League.

When the 2008 season approached, ECSU looked to be on track for another good season. A good core of players was returning, including two-time All-American Shawn Gilblair. They were ranked sixth in the pre-season national poll.

The Warriors were tested immediately when they played three games before their usual spring trip to the southwest. Game one was against Kean University, the 2007 national champion and the third-ranked team coming

into the season. Unfortunately, ECSU started off the way they finished the
prior season by committing five errors and allowing five unearned runs in a
9–4 loss to the Cougars.

In their first game out west, they trounced Rutgers-Camden, 25–6. The
Warriors actually surrendered a lead-off home run and were losing 2–0 after
2½ innings before the onslaught occurred. Six players had multiple RBIs and
Gilblair hit two home runs. Four days later they beat Whittier College (California), 21–5.

One part of the road trip that wasn't encouraging was the game against
Ithaca College (New York) in which Gilblair went but three innings, allowing eight runs (four earned) on seven hits. Because of injuries, he would start
only two more games and pitch just 24-plus innings for the season. He still
continued to make major contributions with his hitting. Gilblair hit .403 for
the season with 12 home runs and 43 RBI's despite not playing in 13 games.

After returning from the West and possessing a 7–5 record, the Warriors
played their first home game on March 30, a full month into the season. They
went 11–3 in the league and entered the Little East tournament 27-11-1. But
ECSU dropped two in the tournament (15–3 to the University of Southern
Maine and 1–0 to Keene State) and the Warriors were denied a third straight
title.

An at-large bid to the NCAA Division III regionals at Auburn, New York
(hosted by Ithaca College), was still provided to the Warriors. They opened
up against Montclair State (New Jersey) and saw a 7–3 seventh-inning lead
evaporate into an 8–7 loss. Falling into the loser's bracket, ECSU battled back
to win three straight, the last an avenging 14–0 victory over Montclair State
after wins over Grove City (Pennsylvania) and Ohio Wesleyan, respectively.

The consecutive wins set up the Warriors to face Rensselaer Polytech-
nic Institute (RPI in Troy, New York). Both offenses got their money's worth.
There were seven lead changes, both squads had 16 hits and each team scored
six runs in an inning. The score was tied at 11 after nine. The Red Hawks
pushed across three runs in the top of the tenth. With the heart of the order
due up, the Warriors still had life. Tristan Hobbes doubled home two runs
before an out was recorded. However, a failed sacrifice, an infield pop-up
and a strikeout ended the threat and the season.

Trinity College (Hartford, Connecticut) won the national championship
and the top ranking. ECSU ended up ranked 27th but it was still a good year.
Of the starting batting order in the final game against RPI, seven of those players are scheduled to return. Three of the four key pitchers should be back for
2009. Bill Holowaty should be moving steadily towards 1,300 career coaching wins.

## *Louisiana State University*

If one were to plot the LSU baseball program, like a corporation's stock history on a line graph, it would bottom out on May 11, 2007. On that evening, the Tigers lost to Florida, 19–3.

Two things happened that changed the trend. The first was the 2007 season simply ended. It ended on May 19. It ended with a loss to Vanderbilt one day after the school mascot, Mike V, died. It didn't end when the LSU schedule indicated it might end. It didn't end in late May after the SEC tournament. It didn't end in the first week in June at the NCAA regionals. It didn't end the following week at the Super Regionals. It didn't end in mid–June during the College World Series. When LSU prints the season schedule each year it includes such dates because of the very real possibility that the Tigers will be playing until the final weekend. However, those dates were irrelevant in 2007.

Once the 2007 season ended, the LSU baseball program had an opportunity for a fresh beginning in 2008. The second significant event occurred on April 20, 2008, when the Tigers tied Georgia, 10–10, in 12 innings (SEC travel rules required the Sunday game to end when it did). After that game, LSU was 23-16-1 overall and 6-11-1 in the SEC. At this point, they were doing worse in conference play than in 2007. They were in 11th place overall.

Then they won their next 23 games.

The memory of 2007 was just about gone, but the 2007 season had been a strange year in general. For the first time in 30 years, neither LSU, nor Texas, nor USC nor Miami were in the College World Series.

There were some genuine reasons for optimism for 2008. The Tigers were returning several players with significant playing time. Their incoming recruiting class was considered by some to be among the best in the country.

The 2007 draft did not deplete the team. Pitcher Charlie Furbush was selected in the fourth round by the Detroit Tigers. He put up solid numbers in the summer of 2007, splitting his time between the Gulf Coast League and the West Michigan Whitecaps (Comstock Park) in the Class A Midwest League. He spent the 2008 rehabbing from Tommy John elbow surgery. J.T. Wise was a late draft pick (45th round, Oakland Athletics) but the catcher opted to transfer to the University of Oklahoma in the last season before the one-year "sit out" rule took effect.

While the Tigers would rely on everyday returning players Blake Dean, Michael Hollander, Jared Mitchell (who also caught 13 passes in the 2007 season for the LSU football team) and Ryan Schimpf, it was the newcomers that boosted the team. Two California junior college transfers, Matt Clark and Derek Helenihi, played a big role. Three freshmen provided the strength up the middle, with Micah Gibbs as catcher, D.J. LeMahieu at shortstop and Leon Landry in center field. Ryan Verdugo and Jordan Brown were also juco transfers and keys to the pitching staff along with returning pitchers Jared Bradford, Blake Martin, Louis Coleman and Paul Bertuccini.

The Tigers finished the regular season 39-16-1 and were 18-11-1 in the SEC. In winning its first SEC tournament since 2000, LSU beat Ole Miss, 8–2, marking the16th time in the then 20-game win streak that they came from behind to pull out a victory. The Tigers then hosted the NCAA regional and took care of Texas Southern and Southern Miss with relative ease.

LSU then hosted a Super Regional series against UC Irvine. These were the final games to be played at Alex Box Stadium. The first game was a largely forgettable 11–5 loss to the Anteaters. It was memorable for LSU fans only for a hidden-ball trick that was miscalled against the Tigers and a spectacular fifth-inning catch by Leon Landry, denying a home run. It was the first time LSU had lost in seven weeks.

Game two progressed into another seemingly anticlimactic contest. LSU, the designated visitor in this game, trailed 7–2 after seven innings. In the eighth, a Jared Mitchell solo home run and a Matt Clark RBI single made the score 7–4; it seemed like, at best, that LSU was earning some "there's no quit in those Tigers" hollow praise. When Leon Landry led off the ninth with a walk, perhaps a few of the partisan fans were thinking fate would not allow the final Alex Box Stadium game to end in unspectacular fashion. It didn't.

The first three Tigers reached base and Mitchell made it four when he walked and forced in a run. In a pitching staff's nightmare, UC Irvine gave up five runs on four hits and three walks in that inning. Louis Coleman held the Anteaters scoreless over the final three innings and LSU ended the day with a 9–7 win.

For those who really believed in fate or the karma of Alex Box's concrete and steel, the final game of the series was a foregone conclusion. An actual body-count crowd of 8,173 saw LSU win by the football score of 21–7. In fact, although the Tigers fell short of matching the 35 points the LSU football team put up against Ohio State in the BCS National Championship, it was an incredible offensive display. For starters, Blake Dean had five hits (one home run) and three RBIs and Ryan Schimpf had four hits and five RBIs (two home runs). As a result, LSU was headed to the College World Series.

In the first game in Omaha, Michael Hollander hit a lead-off home run and Matt Clark hit a solo shot in the second, but it was mostly North Carolina's day as the Tar Heels won, 8–4. Game two was against Rice and, although it took awhile, the 2008 Tiger magic was back. Trailing 5–1 after seven innings, LSU got an unearned run in the eighth, but they were still four runs down going into the bottom of the ninth. After the Tigers scored a run, Blake Dean hit a bases-loaded, walk-off double, driving in all three runs for the 6–5 win. For the season, it was their 30th come-from-behind win.

The College World Series format is two brackets of four teams. Rice was eliminated and LSU had to face North Carolina again, with Fresno State awaiting the winner. Blake Martin started, but he just didn't have it that evening; he lasted but a third of an inning. In another time and place, Martin would likely have had the chance to get into a groove and pitch several innings. Jared Bradford came in and got a double-play grounder. The damage was limited to two runs. He held the Tar Heels to one run in the next five innings and when Matt Clark crushed a two-run homer (his 28th of the year) in the sixth, the game was tied at 3–3. With two outs in the top of the ninth, North Carolina loaded the bases (a double and two intentional walks) before clean-up hitter Tim Federowicz stunned the Tigers (and pitcher Louis Coleman) with a grand slam. There was no miracle finish for LSU that evening. Their season had come to an end.

What a season it was. Just when some LSU supporters were wondering if they would ever see the glory days of former Coach Skip Bertman again, it arrived. Bertman retired as the active athletic director shortly after the season was over. The team finished ranked sixth in the major polls. Blake Dean was a first-team All-American. Micah Gibbs was chosen for the USA Baseball national team. Paul Mainieri was named as Coach of the Year by a couple of respected college baseball websites. Even the school's baseball media guide was awarded as the second best in the country (after the University of Texas).

The major league draft took place before the NCAA Super Regional. Seven Tigers were selected. Two of the players selected did not sign professional contracts before the August 15 deadline: Louis Coleman (Washington Nationals, 14th round) and Jordan Brown (Chicago Cubs, 39th round).

Ryan Verdugo (San Francisco Giants, 9th round) and Matt Clark (San Diego Padres, 12th round) both signed in late July and Verdugo began play in the rookie Arizona League (Scottsdale) while Clark headed to the Eugene Emeralds (Oregon) in the Northwest League. Three other LSU players signed and began their professional careers shortly after the season ended. Pitcher Blake Martin was a 17th round selection by the Minnesota Twins and he split time with the Elizabethton Twins (Tennessee) in the Appalachian League and the Beloit Snappers (Wisconsin) of the Midwest League. The St. Louis Cardinals chose pitcher Jared Bradford in the 18th round and he played with the Quad Cities River Bandits (Davenport, Iowa) in the Midwest League. Third baseman Michael Hollander was selected in the 20th round by the Texas Rangers and played for the Spokane Indians (Washington) of the Northwest League and in the Arizona League.

Although the old Alex Box Stadium saved its powers until the very end, the new stadium may provide magical results beginning in 2009.

## University of Miami

"With the seventh selection in the first round of 2008 first year player draft, the Cincinnati Reds select Yonder Alonso a first baseman from the University of Miami, Coral Gables, Florida," announced Bud Selig on June 5, 2008, to those assembled at The Milk House at Disney's Wide World of Sports Complex near Kissimmee, Florida.

Not long after announcing Alonso's name, Selig approached the podium again and said, "With the twelfth selection in the first round of 2008 first-year player draft, the Oakland Athletics select Jemile Weeks, a second baseman from the University of Miami, Coral Gables, Florida."

Most players have two lofty goals when they become part of a college program: to be part of a team that reaches the College World Series and to be a high draft choice. Alonso and Weeks attained both of those.

After the crushing loss to Florida State on April 27, 2007, Miami finished the regular season on a strong run, winning 10 of their last 12 games. They were 35–20 and ranked 25th in the country.

In the Atlantic Coast Conference (ACC) tournament, the Hurricanes lost the first game on a 13th-inning Clemson squeeze bunt. Miami bounced back from the 5–4 loss and beat Florida State two days later, 9–3, behind a strong Eric Erickson pitching performance. In game three, Richard O'Brien's two-run homer was one of the few highlights in a 7–3 loss to Wake Forest. The loss eliminated Miami from the tournament, but the Hurricanes fully anticipated an at-large bid to the NCAA tournament.

The Hurricanes were selected as the second seed at the regional hosted by the University of Missouri. In the first game against Louisville, the outcome looked very promising when Miami scored seven runs in the first two innings (Weeks' three-run triple was the key hit) and the Hurricanes had Scott Maine on the mound. However, it unraveled when the Hurricanes were held hitless for the last six innings; the Cardinals scored in all but two innings and went on to win, 13–7.

In the second game they survived a scare from Kent State. After Miami held an 8–1 lead going into the bottom of the eighth, the Golden Flashes had 11 at-bats and scored six runs. Miami held on to an 8–7 win. The third game was a rematch against Louisville and this time the Hurricanes played from behind. The Cardinals got their first three batters of the game on base and each of them scored. Despite home runs from Raben, Sobolewski and O'Brien (who went 3 for 4), Miami fell short, 8–7. It was the first time since 1993 that the Hurricanes did not win their NCAA regional. This time they did not even get to play in the final game.

There were some individual bright spots. Yonder Alonso was named to some second- and third-team All-American teams. Eric Erickson and Mark Sobolewski were named to Freshman All-American teams. Former Hurricane Ryan Braun provided some more program bragging material when he won the 2007 National League Rookie of the Year award with the Milwaukee Brewers.

In the major league draft, pitcher Scott Maine was the highest selection; he went to the Arizona Diamondbacks in the sixth round. Thus far he has been used as a reliever, with the Yakima Bears in the Northwest League in 2007 and the Visalia Oaks in the Class A California League in 2008. Pitcher Manny Miguelez was selected in the eighth round by the Detroit Tigers. He was primarily used as a starter in 2007 with the Tigers' Gulf Coast League team and then with Oneonta (New York) in the New York–Penn League. For 2008, he was promoted to the West Michigan Whitecaps (Comstock Park) in the Class A Midwest League. Pitcher Danny Gil was selected in the 30th round by the Houston Astros and played during 2007 with the Tri-City ValleyCats (Troy, New York). He was released by Houston in 2008 and was subsequently picked up by the Washington Nationals who sent him to their Gulf Coast League team.

Third baseman Roger Tomas was not drafted but he signed as a free agent with the Tigers organization in 2007 and played with their Gulf Coast League team. In 2008, he played alongside Manny Miguelez with the West Michigan Whitecaps.

Enrique Garcia was selected in the 34th round by the Chicago Cubs, but he opted to return to the Hurricanes.

For three players who would have finished their junior year at Miami had they not opted to play professional baseball out of high school, their baseball experiences have been very different by the 2008 season. Mark Rogers, a first round pick of the Milwaukee Brewers in 2004, missed minor league seasons in 2007 and 2008 due to shoulder surgeries. Gio Gonzalez, whom the Chicago White Sox selected the supplementary first round, was traded to the Oakland A's organization as part of the Nick Swisher deal and he made his Major League debut with the A's in August 2008. Dexter Fowler followed up an injury-shortened 2007 season with good offensive numbers with the Tulsa Drillers in the Class AA Texas League.

Losing four of its final six games in the 2007 postseason ensured that Miami was kept out of the final 2007 polls. The 2008 season was a different story. Garcia and Erickson gave Miami two experienced starters returning in

2008. Of the six everyday players who hit .280 or better during the 2007 campaign five would return (Roger Tomas was the exception). The various preseason polls had the Hurricanes ranked as high as second and as low as 14th. The baseball community was clearly expecting an improved Miami team.

Not counting their exhibition loss to the Florida Marlins, the Hurricanes won five of their first six games before starting ACC play. By April 7 they advanced to the number one spot in the polls. They ultimately went 23–5 in conference games with the only real blemish the two losses against North Carolina (ranked number two at the time) to end the regular season.

In the ACC tournament, Miami won all four games against different opponents. The Hurricanes trailed in only two innings throughout the entire tournament. They outscored their opponents 35 to 19. To the casual observer, the most surprising result of the tournament was that it was their first conference title. Ever. Before joining the ACC in 2005, the baseball team played as an independent.

There was no suspense with the NCAA selections. Of course, Miami would host regional play. The Hurricanes were still the number one ranked team in the country.

They first drew Bethune-Cookman, a school they beat twice in March. Miami won again, this time 7–4. Freshman Chris Hernandez got the start in the second game and he held off the Missouri Tigers 6–5. His battery mate, another freshman, Yasmani Grandal, got the game-winning hit. The final game was an 11–2 rout of Ole Miss in which the trio of Eric Erickson, Kyle Bellamy and Carlos Gutierrez all pitched well.

Coral Gables was the host site once again, this time for a Super Regional match-up against the University of Arizona. The first game was deadlocked at 3–3 through ten innings. With two outs, Arizona used a hit-by-pitch, a single and a Jon Gaston home run to stun Miami and win 6–3. It was the Hurricanes' first loss in the post-season.

With elimination on the line, Miami found itself down 4–0 after the first inning in game two. However, thanks to the 16 walks Arizona provided (six of them to Dennis Raben) and the four home runs Miami hit (Alonso, Sobolewski, Hagerty and Grandal), the Hurricanes came back to win, 14–10. In the deciding game three, Enrique Garcia got the start and held the Wildcats to two runs over six innings before the bullpen shut them out the rest of the way. The first three Hurricanes got hits to start the game (a Blake Tekotte single, a Weeks double and an Alonso home run), and those three runs would be enough for an eventual 4–2 win. Carlos Gutierrez got his 13th save of the season. They had earned their 23rd trip to the College World Series.

In the first game against Georgia, Miami carried a 4–3 lead into the ninth inning. The Hurricanes scored all of their runs from the home runs provided by Tekotte, Weeks and Alonso. Chris Hernandez pitched a strong 6⅓ innings and Kyle Bellamy handled the Bulldogs through the eighth. Gutierrez came in for the hopeful save but it didn't happen. At one point, he wild-pitched a strikeout and later threw a ground ball wide of first base. Four runs scored and Georgia finished with a 7–4 win.

Game two matched Miami against its interstate and conference rival, Florida State. The Seminoles' national player of the year (the fifth player taken in the draft), Buster Posey, had four of his team's 18 hits and they also received five walks and had one runner via an error. It was not enough for FSU. They left 17 men on base. Tekotte and Weeks got their second home runs of the Series to highlight the Miami offense. Two days after his "I need to forget this" ninth-inning relief appearance, Gutierrez came into the ninth again and gave up four hits and two walks. However, this time he got the clean-up hitter, Jack Rye, to ground out with the bases loaded to end the game and preserve a 7–5 win.

In the next elimination game, Miami had to face Stanford, a team that had a significant turnaround from its 28–28 season in 2007 (40-23-2 coming into the game). Enrique Garcia got the start for the Hurricanes. It was simply a game in which Stanford played better. While both offenses had a similar number of hits and walks, Miami just couldn't put together any sustained rallies.

The fifth inning was a microcosm of the game. In the top half, Miami started with back-to-back walks, but the runners were stranded after a foul-out and two strikeouts. By contrast, Stanford used four hits and a Miami error to score four. Trailing 8–3 going into the bottom of the ninth, it was a predictable ending this day when Miami could not convert a second and third, no-out situation. Miami's season ended.

Fresno State impressively won the College World Series, and that feat pushed them to the number one ranking despite a 31-loss season. Miami, whose final record was 53–11, slipped to fourth or fifth, depending on the particular poll.

Alonso was voted as a *Baseball America* first-team All-American and Hernandez, Tekotte and Weeks were all voted to the second team. *Collegiate Baseball* selected Chris Hernandez as the freshman pitcher of the year (11–0, 2.72 ERA). Reliever Kyle Bellamy was chosen by Rivals.com as a second-team All-American. Shortstop Ryan Jackson joined Hernandez on the prestigious USA Baseball national team.

The day before Miami's Super Regional loss to Arizona State, the 2008 major league draft was held. Besides the selection of Alonso and Weeks, closer Carlos Gutierrez was selected in the first round by the Minnesota Twins. Three other players were selected on the first day of the two-day event:

outfielder Dennis Raben (2nd round, Seattle Mariners), outfielder Blake Tekotte (3rd round, San Diego Padres) and third baseman Mark Sobolewski (4th round, Toronto Blue Jays). Sobolewski, who just finished his sophomore season with the Hurricanes, was draft eligible because, in accordance with draft rules, he turned 21 years old within 45 days of the draft.

Weeks received a signing bonus of $1.9 million and headed off for Kane County Cougars (Geneva, Illinois) in the Class A Midwest League. Gutierrez signed for a bonus just under $1.3 million and reported to the Class A Fort Meyers Miracle in the Florida State League. Cincinnati had until August 15, 2008, to sign the other first round pick, Alonso, or they would lose his rights. Just before the midnight deadline, they provided him with a major league contract and a $2 million signing bonus included in an overall contract reportedly worth $4.5 million. Most draft picks sign a minor league contract which has fewer benefits than the major league version. Alonso became part of the Reds' 40-man roster regardless of what level he is playing. He began his professional career with the final six games of the Sarasota Reds' season in the Florida State League before continuing with the Waikiki Beach Boys in the Hawaii Winter League.

Raben began his professional play with the Everett AquaSox in the Class A Northwest League. Tekotte played with the Eugene Emeralds, also in the Northwest League. Sobolewski played with the Auburn Doubledays (New York) in the New York–Penn League.

Besides the impressive number of first-day draft selections, two other Hurricanes were selected on day two. The first was pitcher Enrique Garcia who was selected in the 24th round by the Cincinnati Reds. Garcia is a veteran of the draft process. He was originally drafted after his freshman year at Potomac State College (a junior college in Keyser, West Virginia, that is affiliated with the University of West Virginia) by the Chicago White Sox in the 17th round. After an outstanding sophomore year at Potomac, he was drafted by the Arizona Diamondbacks in the 20th round. When he completed his junior year at Miami, he was selected in the 34th round by the Chicago Cubs. The 2008 draft made it the fourth time he was selected. He signed and began playing for the Billings Mustangs (Montana) in the Pioneer League.

The other day two selection was Adam Severino, who was picked by the Minnesota Twins in the 26th round. The outfielder started his pro career with the Elizabethton Twins (Tennessee) in the Appalachian League.

Going into the 2009 season, it is natural to speculate that the Hurricanes lost so many good players to the 2008 draft that it is bound to affect the team. That may be. However, some very talented and experienced players return.

No doubt, in the near future, Bud Selig (or his replacement) will walk to the podium and announce the name of another University of Miami player taken in the first round.

# Sources and Resources

## Publications

Cal State Fullerton 2007 Baseball Media Guide
Chico State Wildcat Baseball 2007 Program
Eastern Connecticut State University Baseball Guide 2007
GAMEDAY The Official Game Program of LSU Baseball
Lewis-Clark State College Warriors 2007 Program
LSU Tigers 2007 Baseball Media Guide
Miami Hurricanes 2007 Baseball Media Guide
San Jacinto College Gators Baseball Program 2007
Winters, Manque. *Professional Sports: The Community College Connection.* Winmar Press, 1984.
USC Trojans 2007 Baseball Media Guide

## Websites

Baseball America magazine, http://www.baseballamerica.com.
Boyd Nation's RPI rankings, http://boydsworld.com/baseball/rpi.
California Community College Athletic Assocation, http://coasports.org.
College Baseball Insider, http://collegebaseballinsider.com.
College Baseball — Rivals, http://collegebaseball.rivals.com.
College Baseball Summer Ball, http://collegesummerball.blogspot.com.
Collegiate Baseball magazine, http://collegiatebaseball.com.
Dale's Summer League Central, http://www.geocities.com/dalesslc
Division III Baseball, http://d3baseball.com.
High School Baseball, http://hsbaseballweb.com.
Massey Baseball Ratings, http://mratings.com.
National Association of Intercollegiate Athletics, http://naia.cstv.com.
National Collegiate Athletic Association news, polls and statistics, http://ncaa.com.
National Collegiate Athletic Association rules and regulations, http://www.ncaa.org/wps.
National Junior College Athletic Association, http://njcaa.org.
San Jacinto Gators baseball, http://www.eteamz.com/sanjac.
University of Texas Longhorns athletics, http://www.texassports.com.

# Index